Best

TRUMP

TRUMP

A True American Patriot ... or Not?

GLENN W. FEARN

MIKE BLACKWELL

SOVEREIGN PRESS
DENTON, TEXAS

TRUMP

Copyright © 2020 by Glenn W. Fearn and Mike Blackwell

Published by
Sovereign Press
www.sovereignpress.net

Library of Congress Control Number: 2020915276

Paperback ISBN: 978-1-947360-56-3
eBook ISBN: 978-1-947360-57-0

Typeset by Art Innovations (http://artinnovations.in/)
Cover design by Debbie Lewis

Printed in the United States of America

BOOKS BY GLENN W. FEARN

Trump, A True American Patriot . . . or Not?

BOOKS BY MICHAEL BLACKWELL

Treason By Lies, Deceit and Fraud
Trump, A True American Patriot . . . or Not?

Why would a man who is a self-made billionaire leave his billionaire lifestyle, and subject himself and his family to the humiliation, ridicule, and slander, and potential assassination of being President of the United States?

CONTENTS

PREFACE

Most of the people of the United States are completely oblivious to what I am going to present in this book. Most people have no idea of the threats the people on this planet face, and the threat that The United States of America poses to the powers that be.

We, the citizens of America, are now joined in a great national effort to rebuild our country and restore its promise for all of our people.

Today's ceremony, however, has very special meaning. Because today we are not merely transferring power from one Administration to another, or from one party to another – but we are transferring power from Washington DC and giving it back to you, the people.

For too long, a small group in our nation's Capital has reaped the rewards of government while the people have borne the cost.

Washington flourished – but the people did not share in its wealth.

Politicians prospered – but the jobs left, and the factories closed.

The establishment protected itself, but not the citizens of our country.

Their victories have not been your victories; their triumphs have not been your triumphs; and while they celebrated in our nation's capital, there was little to celebrate for struggling families all across our land.

That all changes – starting right here, and right now, because this moment is your moment: it belongs to you.

It belongs to everyone gathered here today and everyone watching all across America.

This is your day. This is your celebration.

And this, the United States of America, is your country.

What truly matters is not which party controls our government, *but whether our government is controlled by the people.*

January 20, 2017, will be remembered as the day the people became the rulers of this nation again.

The forgotten men and women of our country will be forgotten no longer.

Everyone is listening to you now.

You came by the tens of millions to become part of a historic movement the likes of which the world has never seen before.

At the center of this movement is a crucial conviction: that a nation exists to serve its citizens.[1]

The White House is probably very nice, especially compared to what I am used to. It certainly is full of history, but compared to Trump's $100 million penthouse in Trump tower, or his Mara Lago resort, the White House looks like a bit of a dump, and it is certainly a step down from what Trump is used to.

There are some obvious reasons why Trump wants to transfer the power back to the people, but those reasons are really just symptoms to what the real problem is.

This book is about what is really happening in the District of Columbia and why Donald Trump would want to transfer power back to we the people and what needs to take place to make that happen.

This book goes back into history to lay a foundation for what is happening today.

This book discusses the influence that other countries and international organizations have had and uses official documents for substantiation.

Figure 1 – The Oval Office

Figure 2 – Trump Private Residence in Whitehouse

This book discusses why so many people wanted to leave England and other European countries to face the hardships of life in what is now known as the West.

This book discusses the War of Independence, and the causes of the War of Independence from a different perspective.

This book discusses the Civil War and the results of the Civil War from the view of the courts and how international organizations precipitated the War of Independence, and the Civil War, and everything that Donald Trump is dealing with to put the power back into the hands of the people.

This book uses a lot of court citations, citations from law dictionaries, and international agreements because these things are not the subject of anyone's opinion, and are more likely to be provable, and less likely to be somebody's opinion.

PRELUDE

There is a 2015 YouTube video of Jerome Corsi explaining how five generals told him they were planning a coup on the Obama administration, and Corsi told the generals to go and talk to Donald Trump.

A few months later Corsi got a phone call, and the generals had decided NOT to go ahead with their plans because Donald Trump had agreed to run for President of the United States.

Figure 3 – Donald Trump Hugging the Flag

1

REPUBLIC OR DEMOCRACY

"Those who fail to learn from history are doomed to repeat it!"

—SIR WINSTON CHURCHILL

When he came out of the Constitutional Convention in 1787, Mrs. Powel of Philadelphia asked Benjamin Franklin, "Well, Doctor, what have we got, a republic or a monarchy?" With no hesitation whatsoever Franklin responded, "'A republic, if you can keep it.'"

Many people fail to really understand the significance of the "if you can keep it" statement from Franklin, and yet it seems every day the news media and government officials tell us about our democracy not our republic.

> "The experience of all former ages had shown that of all human governments, democracy was the most unstable, fluctuating and short-lived."
>
> —*John Quincy Adams*

1

"Remember, democracy never lasts long. It soon wastes, exhausts, and murders itself. There never was a democracy yet that did not commit suicide."

—John Adams

"Between a balanced republic and a democracy, the difference is like that between order and chaos."

—John Marshall

"The two enemies of the people are criminals and the government, so let us tie the second down with the chains of the constitution so the second will not become the legalized version of the first."

—Thomas Jefferson

"It has been observed that a pure democracy if it were practicable would be the most perfect government. Experience has proved that no position is more false than this. The ancient democracies in which the people themselves deliberated never possessed one good feature of government. Their very character was tyranny; their figure deformity."

—Alexander Hamilton

"The greatest danger to American Freedom is a government that ignores the Constitution"

—Thomas Jefferson

Democratic Socialism

Obviously, a Republic was the preferred system of government and democracy was the worst form of government, and what you see happening today are the fruits of a type of democracy called socialism.

"The problem with socialism is that eventually you run out of other people's money."

—*Margaret Thatcher*

"When plunder becomes a way of life for a group of men in a society, over the course of time they create for themselves a legal system that authorizes it and a moral code that glorifies it."

—*Frederic Bastiat, The Law*

Under our federal system of government, each state was a sovereign, free, and independent state, with some powers delegated to the federal government.

"His Brittanic Majesty *acknowledges the said* United States, viz., New Hampshire, Massachusetts Bay, Rhode Island and Providence Plantations, Connecticut, New York, New Jersey, Pennsylvania, Maryland, *Virginia*, North Carolina, South Carolina and Georgia, to be *free sovereign and independent states*, that he treats with them as such, and for himself, his heirs, and successors, relinquishes all claims to the government, propriety, and territorial rights of the same and every part thereof."

—*Article I, Definitive Treaty of Peace of 1783 [emphasis added]*

"The term 'Citizen of the United States' must be understood to mean those who were citizens of the State as such after the Union had commenced and the several States had assumed their sovereignty. Before that period there were no citizens of the United States."

—*Inhabitants of Manchester v. Inhabitants of Boston,*
16 Mass. 230, 235

"The governments are but *trustees* acting under derived authority and have no power to delegate what is not delegated to them. But *the people*, as the original fountain *might take away what they have delegated and entrust* to whom they please. ... The sovereignty in every state resides in the people of the state and they may alter and change their form of government at their own pleasure."

—*Luther v. Borden, 48 US 1, 12 Led 581*
[emphasis added]

"There is no such thing as power of inherent Sovereignty in the government of the United States. It is a government of delegated powers, supreme within its prescribed sphere but powerless outside of it. In this country sovereignty resides in the People, and Congress can exercise no power which they have not, *by their Constitution entrusted to it*; All else is withheld."

—*Julliard v Greenman 110 U.S. 421 at p 467*
[emphasis added]

And prior to the Civil War, when people talked about the United States, they talked about *them* not *it*.

The Constitution for the United States and the Articles of Confederation are both trust indentures that establish a trust, and they both continue to exist to this day.

Certain things were put in place to protect the Republican form of government that are NOT in place now:

- A Senate that was appointed by State governors
- ONLY landowners were the electors

Summary

So what happened? How did our republic become a socialist democracy?

"The best argument against democracy is a five-minute conversation with the average voter."

—Winston Churchill

These questions and more are answered in the chapters following.

2

STARE DECISIS

The principle of stare decisis basically says that once something is decided, it is decided for all time:

"STARE DECISIS (Lat.). To abide by, or adhere to, decided cases. *Stare* decisis *et non quieta movere.* It is a general maxim that when a point has been settled by decision, it forms a precedent which is not afterwards to be departed from. The doctrine of stare decisis not always to be relied upon; for the courts find it necessary to overrule cases which have been decided contrary to principle. Many hundreds of such overruled cases may be found in the American and English reports." (*Bouvier's Law Dictionary*, 1883 Edition, Volume 2, page 661)

The Doctrine of Precedent

"doctrine of precedent. 1. The rule that precedents not only have persuasive authority but also must be followed when similar circumstances arise. • This rule developed in the 19th century and prevails today. See STARE DECISIS. [Cases: Courts 88. C.J.S. Courts § 139; Trade-Marks, Trade-

Names, and Unfair Competition§ 187.] 2. A rule that precedents are reported, may be cited, and will probably be followed by courts. • This is the rule that prevailed in England until the 19th century." (*Black's Law Dictionary*, page 1460)

"stare decisis (stahr-ee di-sI-sis orstair-ee), n. [Latin "to stand by things decided"] The doctrine of precedent, under which it is necessary for a court to follow earlier judicial decisions when the same points arise again in litigation. See PRECEDENT; NON QUIETA MOVERE. Cf. RES JUDICATA; LAW OF THE CASE ; (in civil law) jurisprudence constante under JURISPRUDENCE. [Cases: Courts 89. C.J.S. Courts §§ 139–140, 144–146, 161–164, 166–167.]" (*Black's Law Dictionary*, page 4403)

Every court case references other cases which are similar, and they'll say based on *stare decisis*, it is already decided, and it is always "my opinion is...."

We the People Make All Law

The cases I reference here point to older cases, and those cases point to even older cases, and eventually they all go back to a common law jury, because "we the people" are the source of all law and have always been the source of all law.

"A Sovereign is exempt from suit, not because of any formal conception or obsolete theory, but on the logical and practical ground that there can be no legal Right as against the authority that makes the law on which the Right depends."

(Kawananakoa v. Polyblank, 205 U.S. 349, 353, 27 S. Ct. 526, 527, 51 L. Ed. 834 (1907))

"The judicial power is the power to hear those matters which affect life, liberty or property of the Citizens of the State." (Sapulpa v Land, 101 Okla. 22, 223 Pac. 640, 35 A.L.R. 872)

"The very meaning of 'sovereignty' is that the decree of the sovereign makes law." (American Banana Co. v. United Fruit Co., 29 S.Ct. 511, 513, 213 U.S. 347, 53 L.Ed. 826, 19 Ann.Cas. 1047)

"Sovereignty itself is, of course, not subject to law, for it is the author and source of law; but in our system, while sovereign powers are delegated to the agencies of government, sovereignty itself remains with the people, by whom and for whom all government exists and acts." (Yick Wo v Hopkins, 118 US 356, 370)

COURT. The person and suit of the sovereign; the place where the sovereign sojourns with his regal retinue, wherever that may be. (*Black's Law Dictionary*, 5th Edition, page 318)

COURT. An agency of the sovereign created by it directly or indirectly under its authority, consisting of one or more officers, established and maintained for the purpose of hearing and determining issues of law and fact regarding legal rights and alleged violations thereof, and of applying the sanctions of the law, authorized to exercise its powers in the course of law at times and places previously determined by lawful authority. (Isbill v. Stovall, Tex.Civ.App., 92 S.W.2d 1067, 1070; B*lack's Law Dictionary*, 4th Edition, page 425)

"[A]nd because it brings into action, and enforces this great and glorious principle, that the people are the sovereign of this country, *and consequently that fellow citizens and joint sovereigns cannot be degraded by appearing with each other in their own courts to have their controversies determined.*" (Chisolm v Georgia 2 Dall. 419 [emphasis added])

Judges interpret the law, but we the people make the law.

Jury Nullification

Jury nullification is the principle that juries can say: "this is a bad law and it is not just that this guy is even on trial, and we don't care what the law says, we are going to find him not guilty."

"It is presumed, that juries are the best judges of facts; it is, on the other hand, presumed that courts are the best judges of law. But still both objects are within your power of decision....*you have a right to take it upon yourselves to judge of both, and to determine the law as well as the fact in controversy.*" (Chief Judge John Jay, US Supreme Court, State of Georgia vs. Brailsford, 3 Dall 1 (1794) [emphasis added])

IS THIS JUSTICE?

Dennis Hastert – former Speaker of the United States House of Representatives, faces 6 months in jail for raping 5 little boys.

Or

Shona Banda – single mother, faces nearly 30 years in prison for treating her disease with cannabis

The jury has an "unreviewable and irreversible power... to acquit in disregard of the instructions on the law given by the trial judge…" (US vs Dougherty, 473 F 2d 1113, 1139 (1972) US Court of Appeals for the District of Columbia)

"We recognize, as appellants urge, the undisputed power of the jury to acquit, *even if its verdict is contrary to the law as given by the judge, and contrary to the evidence.* This is a power that must exist as long as we adhere to the general verdict in criminal cases, for the courts cannot search the minds of the jurors to find the basis upon which they judge. If the jury feels that the law under which the defendant is accused, is unjust, or that exigent circumstances justified the actions of the accused, *or for any reason which appeals to their logic of passion, the jury has the power to acquit, and the courts must abide by that decision.*" (US vs Moylan, 417 F 2d 1002, 1006 (1969) [emphasis added])

"the pages of history shine on instances of the jury's exercise of its prerogative to disregard uncontradicted evidence and instructions of the judge." (United States v. Dougherty, 473 F.2d 1113, 1130 (D.C. Cir. 1972))

"Jurors should acquit, even against the judge's instruction...if exercising their judgement with discretion and honesty they have a clear conviction that the charge of the court is wrong." (Alexander Hamilton, 1804)

"The judge cannot direct a verdict it is true, and the jury has the power to bring in a verdict in the teeth of both law and facts." (Mr. Justice Holmes, for the majority in Horning v. District of Columbia, 254 U.S. 135, 138 (1920))

Martial Law

Everything changes under Martial Law, because Martial law supersedes and replaces common law:

"statutes have been passed extending the courts of admiralty and vice-admiralty far beyond their ancient limits for depriving us the accustomed and inestimable privilege of trial by jury, in cases affecting both life and property . . . *to supersede the course of common law and instead thereof to publish and order the use and exercise of the law martial.*" (Causes and Necessity of Taking Up Arms (1775) [emphasis added])

"What is called 'proclaiming martial law' is no law at all; but merely for the sake of public safety, in circumstances of great emergency, setting aside all law, and acting under military power; a proceeding which requires to be followed by an act of indemnity when the disturbances are at an end." (8 Atty. Gen. Op. 365, 367, February 3, 1857)

Which is why they have to pass statutes for common law offenses like murder and assault:

"There are no common law offenses against the United States. Only those acts which Congress has forbidden, with penalties for disobedience of its command, are crimes." (United States v. Hudson & Goodwin, 11 U.S. (7th Cr.) 32 (1812); United States v. Coolidge, 14 U.S. (1 Wheat.) 415 (1816); United States v. Britton, 108 U.S. 199, 206 (1883); United States v. Eaton, 144 U.S. 677, 687 (1892))

"Under Texas law, no act or omission is a crime unless made so by statute. Dawson v. Vance, 329 F.Supp. 1320, (D.C.Tex. 1971). The Legislature may create an offense and in same enactment, provide exceptions to its application." (Williams v. State, 176 SW2d 177, Tex.Cr.App., 1943)

"A. *All common law offenses and affirmative defenses are abolished.* No conduct or omission constitutes an offense or an affirmative defense unless it is an offense or an affirmative defense under this title or under another statute or ordinance." (Arizona Revised Statutes 13-103. Abolition of common law offenses and affirmative defenses; definition [emphasis added])

And all statutes are edicts under martial law:
"Martial Law in a hostile country consists in the suspension, by the occupying military authority, of the criminal and civil law, and of the domestic administration and government in the occupied place or territory, and in the substitution of military rule and force for the same, *as well as in the dictation of general laws, as far as military necessity requires this suspension, substitution, or dictation.*

The commander of the forces may proclaim that the administration of all civil and penal law shall continue either wholly or in part, as in times of peace, unless otherwise ordered by the military authority." (Article 3, General Orders 100 (The Lieber Code)

Under the Law-Martial, only the criminal jurisdiction of a military court is the recognized law. But as Article Three of the Constitution says, "the civil courts can continue wholly or in part as long as the civil jurisdiction does not violate the Military orders laid down by the Commander in Chief or one of his Commanders." By this means a military venue, jurisdiction, and authority are imposed upon the occupied populace under disguise of the ordinary civil courts and officers of the occupied district or region, because the so-called civil authorities in an occupied district, or region, only act at the pleasure of a military authority.

It should also be noted here that the several state legislatures, county boards of commissioners, and city councils are constantly legislating to please the edicts of the federal government (the occupying force) and that their legislation, in this sense, is not an exercise of state sovereignty, but instead, a compliance with edicts of the military force which occupies the several States and consequently are edicts of Martial Law Rule. (The Non-Ratification of the Fourteenth Amendment by Judge A.H. Ellett, Utah Supreme Court, Dyett v Turner, 439 P2d 266 @ 269, 20 U2d 403 [1968] [emphasis added])

When I was first introduced to this, I was told that there were only four law schools on the planet that teach law, and they were all located in London. They teach eight hundred years of jury trial decisions in England. All of the rest of the schools that are supposed to teach law, actually teach procedure (jurisprudence):

> jurisprudence, n.1. Originally (in the 18th century), the study of the first principles of the law of nature, the civil law, and the law of nations. . . . . 2. More modernly, the study of the general or fundamental elements of a particular legal system, as opposed to its practical and concrete details. 3. The study of legal systems in general. 4. Judicial precedents considered collectively. 5. In German literature, the whole of legal knowledge. 6. A system, body, or division of law. 7. CASELAW." (*Black's Law Dictionary*, 8th Edition, page 2499)

Summary

All law comes from we the people. Court rulings are just comparing current cases with previous jury trial decisions, and they also make rulings on statutes, which change and which is why court precedents can be overruled, but the underlying law always remains the same because all law comes from the people and no court has anything to say about that, and they won't even try.

3

THE CIVIL WAR

It is well established that the Union army invaded the Confederacy during the US Civil War and eventually put all of the Southern states under martial law, as found in General Order No. 100 (The Lieber Code of April 24, 1863):

> "Instructions for the Government of Armies of the United States in the Field, prepared by Francis Lieber, LL.D., Originally Issued as General Orders No. 100, Adjutant General's Office, 1863, Washington 1898: Government Printing Office." (Title Page, General Orders No. 100, United States War Department Instructions for the Government of Armies of the United States in the Field / Lieber. G.P.O, Washington, 1863, a.k.a., the Lieber Code)

> "Martial Law is the immediate and direct effect and consequence of occupation or conquest. The presence of a hostile army proclaims its Martial Law." (Article 1, General Orders 100 (The Lieber Code) [emphasis added])

"Territory is considered occupied when it is actually placed under the authority of the hostile army." (Law and Customs of War on Land (Hague IV), Article 42)

The *only* way that martial law ends is by specific mention in a peace treaty or by special proclamation by the commander in chief: "Martial Law does not cease during the hostile occupation, *except by special proclamation, ordered by the commander in chief,* or by special mention in the *treaty of peace* concluding the war." (Article 2, General Orders 100 (The Lieber Code) [emphasis added])

There was no treaty of peace with the Confederacy, or any of the Southern states, and there have been no special proclamations ending the martial law by the President of the United States (the commander in chief). Therefore, martial law continues to this day.

MARTIAL LAW

There are three kinds of martial law.

1. Full Martial Law
   a. Declaration of martial law is issued

   b. Troops put on the streets

   c. Used only during war time

   d. Used on foreign country or when actually invaded by foreign power or to put down an armed rebellion

2. Martial Law Proper
   a. Law of the armed forces

   b. When a captain tells a private what to do

   c. Enforced by courts-martial

3. Martial Law Rule
   a. Law of *necessity* and *emergency*

   b. Allows the domestic use of martial law powers

   c. Used during times of peace

Ex Parte Milligan 4 Wall (71 U.S.) 2, 18 L.Ed. 281, p 302, The Non-Ratification of the Fourteenth Amendment by Judge A.H. Ellett, Utah Supreme Court, Dyett v Turner, 439 P2d 266 @ 269, 20 U2d 403 [1968]

"Necessity is the plea for every infringement of human freedom. It is the argument of tyrants; it is the creed of slaves." (William Pitt, the Younger)[2]

"Martial Law affects chiefly the police" and therefore all police are military police:

"Martial Law affects chiefly the police and collection of public revenue and taxes, whether imposed by the expelled government or by the invader, and refers mainly to the support and efficiency of the army, its safety, and the safety of its operations." (Article 10, General Orders 100 (The Lieber Code))

Martial Law affects *only* "subjects of the enemy" and aliens:

"Martial Law extends to property, and to persons, whether they are subjects of the enemy or aliens to that government." (Article 7, General Orders 100 (The Lieber Code))

And subjects are government employees and corporations, and anything created by the government:

"All subjects over which the sovereign power of the state extends are objects of taxation, but those over which it does not extend are exempt from taxation. This proposition may also be pronounced as self-evident. The sovereignty of the state extends to everything which exists by its authority or its permission." (McCullough v Maryland, 17 U.S. [4 Wheat] 316 (1819). [emphasis added])

---

2   Speech in the House of Commons, November 18, 1783.

Subjects are privileged. (The privilege is a contract):

> "*The rights of sovereignty extend to all persons and things,
> not privileged that are within the territory.* They extend to
> all *strangers resident* therein; not only to those who are
> naturalized, and to those who are domiciled therein, having
> taken up their abode with the intention of permanent
> residence, but also to those whose residence is transitory. All
> *strangers* are under the protection of the sovereign while they
> are within his territory and owe a temporary allegiance in
> return for that protection." (Carlisle v United States 83 U.S.
> 147, 154 (1873))

> "Let a State be considered as subordinate to the People: But
> let everything else be subordinate to the State." (Chisholm v
> Georgia, 2 Dall 419 at page 455)

This all comes from the Bible, and a stranger is what is now called
an alien:

> "And if a *stranger* sojourn with thee in your land, ye shall
> not vex him. But the *stranger* that dwelleth with you shall be
> unto you as one born among you, and thou shalt love him
> as thyself; for ye were *strangers* in the land of Egypt: I am the
> LORD your God." (Leviticus 19: 33-34 [emphasis added])

Subjects are subject to the regulations and therefore property and
slaves are property:

> "The Congress shall have power to dispose of and make all
> needful rules and regulations respecting the.... other property
> belonging to the United States." (Article 4, Section 3, Clause
> 2, US Constitution)

And this is true in all nations

> "Section 2 Definitions (1) In this Act, *owned means, subject to the regulations.*" (Canadian Ownership and Control Determination Act [emphasis added])

Edicts under Martial Law

Under Martial Law all statutes, codes, rules, and regulations are edicts under a military dictatorship

---

EXECUTIVE ORDER = EDICTS UNDER MARTIAL LAW
Executive Order 13603
by Barak Obama

- At a time of the presidents choosing, the federal government may take over
- all forms of energy
- all forms of civil transportation
- all useable water from all sources
- all commodities and products that are capable of being ingested by either human beings or animals
- health resources – drugs, biological products, medical devices, materials, facilities, health supplies, services

---

"Martial Law in a hostile country consists in the suspension, by the occupying military authority, of the criminal and civil law, and of the domestic administration and government in the occupied place or territory, and in the substitution of military rule and force for the same, *as well as in the dictation of general laws, as far as military necessity requires this suspension, substitution, or dictation.*

The commander of the forces may proclaim that the administration of all civil and penal law shall continue either wholly or in part, as in times of peace, unless otherwise ordered by the military authority." (Article 3, General Orders 100 (The Lieber Code) [emphasis added])

"NOTE: Under the Law-Martial, only the criminal jurisdiction of a Military Court is the recognized law. But as Article Three says, "the civil courts can continue wholly or in part as long as the civil jurisdiction does not violate the Military orders laid down by the Commander in Chief or one of his Commanders." By this means; a military venue, jurisdiction, and authority are imposed upon the occupied populace under disguise of the ordinary civil courts and officers of the occupied district or region, because the so-called civil authorities in an occupied district, or region, only act at the pleasure of a military authority.

It should also be noted here that the several State Legislatures, County Boards of Commissioners, and City Councils, are constantly legislating to please the edicts of the federal government (the occupying force) and that their legislation, in this sense, is not an exercise of State sovereignty, but instead, a compliance with edicts of the military force which occupies the several States and consequently are edicts of Martial Law Rule."

(The Non-Ratification of the Fourteenth Amendment by Judge A.H. Ellett, Utah Supreme Court, Dyett v Turner, 439 P2d 266 @ 269, 20 U2d 403 [1968] [emphasis added])

All statutes are martial law statutes and apply to subjects only:

"Military jurisdiction is of two kinds: First, that which is conferred and defined by statute; second, that which is derived from the common law of war. Military offenses under the statute law must be tried in the manner therein directed; but military offenses which do not come within the statute must be tried and punished under the common law of war. The character of the courts which exercise these jurisdictions depends upon the local laws of each particular country.

In the armies of the United States the first is exercised by courts-martial, while cases which do not come within the "Rules and Articles of War," or the jurisdiction conferred by statute on courts-martial, are tried by military commissions." (Article 13, General Orders 100 (The Lieber Code),)

No Article 3 Courts

There are no Article III courts (state or federal) which are replaced by military commissioners for statutory matters and general courts-martial for breached of the laws and customs of war, which is consistent with what the courts (military commissioners elsewhere) are saying:

"When acting to enforce a statute and its subsequent amendments to the present date, the judge of the municipal court is acting as an administrative officer and *not in a judicial capacity*; courts administrating or enforcing statutes *do not act judicially*, but merely ministerially . . . but *merely act as an extension as an agent for the involved agency*--but only in a 'ministerial' and not a 'discretionary capacity.'" (Thompson v. Smith, 154 S.E. 579, 583; Keller v. P.E., 261 US 428; F.R.C. v. G.E., 281, U.S. 464 [emphasis added])

"It is the accepted rule, not only in state courts, but, of the federal courts as well, that when a judge is enforcing administrative law they are described as mere 'extensions of the administrative agency for superior reviewing purposes' as a ministerial clerk for an agency." (30 Cal 596; 167 Cal 762)

"Judges who become involved in enforcement of mere statutes (civil or criminal in nature and otherwise), act as mere "clerks" of the involved agency..." K.C. Davis, ADMIN. LAW, Ch. 1 (CTP. West's 1965 Ed.)

When a clerk (masquerading as judge) is an agent for the administrative agency, it is always a kangaroo court and a bill of pains and penalties because it is a nonjudicial proceeding.

Let's define our terms. A "kangaroo court" is "a sham legal proceeding in which a person's rights are totally disregarded and in which the result is a foregone conclusion because of the bias of the court or other tribunal" (*Blacks Law Dictionary*, 6th Edition, page 868).

A "bill of attainder" is a legislative act, no matter what their form, that applies either to named individuals or to easily ascertainable members of a group in such a way as to inflict punishment on them without a judicial trial.[3]

A "bill of pains and penalties" is a legislative act that, though similar to a bill of attainder, prescribes punishment less severe than capital punishment. Bills of pains and penalties are included within the U.S. Constitution's ban on bills of attainder.[4]

So when and a bought-and-paid-for) clerk enforcing administrative law and pretending to be a judge, fails to have the authority to do anything judicial, like issuing orders or warrants, and if any clerk pretending to be a judge attempts to do anything judicial, it is a fraud and a nullity:

> "Ministerial officers are incompetent to receive grants of judicial power from the legislature, *their acts in attempting to exercise such powers are necessarily nullities.*" (Burns v. Sup., Ct., SF, 140 Cal. 1 [emphasis added])

> "Where there is no jurisdiction there is no judge; the proceeding is as nothing. Such has been the law from the days of the Marshalsea, 10 Coke 68; also Bradley v. Fisher, 13 Wall 335,351." (Manning v. Ketcham, 58 F.2d 948)

Void Judgments

All orders, judgments, or warrants issued by any clerk masquerading as a judge are void:

---

3   United States v. Brown, 381 U.S. 437, 448-49, 85 S. Ct. 1707, 1715, 14 L.Ed. 484, 492; United States v. Lovett, 328 U. S. 303, 315, 66 S.Ct. 1073, 1079, 90 L.Ed. 1252

4   U.S. Const. art I, § 9. [Cases: Constitutional Law 82.5. C.J.S. Constitutional Law §§ 429–431.]" Blacks Law Dictionary, 8th Edition, page 499

"A void judgment is one which, from its inception, was a complete nullity and without legal effect." (Lubben v. Selective Service System Local Bd. No. 27, 453 F.2d 645, 14 A.L.R. Fed. 298 (C.A. 1 Mass. 1972). Hobbs v. U.S. Office of Personnel Management, 485 F.Supp. 456 (M.D. Fla. 1980))

"A void judgment is one which has no legal force or effect whatever, it is an absolute nullity, its invalidity may be asserted by any person whose rights are affected at any time and at any place and it need not be attacked directly but may be attacked collaterally whenever and wherever it is interposed." (City of Lufkin v. McVicker, 510 S.W. 2d 141 (Tex. Civ. App. – Beaumont 1973))

"A void judgment, insofar as it purports to be pronouncement of court, is an absolute nullity" Thompson v. Thompson, 238 S.W.2d 218 (Tex.Civ.App. – Waco 1951)

"Void order may be attacked, either directly or collaterally, at any time" (In re Estate of Steinfield, 630 N.E.2d 801, certiorari denied. See also Steinfeld v. Hoddick, 513 U.S. 809, (Ill. 1994))

"A void judgment is one which, from its inception, is and forever continues to be absolutely null, without legal efficacy, ineffectual to bind the parties or to support a right, of no legal force and effect whatever, and incapable of enforcement in any manner or to any degree." (Loyd v. Director, Dept. of Public Safety, 480 So. 2d 577 (Ala. Civ. App. 1985))

"Not every action by any judge is in exercise of his judicial function. It is not a judicial function for a Judge to commit an intentional tort even though the tort occurs in the Courthouse, when a judge acts as a Trespasser of the Law, when a judge does not follow the law, the judge loses subject matter jurisdiction and The Judge's orders are void, of no legal force or effect!" (Yates Vs. Village of Hoffman Estates, Illinois, 209 F.Supp. 757 (N.D. Ill. 1962))

"Brutum fulmen" is an   "empty noise; an empty threat. A judgment void upon its face which is in legal effect no judgment at all, and by which no rights are divested, and from which none can be obtained; and neither binds nor bars anyone. (Dollert v. Pratt-Hewitt Oil Corporation, Tex.Civ. Appl, 179 S.W.2d 346, 348. *See also* Corpus Juris Secundum, "Judgments" §§ 499, 512 546, 549. *Black's Law Dictionary*, 4th Edition).

And all judges operating as bought-and-paid-for clerks are operating in their private capacity and have walked away from their immunity and are personally liable:

"An officer who acts in violation of the Constitution ceases to represent the government". Brookfield Const. Co. v. Stewart, 284 F. Supp. 94

"Officers of the court have no immunity, when violating a constitutional right, for they are deemed to know the law." Owens v Independence 100 S.C.T. 1398 (Ezra 7:23-26)

"...where any state proceeds against a private individual in a judicial forum it is well settled that the state, county, municipality, etc. waives any immunity to counters, cross claims and complaints, by direct or collateral means regarding the matters involved." Luckenback v. The Thekla, 295 F 1020, 226 Us 328; Lyders v. Lund, 32 F2d 308

"Judge loses his absolute immunity from damage actions only when he acts in clear absence of all jurisdiction or performance of an act which is not judicial in nature." Schucker v. Rockwood, 846 F.2d 1202

"In arriving at our decision in this matter we do not depart in any way from our holding in Huendling v. Jensen that the doctrine of judicial immunity extends to courts of limited jurisdiction. But, when a minor magistrate acts wholly without jurisdiction, civil liability attaches for his malicious and corrupt abuse of process and his willful and malicious oppression of any person under the pretense of acting in his official capacity. See Huendling v. Jensen, 168 N.W.2d at 749 and authorities cited."188 N.W.2d 294; 1971 Iowa Sup. LEXIS 863; 64 A.L.R.3d 1242

And they accept all liability for their actions, which is why they are so adamant about operating in their private capacity as revenue officers, by demanding the filing fee extortion because a portion of the filing fee pays for the errors and omissions insurance for the (bought and paid for) Clerk masquerading as a Judge, and once their extortion is paid, it converts a court case into a commercial transaction (because the outcome is insured), and they can sit there and play stupid, and it nullifies their oath of office because the court case becomes nothing more than a commercial transaction.

All of the Civil war States are under a military occupation (dictatorship) that continues to this day. All of the Treaty of Hidalgo States are under a military occupation (dictatorship) that continues to this day.

Lincoln was a BAR member, as described herein.

When the southern states walked out of Congress in 1861, Congress ceased to have a quorum to conduct business and Lincoln ordered Congress to re-convene under his martial law authority.

When the Supreme Court of the United States made some rulings that Lincoln failed to like, he sent military troops to the Supreme Court and to this day, the Supreme Court of the United States operates under executive authority,

> "Process; Mandates - All process of this Court issues in the name of the President of the United States." Rule 45.1 US Supreme Court Rules of Procedure, [emphasis added]

therefore, there is no separation of powers, and Congress and the Supreme Court all operate under executive authority, and the UNITED STATES OF AMERICA is under a full military dictatorship

> "Martial Law in a hostile country consists in the suspension, by the occupying military authority, of the criminal and civil law, and of the domestic administration and government in the occupied place or territory, and in the substitution

of military rule and force for the same, <u>as well as in the dictation of general laws, as far as military necessity requires this suspension, substitution, or dictation.</u>

The commander of the forces may proclaim that the administration of all civil and penal law shall continue either wholly or in part, as in times of peace, unless otherwise ordered by the military authority." Article 3, General Orders 100 (The Lieber Code) [emphasis added]

It is also talked about in the Opinion of the US Attorney General about the Reconstruction Acts, that reverses the principle that the military be subordinate to the civil authority

"There can be no doubt as to the rule of construction according to which we must interpret this grant of power. It is a grant of power to military authority, over civil rights and citizens, in time of peace. <u>It is a new jurisdiction, never granted before, by which, in certain particulars and for certain purposes, the established principle that the military shall be subordinate to the civil authority is reversed.</u>" 12 US Op Atty Gen 182 page 4 [emphasis added]

For those who may remember, it was generally viewed that Obama Care was unconstitutional until Obama came out publicly railing against the Courts, and the Courts fell right into line with what they were being required to do.

Two National Governments

In 1871 Congress created an unconstitutional municipal corporation called UNITED STATES OF AMERICA , to operate as government of the District of Columbia (as an edict under martial law)

> "Two national governments exist, one to be maintained under the Constitution, with all its restrictions, the other to be maintained by Congress outside and independently of that instrument" Dissenting opinion of Justice Marshall Harlan. Downes v. Bidwell, 182 U.S. 244 (1901)

And the unconstitutional municipal corporation fails to be "The United States of America" "The Stile of this Confederacy shall be; "The United States of America"." Article 1, Articles of Confederation, (1781) [emphasis added]and in 1845 the **"State of Texas"** is alleged to have joined both the Confederacy and the Union

> "Be it enacted by the Senate and House of Representatives of the United States of America in Congress assembled, That all the laws of the United States are hereby declared to extend to and over, and to have full force and effect within, the State of Texas, admitted at the present session of Congress *into the Confederacy and Union* of the United States." 9 Stat 1 [emphasis added]

> which fails to be *"The State of Texas"* (a unconstitutional municipal corporation)

> "There shall be a Seal of the State which shall be kept by the Secretary of State, and used by him officially under the

direction of the Governor. The Seal of the State shall be a star of five points encircled by olive and live oak branches, and the words *"The State of Texas."* Section 19. Seal of State, Texas Constitution [emphasis added]

Figure 4 – Indiana and Company

"There has been created a fictional federal State (of) xxxxxx within a State. See Howard v. Sinking Fund of Louisville, 344 U.S. 624, 73 S.Ct. 465, 476, 97 L.Ed. 617 (1953);" Schwarts v. O'Hara TP School District, 100 A 2d. 621, 625, 375, Pa. 440 and nobody has any allegiance to an unconstitutional Roman Cult municipal corporation.

> " 'Civil Law,' 'Roman Law,' and 'Roman Civil Law' are convertible phrases, meaning the same system of jurisprudence. That rule of action which every particular nation, commonwealth, or city has established peculiarly for itself; *more properly called "municipal" law*, to distinguish it from the "law of nature," and from international law. See Bowyer, Mod. Civil Law, 19; Sevier v. Riley, 189 Cal. 170, 244 P. 323, 325" (*Black's Law Dictionary*, Revised 4th Edition, page 312 [emphasis added])

But all government officials have an oath of office to the trust called *"The United States of America"* and the trust called *"State of Texas"* As spelled out clearly in the case of Luther v. Borden, the governments are *"trustees* acting under derived authority and have no power to delegate what is not delegated to them. But *the people*, as the original fountain *might take away what they have delegated and entrust* to whom they please. . . . The sovereignty in every state resides in the people of the state and they may alter and change their form of government at their own pleasure" (Luther v. Borden, 48 US 1, 12 Led 581). For there is no such thing as "power of inherent Sovereignty in the government of the United States. It is a government of delegated powers, supreme within its prescribed sphere but powerless outside of it. In this country sovereignty resides in the People, and Congress can exercise no power which they have not, *by their Constitution entrusted to it*; All else is withheld" (Julliard v Greenman 110 U.S. 421 at p 467 [emphasis added]).

Unconstitutional Acts

Because of the martial law dictatorship, elite leaders have been very busy with unconstitutional things:

Fourteenth Amendment Is Unconstitutional

The so-called Fourteenth Amendment is unconstitutional because an amendment is very limited and specific. It should include only "the power to amend any section in such a manner that such Amendment, if approved, would be complete within itself, relate to one subject and not substantially affect any other section of Articles of the Constitution or require further Amendments to the Constitution to accomplish its purpose" (Adams v Gunter 238 So.2d 824 (Fla. 1970)).

The so-called Fourteenth Amendment is actually a revision changing many things in the Constitution for the United States of America:

> "The wide and diverse range of subject matters proposed to be voted upon, and the *revisional effect* which it would necessarily have on our basic plan of government. *The proposal is offered as a single amendment but it obviously is multifarious.* It does not give the people an opportunity to express approval or disapproval severally as to each major change suggested." (McFadden v Jordan, 196 P.2d 787)

For example it converts citizenship into the opposite of what the founding fathers intended. "While the Fourteenth Amendment does not create a national citizenship, it has the effect of making that citizenship "paramount and dominant" instead of "derivative and dependent" upon state citizenship" (Colgate v Harvey 296 US 404 at p 427).

The unconstitutional Fourteenth Amendment "reversed and annulled the original policy of the constitution" (United States v. Rhodes, 27 Federal Cases, 785, 794). It solemnly established the fictitious debt from forced loans:

> "*The forced loans of 1862 and 1863*, in the form of legal tender notes, were vital forces in the struggle for national supremacy. They formed a part of the public debt of the United States, the validity of which is *solemnly established by the Fourteenth Amendment to the Constitution.*" (Julliard v. Greenman, 110 US 432 [emphasis added])

> "This rule does not interfere with the right of the victorious invader to tax the people or their property, *to levy forced loans*, to billet soldiers, or to appropriate property, especially houses, lands, boats or ships, and churches, for temporary and military uses." (Article 37, General Orders 100 (The Lieber Code) [emphasis added])

And this rogue amendment makes many other changes:

> "It violates the Preamble, which defines the whole intent of all powers granted to Congress, by introducing a foreign member into the sovereign body.

"It is an ex post facto law punishing Southerners in many ways for acts not necessarily illegal at the time of their commission.

"It is a bill of attainder (in its lesser form a bill of pains and penalties) depriving all southern slave holders of property without trial.

"It deprived Southerners of property by unreasonable seizure and without just compensation, bringing Congress beyond limitations set out by the Fourth and Fifth Articles in Amendment (Bill of Rights).

"It lays prohibitions upon the States beyond those known to the original Constitution of the United States and makes inroads upon the Constitutions of the several States, encroaching upon sovereignty belonging to the people of the several States which is prohibited by the Tenth Article in Amendment (Bill of Rights).

"It created purely legislative tribunals without respect to the separation of powers.

"It extended Congress' martial law power, allowing the emission of bills of credit." (The Non-Ratification of the Fourteenth Amendment by Judge A.H. Ellett, Utah Supreme Court, Dyett v Turner, 439 P2d 266 @ 269, 20 U2d 403 [1968]).

The ratification of the so-called Fourteenth Amendment failed as the dissenting opinion in State v. Phillips asserted that "The

Fourteenth Amendment is a part of the Constitution of the United States. While this same assertion has been made by the United States Supreme Court, that court has never held that the amendment was legally adopted. I cannot believe that any court, in full possession of its faculties could honestly hold that the amendment was properly approved and adopted" (State v Phillips 540 Pac. Rep.2d 936). All of which and more is confirmed by the *Congressional Record* on June 13, 1867, pages 15642 – 15646:

THE 14TH AMENDMENT IS UNCONSTITUTIONAL

The purported Fourteenth Amendment to the United States Constitution is and should be held to be ineffective, invalid, null, void, and unconstitutional for the following reasons:

1. The Joint Resolution proposing said Amendment was not submitted to or adopted by a Constitutional Congress, Article I, Section 3, and Article V of the U.S. Constitution.
2. The Joint Resolution was not submitted to the President for his approval. Article I, Section 7.
3. The proposed 14th Amendment was rejected by more than one-fourth of all the States in the Union. Article V.

I. THE UNCONSTITUTIONAL CONGRESS

The U.S. Constitution provides:

Article I, Section 3, "The Senate of the United States shall be composed of two Senators from each State…"

Article V provides: "No State, without its consent, shall be deprived of its equal suffrage in the Senate."

The fact that 23 Senators had been unlawfully excluded from the U.S. senate, in order to secure the two-thirds vote for adoption of the Joint Resolution proposing the 14th Amendment is shown by Resolutions of protest adopted by the following State Legislatures as follows:

The New Jersey Legislature by Resolution of March 27, 1868, protested as follows:

"The said proposed amendment not having yet received the assent of three-fourths of the states, which is necessary to make it valid, the natural and constitutional right of this state to withdraw its assent is undeniable…"

The Alabama Legislature protested against being deprived of representation in the Senate of the U.S. Congress (Alabama House Journal 1866, pp. 210-213)

The Texas Legislature by Resolution on October 15, 1866, protested….

The Arkansas Legislature, by Resolution on December 17, 1866, protested…

The Georgia Legislature, by Resolution on November 9, 1866, protested....

The Florida Legislature, by Resolution of December, 1866, protested.....

The South Carolina Legislature by Resolution of November 27, 1866, protested....

The North Carolina Legislature protested by Resolution of December 6, 1866,....

II. JOINT RESOLUTION INEFFECTIVE

Article I, Section 7 provides that not only every bill which shall have been passed by the House of Representatives and the Senate of the United States Congress, but that:

"Every order, resolution, or vote to which the concurrence of the Senate and House of Representatives may be necessary (except on a question of adjournment) shall be presented to the President of the United States; and before the same shall take effect, shall be approved by him, or being disapproved by him shall be repassed by two-thirds of the Senate and House of Representatives, according to the rules and limitations prescribed in the case of a bill."

The Joint Resolution proposing the 14th Amendment was never presented to the President of the United States for his approval, as President Andrew Johnson states in his message on June 22, 1866. (Senate Journal 39th Congress, 1st Session p. 563, and House Journal p. 889) Therefore the Joint Resolution did not take effect.

III. PROPOSED AMENDMENT NEVER RATIFIED BY THREE-FOURTHS OF THE STATES

Pretermitting the ineffectiveness of said resolution, as above, fifteen (15) States out of the then thirty-seven (37) States of the Union rejected the proposed 14th Amendment between the date of its submission to the States by the Secretary of State on June 16, 1866 and March 24, 1868, thereby further nullifying said resolution and making it impossible for its ratification by the constitutionally required three-fourths of such States, as shown by the rejections thereof by the Legislatures of the following states:

Texas rejected the 14th Amendment on October 27, 1866 (House Journal 1866 pp. 578-584 – Senate Journal 1866, p. 471.)

Georgia rejected the 14th Amendment on November 9, 1866 (House Journal 1866 pp. 68 – Senate Journal 1866, p. 72.)

Florida rejected the 14th Amendment on December 6, 1866 (House Journal 1866 p. 76 – Senate Journal 1866, p. 8.)

Alabama rejected the 14th Amendment on December 7, 1866 (House Journal 1866 pp. 210-213 – Senate Journal 1866, p. 183.)

North Carolina rejected the 14th Amendment on December 14, 1866 (House Journal 1866-1867 pp. 183 – Senate Journal 1866-1867, p. 138.)

Arkansas rejected the 14th Amendment on December 17, 1866 (House Journal 1866 pp. 288-291 – Senate Journal 1866, p. 262.)

South Carolina rejected the 14th Amendment on December 20, 1866 (House Journal 1866 pp. 284 – Senate Journal 1866, p. 230.)

Kentucky rejected the 14th Amendment on January 8, 1867 (House Journal 1867 p. 60 – Senate Journal 1867, p. 62.)

Virginia rejected the 14th Amendment on January 9, 1867 (House Journal 1866-1867 p. 108 – Senate Journal 1866-1867, p. 101.)

Louisiana rejected the 14th Amendment on February 6, 1867 (McPherson, Reconstruction, p. 194 – Annual Encyclopedia, p. 452.)

Delaware rejected the 14th Amendment on February 7, 1867 (House Journal 1867 pp. 223 – Senate Journal 1867, p. 176.)

Maryland rejected the 14th Amendment on March 23, 1867 (House Journal 1867 pp. 1141 – Senate Journal 1867, p. 808.)

Mississippi rejected the 14th Amendment on January 31, 1867 (McPherson, Reconstruction, p. 194.)

Ohio rejected the 14th Amendment on January 15, 1868 (House Journal 1868 pp. 44-50 – Senate Journal 1868, pp. 33-38.)

New Jersey rejected the 14th Amendment on March 24, 1868 (Minutes of the Assembly 1868 p. 743 – Senate Journal 1868, p. 356.)

Fourteenth Amendment Was Forced

In reprisal for some of the southern states failing to ratify the so-called Fourteenth Amendment Congress passed

"WHEREAS no legal State governments or adequate protection for life or property now exists in the rebel States of Virginia, North Carolina, South Carolina, Georgia, Mississippi, Alabama, Louisiana, Florida, Texas, and Arkansas; and whereas it is necessary that peace and good order should be enforced in said States until loyal and republican State governments can be legally established." (Preamble to Chap CLIII – An Act to provide for the more efficient Government of the Rebel States, 14 Stat. 428)

That required the same southern states that failed to ratify the so-called Fourteenth Amendment to ratify the so-called Fourteenth Amendment as a condition to be readmitted to representation in Congress:

"Sec. 5......and Congress shall have approved the same, *and when said State, by a vote of its legislature elected under said constitution, shall have adopted the amendment to the Constitution of the United States, proposed by the Thirty-ninth Congress, and known as article fourteen,* and when said article shall have become a part of the Constitution of the United States, said State shall be declared entitled to representation in Congress, and senators and representatives shall be admitted therefrom on their taking the oath prescribed by law, and then and thereafter the preceding sections of this act shall be inoperative in said State: *Provided That no person excluded from the privilege of holding office by said proposed amendment to the Constitution of the United States, shall be eligible to election as a member of the convention* to frame a constitution for any of said rebel States, nor shall any such person vote for members of such convention." (An Act to provide for the more efficient Government of the Rebel States, 14 Stat. 428)

This prohibited anyone who failed to be a Fourteenth Amendment citizen from participating, which is further evidence that it is for the

Roman cult's unconstitutional municipal corporation *only*, and they overrode the President's veto.

IN THE HOUSE OP REPRESENTATIVES,
March 2, 1867.

The President of the United States having returned to the House of Representatives, in which it originated, the bill entitled a "An act to provide for the more efficient government of the rebel States," with his objections thereto, the House of Representatives proceeded, in pursuance of the Constitution, to reconsider the same; and Resolved, That the said bill do pass, two thirds of the House of Representatives agreeing to pass the same .

Attest :
EDWD. McPHERSON,
Clerk of H. R. U. S.

IN SENATE OF THE UNITED STATES,
March 2, 1867.

The Senate having proceeded, in pursuance of the Constitution, to reconsider the bill entitled " An act to provide for the more efficient government of the rebel States," returned to the House of Representatives by the President of the United States, with his objections, and sent by the House of Representatives to the Senate, with the message of the President returning the bill:

Resolved, That the bill do pass, two thirds of the Senate agreeing to pass the same.

Attest :

J. W. FORNEY,

Secretary of the Senate.

[An Act to provide for the more efficient Government of the Rebel States, 14 Stat. 428]

This reversed the principle that the military authority should be subordinate to the civil power. "There can be no doubt as to the rule of construction according to which we must interpret this grant of power. It is a grant of power to military authority, over civil rights and citizens, in time of peace. *It is a new jurisdiction, never granted before, by which, in certain particulars and for certain purposes, the established principle that the military shall be subordinate to the civil authority is reversed.*" (12 US Op Atty Gen 182 page 4 [emphasis added])

The Vanishing Thirteenth Amendment

They made disappear the true Article Thirteen in the Constitution, which says

"If any citizen of the United States shall accept, claim, receive, or retain any title of nobility or honor, or shall, without the consent of congress, accept and retain any present, pension, office, or emolument of any kind whatever, from any emperor, king, prince, or foreign power, such person shall cease to be a citizen of the United States, and shall be incapable of holding any office of trust or profit under them, or either of them."

The Martial Law Amendments

The current Thirteenth, Fourteenth, and Fifteenth Amendments were martial law amendments for the slaves:

"This court declared in the Slaughter-House cases that the Fourteenth Amendment as well as the Thirteenth and Fifteenth were adopted to protect the Negroes in their freedom." (Madden v. Kentucky 309 US 83 (1940))

"The thirteenth, fourteenth, and fifteenth amendments were designed mainly for the protection of the newly emancipated negroes." (United States v. Anthony, 24 Fed. Cas. 829, Case No. 14,459)

"After the adoption of the 14th Amendment, a bill which became the first Civil Rights Act was introduced in the 39th Congress, the major purpose of which was to secure to the recently freed Negroes all the civil rights secured to white men. . . . (N)one other than citizens of the United States were within the provisions of the Act." (Hague v. C. I. O., 307 U. S. 496, 509)

But the truth of the matter is they were used to enslave everybody under martial law by way of a so-called contract:

"No white person born within the limits of the United States and subject to their jurisdiction, or born without those limits and subsequently naturalized under their laws, owes his status of citizenship to the recent amendments to the Federal Constitution." (Van Valkenburg v. Brown, 43 Cal 43)

All of this is further evidence that the current Thirteenth Amendment and all subsequent so-called amendments apply *only* in the District of Columbia and the territories, and are for the unconstitutional municipal corporation *only:*

"The term 'special maritime and territorial jurisdiction of the United States,' as used in this title, includes:

(1) The high seas, any other waters within the admiralty and maritime jurisdiction of the United States and out of the jurisdiction of any particular State, and <u>any vessel belonging in whole or in part to the United States or any citizen thereof, or to any corporation created by or under the laws of the United States, or of any State, Territory, District, or possession thereof, when such vessel is within the admiralty and maritime jurisdiction of the United States</u> and out of the jurisdiction of any particular State." 18 USC § 7 Special maritime and territorial jurisdiction of the United States defined (edict under martial law)

"And it may embrace also the vehicles and persons engaged in carrying it on. It would be in the power of Congress to confer admiralty jurisdiction upon its courts, over the cars engaged in transporting passengers or merchandise from one State to another, and over the persons engaged in conducting them, and deny to the parties the trial by jury." (Propeller Genessee Chief et al. v. Fitzhugh et al. 12 How. 443 (U.S. 1851))

"This power [of admiralty jurisdiction] is as extensive upon land as upon water. The Constitution makes no distinction in that respect. And if the admiralty jurisdiction, in matters of contract and tort which the courts of the United States may lawfully exercise on the high seas, can be extended to the lakes under the power to regulate commerce, it can with the same propriety and upon the same construction, be extended to contracts and torts on land when the commerce is between different States." (Propeller Genessee Chief et al. v. Fitzhugh et al. 12 How. 443 (U.S. 1851))

"And the forms and modes of proceedings in causes of equity, and of admiralty, and maritime jurisdiction, shall be according to the civil law." (Wayman et al. v. Southard and another, 10 Wall 1, p. 317)

" 'Civil Law,' 'Roman Law,' and 'Roman Civil Law' are convertible phrases, meaning the same system of jurisprudence. That rule of action which every particular nation, commonwealth, or city has established peculiarly for itself; *more properly called 'municipal' law*, to distinguish it from the 'law of nature,' and from international law. See Bowyer, Mod. Civil Law, 19; Sevier v. Riley, 189 Cal. 170, 244 P. 323, 325" (*Black's Law Dictionary*, Revised 4th Edition, page 312 [emphasis added])

No Separation of Powers

The BAR members in the so-called courts go along with all of this as evidence that there is no real separation of powers and the unconstitutional municipal corporation UNITED STATES OF AMERICA is under a full military dictatorship:

"When a State forms a constitution, which is approved by Congress, it is estopped to deny its validity. *The action of Congress cannot be inquired into, for the judicial is bound to follow the action of the political department.* (White v. Hart, 39 Ga., 306; Powell v. Boon, 43 Ala.l, 459 Luther v. Borden, 48 US 1, 12 Led 581)

"Process; Mandates - *All process of this Court issues in the name of the President of the United States.*" (Rule 45.1 US Supreme Court Rules of Procedure)

DeFacto Government

Because Congress has failed to have a quorum, and is operating under executive authority, they become the de facto government. *De facto* is defined by Black's Law Dictionary (8th Edition) as 1. Actual; existing in fact; having effect even though not formally or legally recognized <a de facto contract> 2. *Illegitimate but in effect* <a de facto government>. This is why Congress established the unconstitutional municipal corporation in 1871. "The power that is derived cannot be greater than that from which it is derived" (*Bouvier's Law Dictionary*, 1856 Edition). And everything done by Congress after 1861 is under executive authority.

Summary

The President of the United States wears at least two hats. He is both the President of the trust called *The United States of America* (currently fifty sovereign states) and also the President of the unconstitutional municipal corporation called UNITED STATES OF AMERICA and also UNITED STATES, which includes the District of Columbia, the territories of Guam, Puerto Rico, American Samoa, and the US Virgin Islands, under a full military dictatorship for subjects and aliens *only*.

The Matrix is real. Donald Trump is president (chief executive officer and dictator) of the unconstitutional corporation, and he is also President of the Trust that was established by the Articles of Confederation (1781) and the Constitution for *The United States of America* (1787) the lawful de jure government.

4

MARTIAL LAW = DEMOCRACY

When the southern States walked out of Congress in 1861, Congress ceased to have a quorum. Lincoln ordered them to reconvene under executive authority, and that is how they have been operating ever since, as the unconstitutional municipal corporation. The Republic still exists and is in abeyance (dormancy), but all government officials wear two hats: (1) as an officer of the unconstitutional municipal corporation, and (2) as an official of the Republic under common law. All of the statutes passed by Congress prior to 1861 are still in place, and all government officials that have an oath of office are required to enforce them.

Landowners Were the Electors

Under the original Constitution, no registration was required for elections because by owning land you were automatically registered and the landowners were the electors.

Martial Law = Voter Registration

"Sec. 5......and Congress shall have approved the same, *and when said State, by a vote of its legislature elected under said constitution, shall have adopted the amendment to the Constitution of the United States, proposed by the Thirty-ninth Congress, and known as article fourteen,* and when said article shall have become a part of the Constitution of the United States, said State shall be declared entitled to representation in Congress, and senators and representatives shall be admitted therefrom on their taking the oath prescribed by law, and then and thereafter the preceding sections of this act shall be inoperative in said State: *Provided That no person excluded from the privilege of holding office by said proposed amendment to the Constitution of the United States, shall be eligible to election as a member of the convention* to frame a constitution for any of said rebel States, nor shall any such person vote for members of such convention." (An Act to provide for the more efficient Government of the Rebel States 14 Stat. 428)—and *only* the rebel states.

"WHEREAS no legal State governments or adequate protection for life or property now exists in the rebel States of Virginia, North Carolina, South Carolina, Georgia, Mississippi, Alabama, Louisiana, Florida, Texas, and Arkansas ; and whereas it is necessary that peace and good order should be enforced in said States until loyal and republican State governments can be legally established:" (Preamble to Chap CLIII – An Act to provide for the more efficient Government of the Rebel States, 14 Stat. 428)

Yet today, everybody who wishes to vote in an election is required to "swear under penalty of perjury" that they "are a US citizen" on the registration form, regardless of ownership of any land.

Martial Law Voters = Almost Everybody

Under the current Amendment XVII the senators are elected by popular vote. Under the current Amendment XIX anyone of any sex was allowed to vote. Under the current Amendment XXVI the age to vote was lowered to eighteen years. All of this was being done for the unconstitutional municipal corporation that was operating as the government of the District of Columbia and the territories:

> "Two national governments exist, one to be maintained under the Constitution, with all its restrictions, the other to be maintained by Congress outside and independently of that instrument" Dissenting opinion of Justice Marshall Harlan. Downes v. Bidwell, 182 U.S. 244 (1901)

And for US citizens any of the fifty states or territories:
> "We therefore decline to overrule the opinion of Chief Justice Marshall: We hold that *the District of Columbia is not a state within Article 3 of the Constitution.* In other words cases between citizens of the District and those of the states were not included of the catalogue of controversies over which the Congress could give jurisdiction to the federal courts by virtue of Article 3. In other words *Congress has exclusive legislative jurisdiction over citizens of Washington District of Columbia and through their plenary power nationally covers those citizens even when in one of the several states as though the district expands for the purpose of regulating its citizens wherever they go throughout the states in union"* (National Mutual Insurance Company of the District of Columbia v. Tidewater Transfer Company, 337 U.S. 582, 93 L.Ed. 1556 (1948))

It even covers US citizens internationally as explained by US Supreme Court nominee Brett Kavanagh when Senator Lindsay Graham asked him if a US citizen is subject to US law in Afghanistan, because otherwise Congress would *only* have jurisdiction in federal enclaves:

"The law of Congress… do not extend into the territorial limits of the states, but have force only in the District of Columbia, and other places that are within the exclusive jurisdiction of the national government." (Caha v. United States, 152 U.S. 211 (1894))

"The exclusive jurisdiction which the United States have in forts and dock-yards ceded to them, is derived from the express assent of the states by whom the cessions are made. It could be derived in no other manner; because without it, the authority of the state would be supreme and exclusive therein." (U.S. v. Bevans, 16 U.S. 336, 3 Wheat, at 350, 351 (1818))

Prior to the Civil War, if an act of Congress was intended to apply in the states, the act would say something like the "disappeared" Article XIII in Amendment:

"If any citizen of the United States shall accept, claim, receive, or retain any title of nobility or honor, or shall, without the consent of congress, accept and retain any present, pension, office, or emolument of any kind whatever, from any emperor, king, prince, or foreign power, such person shall cease to be a citizen of the United States, and shall be incapable of holding any office of trust or profit *under them, or either of them.* " (Article Thirteen in Amendment, Constitution for the United States of America, [emphasis added])

The phrase "under them" means the federal government, and the phrase "either of them" means the state governments. The Constitution even does something similar where the phrase "Citizens of each State" means State Citizens, and "Citizens in the several States" means US citizens: "The *Citizens of each State* shall be entitled to all Privileges and Immunities of *Citizens in the several States*" (Article 4, Section 2, Clause 1, US Constitution).

State Citizens

State citizens are unaffected by any of this as seen below: "The rights of (original judicial) Citizens of the States, as such, are not under consideration in the fourteenth amendment. They stand as they did before the fourteenth amendment, and are fully guaranteed under other provisions." (United States v. Anthony, 24 Fed. Cas. 829, 930 (1873))

"[T]hat there was a citizenship of the United States and a citizenship of the states, which were distinct from each other, depending upon different characteristics and circumstances in the individual; that it was only privileges and immunities of the citizens of the United States that were placed by the [Fourteenth] amendment under the protection of the Federal Constitution, and that the privileges and immunities of a citizen of a state, whatever they might be, were not intended to have any additional protection by the paragraph in question, but they must rest for their security and protection

where they have heretofore rested." (Maxwell v Dow, 20
S.C.R. 448, at pg 451)

Martial Law Voters ≠ State Citizens

I have been in discussions with numerous elections officials who
refused to allow me to vote because I failed to become a US citizen.
They prevented me from voting even after I educated them about the
two classes of citizens, and more particularly state citizens.

Summary

When the Southern states walked out of Congress in 1861,
everything changed.

For decades government officials have been saying that the
United States is a democracy, and it is. The republic still exists, but
Congress is still operating under martial law and executive authority
from the Civil War and is therefore operating *only* as the government
of the District of Columbia and the territories:

> "When you become entitled to exercise the right of voting for
> public officers, Let it be impressed on your mind that God
> commands you to choose for rulers, 'just men who will rule
> in the fear of God.' The preservation of [our] Government
> depends on the faithful discharge of this Duty; *if the citizens
> Neglect their Duty and place unprincipled men in office, the
> government will Soon be corrupted*; laws will be made, not for the
> public good so much as for Selfish or local purposes; corrupt
> or incompetent men will be appointed to Execute the Laws;
> the public revenues will be squandered on unworthy men;
> and The rights of the citizen will be violated or disregarded. *If
> [our] government Fails to secure public prosperity and happiness,*

it must be because the Citizens neglect the Divine Commands, and elect bad men to make and administer The Laws." (Noah Webster (1758-1843) American patriot and scholar, author of the first dictionary of American English usage (1806) and the author of the 1828 edition of the dictionary that bears his name.)

"State citizens are the only ones living under free government, whose rights are incapable of impairment by legislation or judicial decision." (Twining v. New Jersey, 211 U.S. 97, 1908)

5

THE BANKRUPTCY
AND THE ROMAN CULT

We are going to start talking about the Roman Cult. This should not be taken to mean anything negative about anyone who happens to be Catholic. I have many wonderful friends who are Catholic and in many cases it was them who were feeding me the information described herein. There are many wonderful people who happen to be Catholic, and in many ways they are victims of the Roman Cult as much or even more than the rest of us. Also, many of the Catholic people are starting to stand up against the Roman Cult, to their credit.

The Bankruptcy

The unconstitutional municipal corporation is now bankrupt. "It is an established fact that the United States Federal Government has been dissolved by the *Emergency Banking Act, March 9, 1933, 48 stat. 1, Public Law 89-719*; declared by President Roosevelt, being bankrupt and insolvent, H.J.R. 192, 73rd Congress in session June 5, 1933 – Joint Resolution To Suspend The Gold Standard and Abrogate The Gold Clause dissolved the Sovereign Authority of the United States and the official capacities of all United States Governmental Offices, Officers, and Departments and is further evidence that *the United States Federal Government exists today in name only*" (United States Congressional Record, March 17, 1993 Vol. 33 [emphasis added]).

Bankruptcy = Martial Law

The BAR members, the lawyers, imposed martial law at the same time they declared their unconstitutional municipal corporation bankrupt:

> "*Since March 9, 1933; the United States has been in a state of declared National Emergency* . . . Under the powers delegated by these statutes, the President may: seize property; organize and control the means of production; seize commodities; assign military forces abroad; institute martial law; seize and control all transportation and communication; regulate the operation of private enterprise; restrict travel; and in a plethora of particular ways, control the lives of all American citizens. . . . *A majority of the people of the United States have lived all of their lives under emergency rule.* For 40 years, freedoms and governmental procedures guaranteed by the Constitution have in varying degrees been *abridged by laws brought into force by states of national emergency . . .*" In Reg: U.S. Senate Report No. 93-549 dated 11/19/73 (73 CIS Serial Set S963-2 - [607 Pages]): [emphasis added]

Bankruptcy = Seizure by Creditors

Bankruptcies resulted in the Roman Cult creditors seizing the bankrupt unconstitutional municipal corporation

"Within twenty years this country is going to rule the world. Kings and Emperors will soon pass away and the democracy of the United States will take their place....When the United States rules the world, *the Catholic Church will rule the world.* . . . Nothing can stand against the church." (Roman Catholic Archbishop James E. Quigley (October 15, 1854 – July 10, 1915) Chicago Daily Tribune May 5, 1903 [emphasis added])

"There are two ways to conquer and enslave a nation. One is by the sword. The other is by debt."

—John Adams 1826

And emergencies require military necessity:

"*Military necessity*, as understood by modern civilized nations, *consists in the necessity of those measures which are indispensable for securing the ends of the war*, and which are lawful according to the modern law and usages of war." (Article 14, General Orders 100 (The Lieber Code) [emphasis added])

Three Kinds of Martial Law

There are three kinds of martial law.[5]

---

5   Ex Parte Milligan 4 Wall (71 U.S.) 2, 18 L.Ed. 281, p 302, The Non-Ratification of the Fourteenth Amendment by Judge A.H. Ellett, Utah Supreme Court, Dyett v Turner, 439 P2d 266 @ 269, 20 U2d 403 [1968]

1. Full Martial Law

a. Declaration of martial law is issued

b. Troops put on the streets

c. Used only during war time

d. Used on foreign country or when actually invaded by foreign power or to put down an armed rebellion

2. Martial Law Proper

a. Law of the armed forces

b. When a captain tells a private what to do

c. Enforced by courts-martial

3. Martial Law Rule

a. Law of *necessity* and *emergency*

b. Allows the domestic use of martial law powers

c. Used during times of peace

The fact that the Roman Cult seized their unconstitutional municipal corporation is evidenced by the Roman fascia that are on each side of the Speaker's podium in the United States House of Representatives and the Roman Aquila military staff that is carried in battle by all Roman commands and that is also planted on all conquered nations, which is located on the right side of the Speaker's podium in the United States House of Representatives, but all government officials have an oath of office which is to the lawful de jure government of The United States of America, "the power which is derived cannot be greater than that from which it is derived" (*Derativa potestas non potest esse major primitiva* – Bouviers Law Dictionary, 1856 Edition).

All uniforms are military uniforms and evidence that the public servant is owned and operated by the Roman Cult: "The wearing of clerical dress or of a religious habit on the part of lay folk . . . is liable

Figure 5 – US House Speakers Podium

to the same penalty on the part of the State as the misuse of military uniform" (Article 10, Concordat of 1933—between Hitler and the Roman Cult). And the Concordat of 1933 has been acceded to by the United States, Canada and many other countries.

In the old days, what did a county sheriff have to identify that he was county sheriff? He had a star and that was all. There were no uniforms. That is common law!

> "Posse comitatus. Latin. The power or force of the county. The entire population of a county above the age of fifteen, which a sheriff may summon to his assistance in certain cases, as to aid him in keeping the peace, in pursuing and arresting felons, etc. Williams v. State, 253 Ark. 973, 490 S.W.2d 117, 121." (*Black's Law Dictionary*, 6th Edition, page 1990)

Cestui que Trust

All wars are fought by the Roman Cult's military. On both sides of the battle are giant commercial transactions, and actual satanic blood sacrifices to the Roman Cult's god BAAL. They get gangs of people from each country to go to some field and murder each other, and they always get to impose the Roman Cults martial law no matter who wins.

All warfare is used to pay off government alleged debt through the Roman Cult's cestui que trust estates:

> "*Yet still it was found difficult to set bounds to ecclesiastical ingenuity*; for when they were driven out of all their former holds, they devised a new method of conveyance, by which the lands were granted, not to themselves directly, but to nominal feoffees *to the use* of the religious houses; thus distinguishing between the *possession* and the *use*, and receiving the actual profits, while the seisin of the lands remained in the nominal feoffee, *who was held by the courts of equity (then under the direction of the clergy)* to be bound in conscience to account [taxes] to his *cestui que use* for the rents and emoluments of the estate: *and it is to these inventions that our practitioners are indebted for the introduction of uses and trusts, the foundation of modern conveyancing.*" (Tomlins Law Dictionary, 1835 Edition, Volume 2 under the definition of Mortmain [emphasis added])

The Roman Cult's cestui que trust (JOHN HENRY SMITH), is created by the birth certificate and social security number and is recognized under the Convention of the Law Applicable to Trusts and on their Recognition which was concluded July 1, 1985, and entered into force on January 1, 1992, which is also considered Private International Law which was originated with the Roman Cult, as described herein:

The unconstitutional corporation that was set up in 1871 has not had a treasury since 1921 (41 Stat. Ch.214 pg. 654). Its treasury is now the International Monetary Fund (Presidential Documents Volume 29-No.4 pg. 113, 22 U.S.C. 285-288), which is an agency of the Roman Cult's World Bank and United Nations.

All Social Security Numbers are issued by the International Monetary Fund through the treasury, which maintains an account for each Roman Cult cestui que trust (JOHN HENRY SMITH) under the social security number which is claimed under the Convention Concerning the International Administration of the Estates of Deceased Persons, which was concluded on 2 October 1973, and is part of the <u>Hague Conference on Private International Law</u>:

> "Any person who pays, or delivers property to, the holder of the certificate drawn up, and, where necessary, recognized, in accordance with this Convention shall be discharged, unless it is proved that the person acted in bad faith." (Article 22, Convention Concerning the International Administration of the Estates of Deceased Persons)

> "Any person who has acquired assets of the estate from the holder of a certificate drawn up, and, where necessary, recognized, in accordance with this Convention shall, unless it is proved that he acted in bad faith, be deemed to have acquired them from a person having power to dispose of them." (Article 23, Convention Concerning the International Administration of the Estates of Deceased Persons)

Bank Loans

There is no such thing as a bank loan as found in *Modern Money Mechanics*, a booklet that was published by the Chicago Federal Reserve in May 1961. It says that "the money creation process takes place principally through transaction accounts" (Modern Money Mechanics, page 2). And the booklet goes on to explain that "*Of course, they do not really pay out loans from the money they receive as deposits.* If they did this, no additional money would be created. What they do *when they make loans is to accept promissory notes in exchange for credits to the borrowers' transaction accounts"* (Modern Money Mechanics, page 6, emphasis added). An unconditional promise to pay is itself money and even though it says it is a promise to pay, the bank is paid with their acceptance of the promissory note

The Federal Reserve

The Fed, as it's called, is a privately owned, Rothschild, Central banking cartel charging taxpayers interest on money they print out of thin air since 1913. Regarding money, we read that "What is said to be *an unconditional promise to pay* a sum certain in money *is itself money.* The words on the face of the paper money, 'will pay to the bearer on demand", cannot alter its character as money and turn it into a different document which calls for the payment of money' " (Bank of Canada v. Bank of Montreal, [1978] 1 S.C.R. 1148 at page 1155 [emphasis added]). A case against an insurance company further speaks to the use of paper money, this time in the form of cashier's checks:

> *"A cashier's check differs in that it is a bill of exchange drawn by the bank upon itself and is accepted by the act of issuance. A cashier's check is the primary obligation of the remitting bank.* See RCW 62A.4211(1)(b). ...An ordinary check is considered as merely a promise to pay, but a cashier's check is regarded substantially as money, which it represents. The gift of such a check is completed upon delivery of the check. Pikeville Nat'l Bank & Trust Co. v. Shirley, 281 Ky. 150, 135 S.W.2d 426, 126 A.L.R. 919 (1939). See also Scott v. Seaboard Sec.

Co., 143 Wash. 514, 255 P. 660 (1927), which quoted with approval extensively from Drinkall, and then quoted from Hathaway v. Delaware Cy., 185 N.Y. 368, 78 N.E. 153 (1906) as follows: '*That by reason of the peculiar character of cashiers' checks and their general use in the commercial world they were to be regarded substantially as the money which they represented.*'" (Crunk v State Farm Fire and Casualty 719 P.2d 1338 [emphasis added])

When a deposit is made into a bank, the deposit becomes the property of the bank, but the bank has a contract to give it back. And banks are *not* allowed to loan their own money: "GENERAL PROHIBITION - No national bank shall make any loan or discount on the security of the shares of its own capital stock" (12 U.S. Code § 83 - Loans by bank on its own stock).

No Such Thing as National Debt

If there is no such thing as a bank loan, then the entire national debt is a fraud and nothing more than a debt slavery scam. Don't you think the Roman Cult's BAR members in the so-called courts know this? You don't think the Roman Cult's BAR members who are supposed to be working for the attorney with the rank of general know this?

"It is true that at common law the duty of the Attorney General is to represent the King, he being the embodiment of the state. But under the democratic form of government now prevailing the People are King so the Attorney General's duties are to that Sovereign rather than to the machinery of government." (Hancock V. Terry Elkhorn Mining Co., Inc.,

KY., 503 S.W. 2D 710 KY Const. §4, Commonwealth Ex
Rel. Hancock V. Paxton, KY, 516 S. W. 2D. PG 867)

Forced Loans = Negotiable Instruments = Military Script

Lincoln issued US treasury notes (military script), which are
forced loans, during the Civil War where government employees and
contractors (subjects of the enemy and aliens under General Orders
100 Lieber Code) were forced to loan the government money:

> "This rule does not interfere with the right of the victorious
> invader to tax the people or their property, *to levy forced
> loans*, to billet soldiers, or to appropriate property, especially
> houses, lands, boats or ships, and churches, for temporary
> and military uses" (Article 37, General Orders 100 (The
> Lieber Code) [emphasis added])

And there were vital forces in the struggle for national supremacy:

> "The forced loans of 1862 and 1863, in the form of legal
> tender notes, *were vital forces in the struggle for national
> supremacy*. They formed a part of the public debt of the
> United States, *the validity of which is solemnly established by
> the Fourteenth Amendment to the Constitution*." (Julliard v.
> Greenman, 110 US 432 [emphasis added])

Congress was running its owned and operated municipal
corporation it had set up in 1871. "Two national governments exist,
one to be maintained under the Constitution, with all its restrictions,
the other to be maintained by Congress outside and independently
of that instrument" (Dissenting opinion of Justice Marshall Harlan.
Downes v. Bidwell, 182 U.S. 244 (1901)). And the banksters have
always been owned and operated by the Roman Cult:

"It is a somewhat curious sequel to the attempt to set up a Catholic competitor to the Rothschilds that at the present time the latter are the guardians of the papal treasure." (Jewish Encyclopedia 1901 – 1906, Volume 2, page 497)

Forced loans (legal tender) falls under negotiable instrument law, which is a branch of the Roman Cults Roman Law. Congress knew it was not required to "borrow" the banksters fake money, because it could just issue it (like Lincoln did), but the Roman Cult's owned-and-operated banksters and BAR members had infiltrated Congress. They created the Rothschilds owned-and-operated Federal Reserve in the middle of the night on Christmas Eve 1913. Then Congress borrowed their fake money, and it took less than twenty years to bankrupt their unconstitutional municipal corporation. On March 9, 1933, as part of Roosevelt's communist New Deal, they intended to convert their unconstitutional municipal corporation over to the Roman Cult using their fake money, and their BAR members love to degrade the people by dragging them into their so-called court "because it brings into action, and enforces this great and glorious principle, that the people are the sovereign of this country, and consequently that fellow citizens *and joint sovereigns cannot be degraded by appearing with each other in their own courts to have their controversies determined*" (Chisolm v Georgia 2 Dall. 419 [emphasis added]).

The recent so-called subprime crisis was a theft by the Roman Cult's banksters because they were not out one penny with any of their so-called "loans," but the unconstitutional municipal corporation was coerced into paying their $700 billion extortion, which is part of their agenda to set up the next fraudulent fictitious bankruptcy as part of the Roman Cult's debt slavery scam.

Summary

The Roman Cult's owned-and-operated banksters, in conspiracy with some members of Congress, created a fictitious debt to force unconstitutional municipal corporation into bankruptcy. The unconstitutional municipal corporation set up by Congress in 1871 is now bankrupt and owned and operated by the Roman Cult. Donald Trump left his billionaire's lifestyle to become President (and chief executive officer) of the unconstitutional corporation that is owned by the Roman Cult.

6

THE BAR AND THE ROMAN CULT

British Accredited Regency

The BAR is an acronym which stands for British Accredited Regency. A regent is somebody who acts on behalf of somebody else:

"REGENCY 1. The office or jurisdiction of a regent or body of regents. 2. A government or authority by regents.

REGENT 1. A person who exercises the ruling power in a kingdom during the minority, absence, or other disability of the sovereign. 2. A governor or ruler." (*Black's Law Dictionary*, 8th Edition, page 4010 [emphasis added])

All BAR members have an exclusive privilege from the Inns of Court, which are certain private unincorporated associations, in the nature of collegiate houses, *located in London*, and invested with the *exclusive privilege of calling men to the bar*" (*Black's Law Dictionary*, 5th Edition, page 709).

The Inns of Court are comprised of four of these associations located in London, England, (Grey's Inn, Lincoln's Inn, Inner

Temple, and Middle Temple), and they are all located in downtown London near the Parliament buildings, (the City of London) in an area that has a wall around it and was never conquered by William the Conqueror (circa 1066) but was seized in a bankruptcy because King John agreed to pay the Roman Cult tribute:

> "[W]e will and establish perpetual obligation and concession we will establish that from the proper and especial revenues of our aforesaid kingdoms, for all the service and customs which we ought to render for them, saving in all things the penny of St. Peter, *the Roman church shall receive yearly a thousand marks sterling*, namely at the feast of St. Michael five hundred marks, and at Easter five hundred marks-seven hundred, namely, for the kingdom of England, and three hundred for the kingdom of Ireland." (Concessions of England to the Pope, 1213)

Figure 6 – City of London

King John failed to make his payments because the Welsh Barons rose up in rebellion and compelled him to agree to the Magna Carta:

> "The Magna Carta is not a unilateral act, emanating solely from the spontaneous will of the King, as the Charters of the predecessors of John; neither is it a treaty; for we cannot say it was concluded between two legitimate and independent sovereignties; nor between nations, nor is it a law. The

Barons do not appear in it as subjects, for they are freed from their promise of fidelity, and the King, brought captive, placed before them, submitted to the conditions which the conquerors imposed upon him. Magna Carta is therefore a contract, but resembles a treaty concluded between two nations, in that one of the parties, in virtue of the law of war, can impose its will upon the other." (Perlman v Piche and Attorney General of Canada, Intervenant, Re Habeus Corpus, 4 D.L.R. 147).

There is an American Inns of Court foundation and chapters in every state, which makes all BAR members foreign agents of the Roman Cult, and Congress is full of BAR members (up to 90 percent) and all legislation (edicts under martial law) passed by Congress is approved by BAR members.

BAR Members = BAAL Priests

All BAR members are BAAL priests for their Roman Cult handlers. The BAR members in Congress passed legislation (edicts under martial law) requiring all judges to be BAR members, and the black robe they wear is a BAAL priest uniform. All of the state legislatures are also populated with BAR members (70-90 percent), and before any legislation (edicts under the Roman Cult's martial law) can be submitted to the legislature for review, or a vote, it has to be reviewed by BAR members, and the BAR members in the legislatures have passed legislation (edicts under the Roman Cult's martial law) requiring all appointed judges and almost all elected judges to be BAR members.

All BAR members (BAAL priests) have received and accepted an honor from a foreign power (the Roman Cult) in violation of the true Article XIII in the Thirteenth Amendment:

> "If any citizen of the United States *shall accept, claim, receive, or retain any title of nobility or honor,* or shall, without the consent of congress, accept and retain any present, pension, office, or emolument of any kind whatever, *from any emperor, king, prince, or foreign power,* such person shall cease to be a citizen of the United States, and *shall be incapable of holding any office of trust* or profit under them, or either of them." (Article Thirteen in Amendment, Constitution for the United States of America, [emphasis added])

Because all BAR members are part of the Roman Cult, that is why they wanted to facilitate its "disappearance" during the time between the War of 1812 and the Civil War. It is also why few BAR members register themselves as foreign agents under their own Foreign Agents Registration Act under their 52 Stat. 631, (edict under martial law). These satanic Roman Cult BAR member/BAAL priests, who are bought-and-paid-for clerks masquerading as judges (military commissioners), do everything they can to assault you with their so-called court. For example, they give you a free attorney as ""an officer of the state with an obligation to the Court" (7 Corpus Juris Secundum § 4 Attorneys). They also compel you to have an attorney in their star chamber, "The corrupt Star Chamber Courts of England *required defendants to have counsel.* Star Chamber stood for swiftness and arbitrary power, [Admiralty Maritime Law] *it was a limitation on the common law*" (Faretta v. California, 422 U.S. 806, 821 [emphasis added]):

"His first duty is to the courts and to the public, *not to the client*, and whenever his duties to his client conflict with those as an officer of the court, in the administration of justice, the former must yield to the latter." (7 Corpus Juris Secundum § 4 Attorneys)

Since "Clients are also called 'wards of the court'" (7 Corpus Juris Secundum § 4 Attorneys) and wards of the court are "Infants and persons of unsound mind. Davis" (Committee v. Loney, 290 Ky. 644, 162 S.W.2d 189, 190. Their rights must be guarded jealously. Montgomery v. Erie R. Co., C.C.A.N.J., 97 F.2d 289, 292), only an imbecile would hire a member of the BAR.

BAR Member = Jurisdiction

Bar members are equal to jurisdiction, so they can deny your challenges to jurisdiction:

"IN PROPRIA PERSONA. In one's own proper person. It is a rule in pleading that pleas to the jurisdiction of the court must be plead *in propria persona, because if pleaded by attorney they admit the jurisdiction, as an attorney is an officer of the court, and he is presumed to plead after having obtained leave, which admits the jurisdiction.* (Lawes, PI. 91." Blacks Law Dictionary, 4th Edition, page 899-900)

"[A]nd because it brings into action, and enforces this great and glorious principle, that the people are the sovereign of this country, and consequently that fellow citizens and joint sovereigns *cannot be degraded by appearing with each other*

in their own courts to have their controversies determined."
(Chisholm v Georgia, 2 Dall 419, at p 479, [emphasis added])

BAR Member = Liar

All attorneys are actually liars because they make all sorts
of statements to their Roman Cult BAR member/BAAL priests
(bought-and-paid-for) clerks masquerading as judges (military
commissioners) and thereby give testimony even though none of
them has any firsthand knowledge of anything:

> "An attorney for the plaintiff cannot admit evidence into
> the court. He is either an attorney or a witness." (Trinsey v.
> Pagliaro D.C.Pa. 1964, 229 F. Supp. 647)

> "Manifestly, [such statements] cannot be properly considered
> by us in the disposition of [a] case." (U. S. v. Lovasco
> (06/09/77) 431 U.S. 783, 97 S. Ct. 2044, 52 L. Ed. 2d 752)

And I have had friends sold into slavery by attorneys for simple
things like fraudulent indictments that fail to say it is a "TRUE
BILL" which means it is *not* a true bill of indictment, which means
there was no probable cause of a crime having been committed.
Therefore, it was a malicious prosecution. "Although probable cause
may not be inferred from malice, malice may be inferred from lack
of probable cause" (Pauley v. Hall, 335 N. W. 2d 197, 124 Mich
App 255), they call this justice. But it would be more correctly called
justus "because it brings into action, and enforces this great and
glorious principle, that the people are the sovereign of this country,
and consequently that fellow citizens and joint sovereigns *cannot be
degraded by appearing with each other in their own courts to have their*

controversies determined" (Chisholm v Georgia, 2 Dall 419, at p 479, [emphasis added]).

Trump Administration

It is called the Trump administration. Therefore Donald J. Trump is the administrator of the estates (*cestui que trust*) of the American people under the direction of the Roman Cult:

> "ADMINISTRATOR. A person authorized to manage and distribute the *estate of an intestate*, or of a *testator who has no executor*. In English law, *administrators are the officers of the Ordinary* appointed by him in pursuance of the statute, and *their title and authority are derived exclusively from the ecclesiastical judge*, by grants called letters of administration. Williams, Ex. 331. At First the Ordinary was appointed administrator under the statute of Westm. 2d. Next, the 31 Edw. III. c. 11, *required the Ordinary to appoint the next of kin and the relations by blood of the deceased.* Next, under the 21 Hen. VIII., he could appoint the widow, or next of kin, or both, at his discretion." (*Bouvier's Law Dictionary*, 1883 Edition, page 119)

Trump is an officer of the ordinary. In American Law. A court "*which has jurisdiction of the probate of wills and the regulation of the management of decedents' estates.* Such courts exist in Georgia, New Jersey, South Carolina, and *Texas.* See 2 Kent, Comm. 409; *Ordinary*" (*Bouvier's Law Dictionary*, 1856 Edition, page 383). And his "title and authority are derived exclusively from" an "ecclesiastical judge":

> "ORDINARY, *ordinarius.*] A civil law term for any judge who hath authority to take cognizance of causes in his own

right, and not by deputation: *by the common law it is taken for him who hath ordinary or exempt and immediate jurisdiction in causes ecclesiastical. (Co. Litt. 344; Stat. Westm. 2. 13 Edw. 1. st. 1. c. 19)*

This name is applied to a bishop who hath original jurisdiction, and an archbishop is the *ordinary* of the whole province, to visit and receive appeals from inferior jurisdictions (&c. *2 Inst. 398; 9 Rep. 41; Wood's Inst. 25).* The word *ordinary* is also used for every commissary or official of the bishop or other ecclesiastical judge having judicial power. An archdeacon is an ordinary, and ordinaries may grant administration of intestates' estates (&c. *31 Edw. 3. c. 11; 9 Rep. 36).* But the bishop of the diocese is the true and only ordinary to certify excommunications, lawfulness of marriage, and such ecclesiastical and spiritual acts to the judges of the common law, for he is the person to whom the court is to write in such things *2 Shep. Abr. 472."* (*Tomlins Law Dictionary*, 1835 Edition, Volume 2).

Ecclesiastical Courts

Their military police issue a citation for an offense against the martial law, to drag you into their ecclesiastical court. A citation is a summons "to appear, *applied particularly to Process in the Spiritual Court. The Ecclesiastical Courts proceed according to the Course of the Civil and Canon Laws, by Citation, Libel,* &c." (*Tomlins Law Dictionary*, 1835 Edition, Volume 1 [emphasis added]). A citation is also "the name of the process used in the *English ecclesiastical, probate, and divorce courts* to call the defendant or respondent before them. 3 Bl. Comm. 100. 3 Steph. Comm. 720" (*Black's Law Dictionary*, 2nd Edition, at page 202).

The courts are spiritual entities that subject you to their satanic religious ceremony. They are "held by the king's authority as supreme governor of the church, for matters which chiefly concern religion. 4 Inst. 321. And the *laws and constitutions whereby the church of England is governed*, are, *1. Divers immemorial customs*. 2. Our own provincial constitutions; and the *canons made in convocations*, especially those in the year 1603. . . . Much oppression having been exercised through the channel of these courts, on persons charged with trifling offences within their spiritual jurisdiction" (*Tomlins Law Dictionary*, 1835 Edition, Volume 1, [emphasis added]).

> COURTS ECCLESIASTICAL …The proceedings in the Ecclesiastical Courts are, *according to the civil and canon law* by *citation, libel*, answer upon oath, *proof by* witnesses, and *presumptions*, &c., and after sentence, for contempt, by excommunication: and *if the sentence is disliked, by appeal*. (Tomlins Law Dictionary, 1835 Edition, Volume 1, [emphasis added])

Jail = Roman Cult = Slavery

When you submit to the system an violate one of their so-called bills of indictment, the BAR will sell you into slavery. Such a person becomes a prisoner and "as a consequence of his crime, not only forfeited his liberty but all his personal rights except those which the law in its humanity affords him. *He is for the time being a slave of the state*" (62 Va. (21 Gratt.) 790, 796 (1871) [emphasis mine]).

> "Penitentiary has meant: a penitent, an ordainer of penances, and *a place for penitents*. See Locus, Penitentias." (*Andersons Law Dictionary*, 1889 Edition, page 764)

This is why they have to get rid of their common law problem with martial law, because at common law "If a man be found stealing any of his brethren of the children of Israel, and maketh merchandise of him, or selleth him; then that thief shall die; and thou shalt put evil away from among you" (Deuteronomy 24:7).

"And through covetousness shall they with feigned words make merchandise of you: whose judgment now of a long time lingereth not, and their damnation slumbereth not." (2 Peter 2:3)

But the Roman Cult's penance was always for sale for penance is " a Punishment imposed for a Crime by the Ecclesiastical Laws. It is an Acknowledgment of the Offence. . . . *Penance may be changed into a Sum of Money* to be applied to pious Uses, called Commuting. 3 Inst. 150. 4 Inst. 336." (A New Law Dictionary, 1750 Edition).

The Roman Cult's BAR members are creating more business for their BAR member buddies by selling people into slavery. In the Thirteenth Amendment is says neither "slavery nor involuntary servitude, *except as a punishment for crime whereof the party shall have been duly convicted*, shall exist within the United States, or any place subject to their jurisdiction" (Section 1). And in Section 2 it says "Congress shall have power to enforce this article by appropriate legislation" [emphasis added].

With their green card scam, they know that at common law the wife and minor children take on the nationality of the husband.

"It is however, true that in all common-law countries it has always and consistently been held that the wife and minor children take the nationality of the husband and father. That is common-law doctrine" (In Re Page 12 F (2d) 135). But these (bought-and-paid-for) whores, selling their "Justus," would rather sit there and play stupid, so they can convert rights into privileges:

"The claim and exercise of a constitutional [common law] *right* cannot be converted into a crime." (Miller v. U.S. 230 F. 486 at 489)

"There can be no sanction or penalty imposed upon one because of his exercise of constitutional [common law] *rights*." (Sherar v. Cullen, 481 F. 946)

"No State shall convert a liberty into a privilege, license it, and charge a fee therefore." (Murdock v. Pennsylvania, 319 US 105)

"If the State converts a right (liberty) into a privilege, the citizen can ignore the license and fee and engage in the right (liberty) with impunity." (Shuttlesworth v. City of Birmingham Alabama, 373 US 262)

They keep it up because their BAR member buddies and their so-called courts get the divorce business when they break up families, and they get the business when they sell the children into slavery because they become a juvenile delinquent when their father is in prison. So the Roman Cult's BAR members get all sorts of business any way you want to look at it! "Destroy the family, you destroy the country," said Vladimir Ilyich Lenin (1870-1924), first leader of the Soviet Union and a psychopath.

Article 3 Courts

The Constitution for the United States of America, Article 3 sets up the Supreme Court and inferior courts *only*. It says that "judicial power of the United States shall be vested in one supreme court, and in such inferior courts as the Congress may from time to time ordain and establish" (Article 3, Section 1, US Constitution). And an inferior court is one of limited jurisdiction defined by statute:

"Also nothing shall be intended to be within the jurisdiction of an inferior court, but what is expressly so alleged: *and if part of the cause arises within the inferior jurisdiction, and part thereof without it, the inferior court ought not to hold plea. 1 Lev. 104: 2 Rep. 16. See tit Abatement, I. 1. An inferior court, not of record, cannot impose a fine, or imprison: but the courts of record at Westminster may fine, imprison, and amerce. 1 1 Rep. 43.;* The king, being the supreme magistrate of the kingdom, and intrusted with the executive power of the law, all courts, superior or inferior, ought to derive their authority from the crown; Staundf. 54." (*Tomlins Law Dictionary*, 1835 Edition, [emphasis added])

The Supreme Court of the United States is the *only* court of general jurisdiction, but the federal courts have been operating as courts of general jurisdiction by putting on show trials that appear to be "of record" and issuing fines and imprisoning people. A court of general jurisdiction, however, "is *presumed* to be acting within its jurisdiction *till the contrary is shown*" (Brown, Jur Section 202;

Wright v. Douglas, 10 Barb. (N.Y.) 97; Town of Huntington v. Town of Charlotte, 15 Vt. 46). "[A]and because it brings into action, and enforces this great and glorious principle, that the people are the sovereign of this country, and consequently that fellow citizens and joint sovereigns *cannot be degraded by appearing with each other in their own courts to have their controversies determined*" (Chisholm v Georgia, 2 Dall 419, at p 479 [emphasis added]).

Territorial Courts under Martial Law

For the courts to operate as a general jurisdiction is *only* allowed in the territories under Article 4, Section 3, Clause 2, US Constitution, which says that "Congress shall have power to dispose of and make all needful rules and regulations respecting the territory or other property belonging to the United States."

> "The United States District Court . . . . is not a true United States court established under Const, art. 3, to administer the judicial power of the United States, but was created by virtue of the sovereign congressional faculty, granted under Article 4, § 3, of making all needful rules and regulations respecting the territory belonging to the United States." (Balzac v People of Puerto Rico, 258 U.S. 298)

> "*The United States district court* hereby established shall be the successor to the United States provisional court established by General Orders, Numbered Eighty-eight, promulgated by Brigadier-General Davis, United States Volunteers, and shall take possession of all records of that court, and take jurisdiction of all cases and proceedings pending therein, and

said United States provisional court is hereby discontinued."
(31 Stat. 85 [emphasis added])

Because of the Roman Cult's martial law and bankruptcy, it fails
to make a difference that a US citizen is not entitled to an Article 3
court because there are no Article 3 courts (state or federal) because
they are all inferior courts defined by statutes (legislative courts) and
have foreign agents of the Roman Cult BAR member (BAAL priests)
as officers of the so-called courts. The inferior courts only perpetuate
the fraud with their decisions (that are advisory *only*, as described
herein) and all so-called courts (state or federal) are actually military
tribunals under martial dictatorship with military commissioners
masquerading as judges who are in fact (bought-and-paid-for)
whores selling their "justus," and the BAR (British Accredited
Regency) members are a critical part of the military occupation,
which must end.

According to the US Constitution "The accused *has the right to
be represented* in his defense before a *general or special court-martial*
or at an investigation under section 832 of this title (article 32) as
provided in this subsection" (10 USC § 838(a)(1)). And all appeals
are taken in admiralty, which is why there are all these courts of
appeal. "A writ of error doth not lie upon a sentence in the admiralty,
but an appeal. *4 Inst.* 135. 339" (Tomlins Law Dictionary, 1835
Edition, Volume 1, under the definition of Admiralty).

The US Constitution provides for judges to hold office
"during good behavior." Article 3, Section 1 says, the "judges,
of both of the supreme and inferior courts, shall hold their
offices their offices *during good behavior*" Article 3, Section 1,
US Constitution [emphasis added]

and the two classes of citizens are found in several places in the
Constitution

> "The judicial power shall extend to all cases, in law and
> equity, arising under this constitution, the laws of the United
> States,....; to controversies to which the United States shall
> be a party; to controversies between two or more states;
> between a state and citizens of another state, between citizens
> of different states, between citizens of the same state, claiming
> lands under grants of different states, and between a state, or
> the citizens thereof and foreign states citizens or subjects."
> Article 3, Section 2, Clause 1, US Constitution

and when any Judge engages in fraud upon the court, "Fraud
upon the court is fraud which is directed to the judicial machinery
itself and is not fraud between the parties or fraudulent documents,
false statements or perjury. ... It is where the court or a member
is corrupted, or influenced, or influence is attempted, or where
the judge has not performed his judicial function --- i.e., where
the impartial functions of the court have been directly corrupted."
Bulloch v. United States, 763 F.2d 1115, 1121 (10th Cir. 1985)

by choosing to be a (bought and paid for) Clerk masquerading
as a Judge, as described herein, and thereby engage in honest services
fraud in violation of their District of Columbia codes

> "For the purposes of this chapter, the term "scheme or artifice
> to defraud" includes a scheme or artifice to deprive another
> of the intangible right of honest services." 18 USC § 1346
> Definition of "Scheme or Artifice to defraud

"It is a fundamental right of a party to have a neutral and detached judge preside over the judicial proceedings." Ward v Village of Monroeville, 409 U.S. 57, 61-62, 93 S.Ct 80, 83, 34 L.Ed. 2d 267 (1972); Tumey v Ohio, 273 U.S. 510, 5209, 47 S. Ct. 437, 440, 71 L.Ed. 749 (1927)

and does anything to criminally convert somebody into one of their US citizen slaves, for their extortion racket called filing fees, it fails to be "good behavior" and since they are required to recuse themselves at even the appearance of impropriety under their 28 USC § 455 and yet they fail to do so, it goes to their malicious intent;

All state statutes are actually federal statutes that apply ONLY to the criminally converted US citizens or Resident Aliens under the Roman Cult's *International Law*, especially since all of the 50 fifty states are under a Roman Cult military dictatorship because of the bankruptcy emergency, and Texas in particular, in my case, is under a military occupation (Roman Cult military dictatorship):

"INTERNATIONAL LAW RULE: *Adopted for areas under Federal legislative jurisdiction*" "*Federalizes State civil law, including common law.--The rule serves to federalize not only the statutory but the common law of a State.* ...STATE AND FEDERAL VENUE DISCUSSED: *The civil laws effective in an area of exclusive Federal jurisdiction are Federal law,* notwithstanding their derivation from State laws, and a cause arising under such laws may be brought in or removed to a Federal district court under sections 24 or 28 of the former Judicial Code (now sections 1331 and 1441 of title 28, United States Code), giving jurisdiction to such courts of

civil actions arising under the "* * *laws * * * of the United
States." (Jurisdiction over Federal Areas Within the States –
Report of the Interdepartmental Committee for the Study
of Jurisdiction over Federal Areas Within the States, Part II,
A Text of the Law of Legislative Jurisdiction Submitted to
the Attorney General and Transmitted to the President June
1957, page 158-165)

"*The statute creates a rebuttable presumption* of residency for
anyone who meets the following criteria: .... however no
such person shall be considered a resident for purposes of this
chapter unless such person is either a United States citizen or
an alien with legal authorization from the U.S. Immigration
and Naturalization Service." (Letter from Jennifer Ammons,
General Counsel, Georgia Department of Driver Services,
dated 5 September 2012)

"and because it brings into action, and enforces this great
and glorious principle, that the people are the sovereign of
this country, and consequently that fellow citizens and joint
sovereigns *cannot be degraded by appearing with each other
in their own courts to have their controversies determined.*"
(Chisholm v Georgia, 2 Dall 419, at p 479, [emphasis added])

BAR members = Conjuration

Conjuration is "a plot or compact made by persons combining
by *oath* to do any public harm" (Tomlins Law Dictionary, 1835
Edition, Volume 1).

United States Code = District of Columbia Code

All United States codes are actually District of Columbia code, and there is no separation of powers under the military dictatorship since the Roman Cults order followers assault people with it anyway, and the Roman Cult BAR member/BAAL priests (bought-and-paid-for) clerks masquerading as judges (military commissioners) whores selling their "justus" and call it a contract:

> "The exclusive jurisdiction which the United States have in forts and dock-yards ceded to them, is derived from the express assent of the States by whom the cessions are made. It could be derived in no other manner; because without it, the authority of the State would be supreme and exclusive therein." (U.S. v Bevans, 16 U.S. 336, 3 Wheat, at 350, 351 (1818))

> "The law of Congress do not extend into the territorial limits of the states, but have force only in the District of Columbia, and other places that are within the exclusive jurisdiction of the national government." (Caha v. United States, 152 U.S. 211 (1894))

The Roman Cult BAR member/BAAL priests (bought-and-paid-for) clerks masquerading as judges (military commissioners) whores selling their "justus" cheer the order followers on BECAUSE IT IS SO GOOD FOR BUSINESS!! "In doing this, I shall have occasion incidentally to evince, how true it is that States and Governments were made for man, and, at the same time, how true it is that his creatures and servants have first deceived, next vilified, and, at last oppressed their master and maker" (Chisholm v Georgia, 2 Dall 419 at p 455).

"A state like a merchant makes a contract. A dishonest state, like a dishonest merchant willfully refuses to discharge it." (Chisholm v Georgia, 2 Dall 419 at p 456)

The Roman Cult BAR member/BAAL priests (bought-and-paid-for) clerks masquerading as judges (military commissioners) whores selling their "justus" love to degrade the people by dragging them into their so-called courts "and because it brings into action, and enforces this great and glorious principle, that the people are the sovereign of this country, and consequently that fellow citizens and joint sovereigns *cannot be degraded by appearing with each other in their own courts to have their controversies determined*" (Chisholm v Georgia, 2 Dall 419, at p 479, [emphasis added]).

It is all ultra vires.

"Ultra vires. An act performed without any authority to act on subject. Haslund v. City of Seattle, 86 Wash.2d 607, 547 P.2d 1221, 1230. Acts beyond the scope of the powers of a corporation, as defined by its charter or laws of state of incorporation. State ex rel. v. Holston Trust Co., 168 Tenn. 546, 79 S.W.2d 1012, 1016. The term has a broad application and includes not only acts prohibited by the charter, but acts which are in excess of powers granted and not prohibited, and generally applied either when a corporation has no power whatever to do an act, or when the corporation has the power but exercises it irregularly." (People ex rel. Barrett v. Bank of Peoria, 295 Ill.App. 543, 15 N.E.2d 333, 335)

Act is ultra vires when corporation is without authority to perform it under any circumstances or for any purpose. By doctrine of ultra vires a contract made by a corporation beyond the scope of its corporate powers is unlawful. Community Federal Sav. & Loan Ass'n of Independence, Mo. v. Fields, C.C.A. Mo., 128 F.2d 705, 708. *Ultra vires act of municipality is one which is beyond powers conferred upon it by law.* Charles v. Town of Jeanerette, Inc., La.App., 234 So.2d 794, 798." (*Black's Law Dictionary*, 6th Edition page 1522, [emphasis added])

"The power that is derived cannot be greater than that from which it is derived" (*Derativa potestas non potest esse major primitive.* Bouviers Law Dictionary, 1856 Edition)

"And because it brings into action, and enforces this great and glorious principle, that the people are the sovereign of this country, and consequently that fellow citizens and joint sovereigns *cannot be degraded by appearing with each other in their own courts to have their controversies determined.*" (Chisholm v Georgia, 2 Dall 419, at p 479, [emphasis added])

Congress uses their unconstitutional municipal corporation, and their *international law rule* to assault any man or (wo)man with their Roman Cult UNIDROIT controlled and regulated uniform commercial code like their (bought-and-paid-for) clerks masquerading as judges do in their (so-called) courts every day. But Founding Father Madison insisted that just "because this power is given to Congress," it did not follow that the Treaty Power was "absolute and unlimited." The President and the Senate lacked the power "to dismember the empire." For example, because "[t]he exercise of the power must be consistent with the object of the delegation." "The object of treaties," in Madison's oft-repeated formulation, "is the regulation of intercourse with foreign nations, *and is external*" (Bond v United States 572 US _____ (2014) case number 12-158 [emphasis added]).

> "Today, it is enough to highlight some of the structural and historical evidence suggesting that the Treaty Power can be used to arrange intercourse with other nations, but not to regulate purely domestic affairs." (Bond v United States 572 US _____ (2014) case number 12-158 [emphasis added])

> "The government of the United States . . . is one of limited powers. *It can exercise authority over no subjects, except those which have been delegated to it.* Congress cannot, by legislation, enlarge the federal jurisdiction, *nor can it be enlarged under the treaty-making power*" (Mayor of New Orleans v. United States, 10 Pet. 662, 736 [emphasis added])

> "The power that is derived cannot be greater than that from which it is derived" (*Derativa potestas non potest esse major primitive.* Bouviers Law Dictionary, 1856 Edition)

> "But in considering the question before us, it must be borne in mind that *there is no law of nations standing between the people of the United States and their Government,* and interfering with their relation to each other. The powers

of the Government, and the rights of the citizens under it, are positive and practical regulations plainly written down. The people of the United States *have delegated to it certain enumerated powers, and forbidden it to exercise others.*" (Dred Scott v. Sandford, 19 How (60 U.S.) 393, 452, 15 L.Ed. 691 (A.D. 1856-1857) [emphasis added])

"[A]nd because it brings into action, and enforces this great and glorious principle, that the people are the sovereign of this country, and consequently that fellow citizens and joint sovereigns *cannot be degraded by appearing with each other in their own courts to have their controversies determined.*" (Chisholm v Georgia, 2 Dall 419, at p 479, [emphasis added])

Summary

The BAR (British Accredited Regency) has infiltrated America to the point that almost all Judges are BAR members. There are statutes requiring all appointed judges to be BAR members. All governments—local, state, and federal—are all controlled by BAR members, and all major corporations are either directly run by BAR members or are controlled by BAR members as chief counsel. And they are thieves and pirates engaged in chicanery

7

THE WAR OF INDEPENDENCE & THE ROMAN CULT

The reason so many people were so eager to leave Europe in the seventeenth, eighteenth, and nineteenth centuries, is because of the Roman Cult and because they would send out summoners " who were "petty officers that *cite* and warn men to appear in any court; and these ought to be *boni homines,* &c. *Fleta, lib.* 4. The *summonitores* were properly the apparitors who warned in delinquents at a certain time and place to answer any charge *or complaint* exhibited against them; *and in citations from a superior court* they were to be equals of the party cited; at least the barons were to be summoned by none under the degree of knights." (Tomlins Law Dictionary, 1835 Edition, Volume 2 [emphasis added]).

The summoners would make a complaint by way of a libel, which meant was an "ARTICULUS. or *complaint*," exhibited by way of libel, in "a court Christian. Sometimes the religious bound themselves to obey the ordinary, without such formal process. Paroch. Antiq. p. 344" (*Tomlins Law Dictionary*, 1835 Edition, Volume 1, [emphasis added]).

When there was libel in the spiritual court, it meant that "If upon a Libel for any Ecclesiastical Matter, the Defendant make a Surmise in B. R. *to have a Prohibition*, and such Surmise be insufficient, the other Party may shew it to the Court, and the Judges will discharge it. 1 Leon 10. 128. *This Libel used in Ecclesiastical Proceedings*, consists of three Parts. I. The major Proposition, which shews a just Cause of the Petition. 2. The Narration or minor Proposition. 3. The Conclusion, or conclusive Petition, which conjoins both Propositions, &c" (Jacob A New Law Dictionary, 1750 Edition [emphasis added]).

A summoner could also issue a summons by way of citation, or *citatio*, which is " a Summons to appear, *applied particularly to Process in the Spiritual Court. The Ecclesiastical Courts proceed according to the Course of the Civil and Canon Laws*, by *Citation, Libel*" (*Tomlins Law Dictionary*, 1835 Edition, Volume 1 [emphasis added]). This is also used in the "English ecclesiastical, probate, and divorce courts to call the defendant or respondent before them. 3 Bl. Comm. 100. 3 Steph. Comm. 720" (*Black's Law Dictionary*, 2nd Edition, at page 202).

These types of summons are to subject you to their satanic religious ceremony:

"COURTS ECCLESIASTICAL, Curia Ecclesiasticae, [Spiritual Courts.] Are those courts which are held by the king's authority as supreme governor of the church, for matters which chiefly concern religion. 4 Inst. 321. And the *laws and constitutions whereby the church of England is governed*, are, *1. Divers immemorial customs. 2.* Our own provincial constitutions; and the *canons made in convocations*, especially those in the year 1603. ....Much oppression having been exercised through the channel of these courts, on persons charged with trifling offences within their spiritual jurisdiction. (Tomlins Law Dictionary, 1835 Edition, Volume 1, [emphasis added])

"COURTS ECCLESIASTICAL. The proceedings in the Ecclesiastical Courts are, *according to the civil and canon law* by *citation, libel,* answer upon oath, *proof by* witnesses, and *presumptions,* &c., and after sentence, for contempt, by excommunication: and *if the sentence is disliked, by appeal.* (Tomlins Law Dictionary, 1835 Edition, Volume 1, [emphasis added])

And then they would hold an inquisition, or *ex officio mero,* which is "one Way of proceeding in Ecclesiastical Court. Wood's lnst. 596" (Jacob A New Law Dictionary, 1750 Edition).

Mandatory BAR Member = Star Chamber

Summoners compel you to have an attorney in their star chamber. The corrupt Star Chamber Courts of England "*required defendants to have counsel.* Star Chamber stood for swiftness and arbitrary power [admiralty maritime law]; *it was a limitation on the common law*" (Faretta v. California, 422 U.S. 806, 821 [emphasis added]). The attorney's first duty is "to the courts and to the public, *not to the client,* and whenever his duties to his client conflict with those as an officer of the court, in the administration of justice, the former must yield to the latter" (7 Corpus Juris Secundum § 4 Attorneys [emphasis added]). So they can convert you into an imbecile:

"Clients are also called "wards of the court" (7 Corpus Juris Secundum § 4 Attorneys)

"Wards of court. Infants and persons of unsound mind. Davis' Committee v. Loney, 290 Ky. 644, 162 S.W.2d 189, 190. Their rights must be guarded jealously. Montgomery v. Erie R. Co., C.C.A.N.J., 97 F.2d 289, 292." (*Black's Law Dictionary*, 4th Edition, page 1755)

They can deny your challenges to jurisdiction:
"IN PROPRIA PERSONA. In one's own proper person. It is a rule in pleading that pleas to the jurisdiction of the court must be plead *in propria persona, because if pleaded by attorney they admit the jurisdiction, as an attorney is an officer of the court, and he is presumed to plead after having obtained leave, which admits the jurisdiction.* (Lawes, Pl. 91." Black's Law Dictionary, 4th Edition, page 899-900 [emphasis added])

And they would forge your signature onto a contract:
"CAPIAS AD SATISFACIENDUM (shortly termed a CA. SA.) A judicial writ of execution which issues out on the record of a Judgment, where there is a recovery in the courts…, of debt, damages, &c. And by this writ the sheriff is commanded to take the body of the defendant in execution, and him safely to keep, so that he have his body in court at the return of the writ, *to satisfy the plaintiff his debt and damages. Vide* 1 *Litt Abr.* 249." (*Tomlins Law Dictionary*, 1835 Edition, Volume 1 [emphasis added])

And sell you into slavery:
"He [the prisoner] has as a consequence of his crime, not only forfeited his liberty but all his personal rights except

those which the law in its humanity affords him. *He is for the time being a slave of the state.*" (62 Va. (21 Gratt.) 790, 796 (1871) [emphasis added])

"Penitentiary has meant: a penitent, an ordainer of penances, and *a place for penitents.* See Locus, Penitentias." (*Anderson's Law Dictionary*, 1889 Edition, page 764 [emphasis added])

And the Roman Cult's penance was always for sale, which means it was an extortion racket:

"Penance, (Paenitentia) Is a Punishment imposed for a Crime by the Ecclesiastical Laws. It is an Acknowledgment of the Offence... *Penance may be changed into a Sum of Money* to be applied to pious Uses, called Commuting. 3 lnst. 150. 4 Inst. 336." (Jacob A New Law Dictionary, 1750 Edition [emphasis added])

This was why people were so eager to leave England for the new world, because all inquisitions, which are "**one Way of proceeding in Ecclesiastical Court**" (**Wood's lnst. 596.**", Jacob A New Law Dictionary, 1750 Edition) were originated with the Roman Cult, and if you didn't like your sentence you could appeal.

If someone was "cited out of their diocese, and live out of the jurisdiction of the bishop, a *prohibition,* or *consultation,* may be granted: but where persons live in the diocese, *if when they are cited they do not appear, they are to be excommunicated*" (Tomlins Law Dictionary, 1835 Edition, Volume 1 [emphasis added]), and imprisonment is an ecclesiastical censure.

Excommunication is an "ecclesiastical censure, divided into the greater and the lesser; by the former a person was excluded from the communion of the church; from the company of the faithful; and incapacitated from performing any legal act; the latter merely debarred him from the service of the church, and this is now the only incapacity that arises from a sentence of excommunication. *The sentence of excommunication was instituted originally for preserving the purity of the church; but ecclesiastics did not scruple to convert it into an engine for promoting their own power, and inflicted it on the most frivolous occasions"* (Tomlins Law Dictionary, 1835 Edition, Volume 1 [emphasis added]). And an excommunicated person had no rights:

> "An excommunicated person was disabled to do any act required to be done by one that that is *probus* and *legalis homo.* He could not serve upon juries, nor be a witness in any court, nor bring an action, either real or personal, to recover lands or money due to him. *Litt.*" (Tomlins Law Dictionary, 1835 Edition, Volume 1 [emphasis added])

Excommunicated people were put in jail until they submitted to the Roman Cult as an ecclesiastical censure:

> "EXCOMMUNICATO CAPIENDO. A writ directed to the sheriff for apprehending him who stands obstinately excommunicated. *If within forty days, after sentence of excommunication* has been published in the church, *the offender does not submit* and abide by the sentence of the Spiritual Court, the bishop may *signify* i. e. certify, such contempt to the king in Chancery. Upon which there issues out this writ to the sheriff of the county, called, from the bishop's certificate, a *signjficavit:* or, from its effect, a writ *de excommunicato capiendo. And the sheriff shall thereupon take the offender and imprison him in the county gaol till he is*

reconciled to the church, and such reconciliation certified by the bishop. F.N.B.62." (Tomlins Law Dictionary, 1835 Edition, Volume 1 [emphasis added])

Martial Law in Colonial Days

The scenario for martial law was set up during and even before colonial days, and it has probably been going on from the beginning of time:

"YIELDING AND PAYING yearly, to us, our heirs and Successors, for the same, the *yearly Rent of Twenty Marks of Lawful money of England, at the Feast of All Saints, yearly, forever,* The First payment thereof to begin and be made on the Feast of All Saints which shall be in the year of Our Lord One thousand six hundred Sixty and five; AND also, *the fourth part of all Gold and Silver Ore* which, with the limits aforesaid, shall, from time to time, happen to be found." (The Carolina Charter, 1663 [emphasis added])

And the resulting bankruptcy precipitated Martial Law and then the revolution:

"[S]tatutes have been passed extending the courts of admiralty and vice-admiralty far beyond their ancient limits for depriving us the accustomed and inestimable privilege of trial by jury, in cases affecting both life and property. . . . *to supersede the course of common law and instead thereof to publish and order the use and exercise of the law martial.*" (Causes and Necessity of Taking Up Arms (1775) [emphasis added])

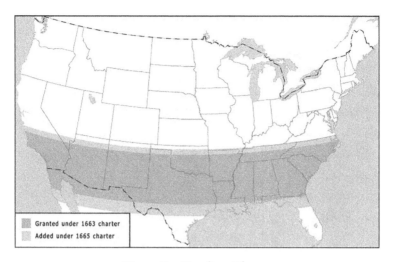

Figure 7 – Carolina Charter

"But when a long train of abuses and usurpations, pursuing invariably the same Object evinces a design to reduce them under absolute Despotism, it is their right, *it is their duty*, to throw off such Government, and to provide new Guards for their future security...

"He has erected a multitude of New Offices, and sent hither swarms of Officers to harass our people, and eat out their substance:"

"He has kept among us, in times of peace, Standing Armies..."

"He has affected to render the Military independent of and superior to the Civil power:"

"For imposing Taxes on us without our Consent:"

"He has combined with others to subject us to a jurisdiction foreign to our constitution, and unacknowledged by our laws; giving his Assent to their Acts of pretended Legislation:"

"For transporting us beyond Seas to be tried for pretended offences:"

"For abolishing the free System of English Laws in a neighbouring Province, *establishing therein an Arbitrary government*, and enlarging its Boundaries so as to render it at once an example and fit instrument for *introducing the same absolute rule* into these Colonies:"

"For taking away our Charters, abolishing our most valuable Laws, and *altering fundamentally the Forms of our Governments*:"

"He has abdicated Government here, by declaring us out of his protection, and *waging War against us.*" Declaration of Independence, (1776) [emphasis added]

And it was all about a military occupation and an extortion racket as evidenced by Patrick Henry when he coined the phrase "Give me liberty or give me death" after witnessing a man flogged to death for refusing to take a license (a contract), and the exact same thing is going on today:

"License, *contracts*, is a right given by some competent authority to do an act, which without such authority would be illegal. The instrument or writing which secures this right is also called a license. Vide Ayl.Parerg. 353; 15 Vin. Ab 92; Ang. Wat. Co. 61, 85. *A license is express or implied.* An express license is one in which in direct terms authorizes the performance of a certain act; as a license to keep a tavern by public authority. An implied license is one which though not expressly given, *may be presumed from the acts of the party having the right to give it.*" (*Bouvier's Law Dictionary*, 1843 Edition, Volume 2, page 53 [emphasis added])

"2. The requirement of payment for such *licenses is only a mode of imposing taxes* on the licensed business, and the prohibition, under penalties, against carrying on the business without *license is only a mode of enforcing the payment of such taxes.*

"5. The recognition by the acts of Congress of *the power and right of the states to tax, control, or regulate any business* carried on within its limits is entirely consistent with an intention on the part of Congress to tax such business for national purposes." (License Tax Cases 72 U.S. (5 Wall.) 462 (1866) [emphasis added])

Shortly after independence the courts declared that "States and Governments were made for man, and, at the same time, how true it is that his creatures and servants have first deceived, next vilified, and, at last oppressed their master and maker . . . "A state like a merchant makes a contract. *A dishonest state, like a dishonest merchant willfully refuses to discharge it*" (Chisholm v Georgia, 2 Dall 419 at p 455, 456 [emphasis added]).

And the colonists agreed with Patrick Henry's sentiment, that they would rather be dead than be a slave, as evidenced by the pile of bodies found in the morning below Betsy Ross' flag that Francis Scott Key was trying to see in his poem that became the national anthem, "Oh say can you see", all of which was a satanic blood sacrifice to the Roman Cult's god BAAL.

King George financed both sides of War of Independence

King George financed both sides of the War of Independence on behalf of the Roman Cult. The tyrant King George signed the *Definitive Treaty of Peace of 1783* as arch treasurer and prince elector of the Holy Roman Empire and the United States of America. Therefore, Queen Elizabeth, as successor to King George, is now arch treasurer, and prince elector of the Holy Roman Empire and the United States of America.

The Definitive Treaty of Peace of 1783 says that King George was "King of Great Britain, France and Ireland," and the contract between the king and the Thirteen United States of North America signed at Versailles, July 16, 1782, is as follows:

"ARTICLE 1 It is agreed and certified that the sums advanced by His Majesty to the Congress of the United States under the title of a loan, in the years 1778, 1779, 1780, 1781, and the present 1782, *amount to the sum of eighteen millions of livres, money of France*, according to the following twenty-one receipts of the above-mentioned underwritten Minister of Congress, given in virtue of his full powers. . .

"By which receipts the said Minister has promised, in the name of Congress and in behalf of the thirteen United States, *to cause to be paid and reimbursed to the royal treasury of His Majesty, on the 1st of January, 1788, at the house of his Grand Banker at Paris, the said sum of eighteen millions, money of France, with interest at five per cent per annum*" (Treaties and Other International Acts of the United States of America. Edited by Hunter Miller Volume 2 Documents 1-40: 1776-1818 Washington: Government Printing Office, 1931. [emphasis added])

Therefore, the tyrant King George financed both sides of the War of Independence, and under instructions from the Roman Cult and the War of Independence it was a debt slavery scam and a Satanic blood sacrifice perpetrated by the tyrant King George for his Roman Cult god BAAL. John Adams declared, "There are two ways to conquer and enslave a nation. One is by the sword. The other is by debt."

It was *only* two years after the Declaration of Independence that the Imperial Parliament passed the following act:

"Whereas *taxation by the parliament of Great Britain*, for the purpose of raising a revenue in his Majesty's colonies, provinces, and plantations, in North America, *has been found by experience to occasion great uneasiness and disorders*…That from and after the passing of this act *the King and Parliament of Great Britain will not impose any duty, tax, or assessment whatever*, payable in any of the colonies, provinces, or plantations, in North America or the West Indies; *except only such duties as it may be expedient to impose for the regulation of commerce.*" (George III, CAP XII 1778 [emphasis added])

The tyrant King George, as a servant for his Roman Cult handlers, perjured his oath of office in the process. Benjamin Franklin explained it well: "The refusal of King George the Third to allow the colonies to operate an honest money system which freed the ordinary man from the clutches of the money manipulators was probably the prime cause of the revolution." And they set up the scenario for the next bankruptcy and the next Roman Cult satanic blood sacrifice with the civil war:

> "And provided further, that nothing herein contained shall affect the titles or possessions of individuals holding or claiming under the laws heretofore in force, or grants heretofore made by the late King George II, or his predecessors, or the late lords proprietors, or any of them." (Declaration of Rights 1776, North Carolina Constitution)

And the courts even agreed with it. In Terrett v. Taylor, it was stated that "*the dissolution of the regal government, no more destroyed the rights of the church to possess and enjoy the property which belonged to it, than it did the right of any other corporation or individual to his or its own property.*" Later, the chief justice, in reference to the corporation of the college, observed that "*all contracts and rights respecting property remained unchanged by the revolution*; and the same sentiment was enforce, more at length, by the other judge who noticed this point in the cause" (The Society, &c., v. The Town of New Haven. Et Al. 8 Wheat. 464; 5 Cond. Rep. 489 [emphasis added]).

Amistadt

There was a slave ship that the slaves (black people from Africa) were able to get control of the ship and they killed everybody (their captors) except one man because they didn't know how to sail, and they told him to take them back to Africa, and he sailed in circles off the coast of Virginia until the US Navy captured the ship and brought them to the US and put them on trial for murder. The case went all the way to the US Supreme Court (United States v Amistadt 40 US 518 (1841)). They were put on trial for murder and their defense arguments were two. Either they were property like a dog or a cat and a dog or a cat can't murder anyone, or they were free men and had every right to do what they did. The court ruled that they were free men and had every right to do what they did, and they sent them back to Africa. This case is proof that everybody of all races are free, and slavery is all about divide and conquer by the Roman Cult and slavery promotes the Roman Cult's satanic agenda, which is why it was introduced into America in colonial days.

Summary

The people of Europe were subjected to inquisitions, star chambers, and numerous other extortion scams by the Roman Cult to the point that they were leaving en masse to get away from the tyranny.

The War of Independence was orchestrated by the tyrant King George under the direction and supervision of the Roman Cult as part of a debt slavery scam, and bankruptcy, which precipitated a satanic blood sacrifice to the Roman Cult god BAAL, and the seeds for next debt slavery scam and bankruptcy were put in place.

8

THE LAW OF NATIONS
& THE ROMAN CULT

Law of Nations = Roman Cult

The Roman Cult is responsible for slavery in America when Pope Nicholas V issued the papal bull Dum Diversas on 18 June 1452, which authorized Alfonso V of Portugal to reduce any "Saracens (Muslims) and pagans and any other unbelievers" [failed to be catholic] to perpetual slavery. This facilitated the Portuguese slave trade from West Africa. The same pope wrote the bull *Romanus Pontifex* on January 5, 1455, to the same Alfonso. As a follow-up to the *Dum diversas*, the *Romanus Pontifex* extended to the Catholic nations of Europe dominion over discovered lands during the age of discovery. Along with sanctifying the seizure of non-Christian [failed to be Catholic] lands, the papal bull encouraged the enslavement of native, non-Christian [failed to be Catholic] peoples in Africa and the New World:

"We weighing all and singular the premises with due meditation, and noting that since we had formerly by other letters of ours granted among other things free and ample faculty to the aforesaid King Alfonso to invade, search out, capture, vanquish, and subdue [assault, kidnap, and falsely imprison] all Saracens and pagans whatsoever, and other enemies of Christ [non-Catholics] wheresoever placed, and the kingdoms, dukedoms, principalities, dominions, possessions, and all movable and immovable goods whatsoever held and possessed by them and to reduce their persons to perpetual slavery, and to apply and appropriate to himself [steal] and his successors the kingdoms, dukedoms, counties, principalities, dominions, possessions, and goods, and to convert them to his and their use and profit by having secured the said faculty, the said King Alfonso, or, by his authority, the aforesaid infante, justly and lawfully has acquired [stolen] and possessed, and doth possess, these islands, lands, harbors, and seas, and they do of right belong and pertain to the said King Alfonso and his successors." (Dum diversas)

The Roman Cult was responsible for establishing the Law of Nations when Pope Alexander VI issued the bull *Inter Caetera* in 1493, stating one Christian nation failed to have the right to establish dominion over lands previously dominated by another Christian nation, *thus establishing the Law of Nations.* Together, the *Dum Diversas,* the *Romanus Pontifex,* and the *Inter Caetera* came to serve as the basis and justification for the doctrine of discovery, the global slave trade of the fifteenth and sixteenth centuries, and the age of imperialism. A Canadian publisher and civil servant said, "If therefore we put aside the conventional law or treaty law of nations, it will be seen that *modern international law is founded on the Roman Law and on the Canon Law,* which latter was carried over Europe by the Roman Church; for even in England up to the time of Edward III the Lord Chancellor was always an ecclesiastic" (*The Transactions of the Royal Society of Canada, Second Series – 1899-1900*, Volume V, Section II, *The Lines of Demarcation of Pope Alexander VI and the Treaty of Tordesillas A.D. 1493 and 1494* by Samuel Edward Dawson, Lit.D (Laval) [emphasis added]).

And slavery continues to this day in the prisons of America under the current (so-called) Thirteenth Amendment:

"Section 1. Neither slavery nor involuntary servitude, *except as a punishment for crime whereof the party shall have been duly convicted,* shall exist within the United States, or any place subject to their jurisdiction.

Section 2. Congress shall have power to enforce this article by appropriate legislation." (Article Thirteen of the US Constitution [emphasis added])

Law of Nations = International Law

The Law of Nations and International Law are convertible phrases. According to *Black's Law Dictionary* international law or the law of nations must be "defined as law applicable to states in their mutual relations and to individuals in their relations with states. International law may also, under this hypothesis, be applicable to certain interrelationships of individuals themselves, where such interrelationships involve matters of international concern" (*Black's Law Dictionary*, 8th Edition, page 2392 [emphasis added].

Roman Cult = Slavery & Murder

The Roman Cult was responsible for all of the slavery today, and perpetuated under their Law of Nations:

> "Residents, as distinguished from citizens, *are aliens* who are permitted to take up a *permanent* abode in the country. Being bound to the society by reason of their dwelling in it, they are *subject* to its laws so long as they remain there, and, being protected by it, *they must defend it*, although they do not enjoy all the rights of citizens. They have only certain privileges which the law, or custom, gives them. *Permanent residents* are those who have been given the right of perpetual residence. They are a sort of citizen of a less privileged character, *and are subject to the society* without enjoying all its advantages. *Their children succeed to their status; for the right of perpetual residence given them by the State passes to their children."* (The Law of Nations, Vattel, Book 1, Chapter 19, Section 213, p. 87)

Martial law or the *"law of war can no more wholly dispense with retaliation than can the law of nations, of which it is a branch.* Yet civilized nations acknowledge retaliation as the sternest feature of war" (Article 12, General Orders 100 (The Lieber Code) [emphasis added]). It is a branch of the Roman Cult's Law of Nations, and all Roman Cult BAR member/BAAL priests (bought-and-paid for) clerks masquerading as judges (military commissioners) are there to facilitate the warfare as agents of the Roman Cult. Therefore, it is the Roman Cult's martial law (see page 25 for the three kinds of martial law), and all law enforcement officers enforcing martial law are agents of the Roman Cult (Roman Cult military police), all

BAR members are BAAL priests, all so-called court cases are satanic religious ceremonies, all warfare is commerce and all commerce is warfare, and all wars are a Satanic blood sacrifice to the Roman Cult's god, BAAL.

Martial Law = Millions of Rules and Regulations

Martial law gives the Roman Cult's BAR members in Congress and the legislatures an excuse to pass literally millions of codes, rules, and regulations. "The more corrupt the state, the more numerous the laws," said Cornelius Tacitus (AD 55-117).

According to one ruling "Every citizen & freeman is endowed with certain rights & privileges to enjoy *which no written law or statute is required*. These are the fundamental or natural rights, recognized among all free people" (U.S. v. Morris, 125 F 322, 325 [emphasis added]). This is why the Roman Cult BAR member/BAAL priests (bought-and-paid-for) clerks masquerading as judges (military commissioners) whores selling their "justus" sit there and play stupid. No justice will ever come at the hands of them unless it is their political agenda, and they come up with all sorts of schemes about how they can ignore (perjure) their oaths and take advantage of people who fail to mention some obscure code, rule, or regulation, and use that as an excuse to sell them into slavery or deny them justice for their personal profit and gain.

Martial Law = Satanic Equity

The Roman Cult's martial law supersedes and replaces common law and laws have extended far beyond their limits "*to supersede the course of common law and instead thereof to publish and order the use and exercise of the law martial.*" (Causes and Necessity of Taking Up

Arms (1775)). Therefore, under equity the so-called judges can do anything they want:

> "In the meantime, "Civil Law" was the form of law imposed in the Roman Empire which was largely (if not wholly) governed by martial law rule. "Equity" has always been understood to follow the law; to have "superior equity," is to turn things on their head. This is exactly what happens when martial law is imposed. If "equity" is the law, then it follows its own course rather than following the common law, *thereby destroying the common law and leaving what is called "equity" in its place*" (The Non-Ratification of the Fourteenth Amendment by Judge A.H. Ellett, Utah Supreme Court, Dyett v Turner, 439 P2d 266 @ 269, 20 U2d 403 [1968], [emphasis added]).

This is why the Roman Cult BAR member/BAAL priests (bought-and-paid-for) clerks masquerading as judges (military commissioners) whores selling their "justus" will tell you in their so-called court rooms: "I can do anything I want in here," which is why they routinely make up fake contracts or quasi contracts.

Quasi Contracts

Both in Roman and English law there are certain obligations that are "not in truth contractual, but which the law treats as IF they were. They are contractual in law, but not in fact, being the subject-matter of a *fictitious extension of the sphere of contract* to cover obligations which do not in reality fall within it" (Salmond, Salmond on Jurisprudence, p. 642 (9th Edition, 1937, Sweet & Maxwell, Ltd. England), [emphasis added]).

A quasi contractual action "presupposes acceptance and retention of a benefit by one party with full appreciation of the facts, under circumstances making it *inequitable* for him to retain the benefit without payment of its reasonable value" (Major-Blakeney Co. v. Jenkins (1953), 121 C.A.2d 325, 263 P.2d 655, hear den.; Townsend Pierson, Inc. v. Holly-Coleman Co. (1960), 178 C.A.2d 373, 2 Cal. Rptr. 812. [emphasis added]).

And the Roman Cult BAR member/BAAL priests (bought-and-paid-for) clerks masquerading as judges (military commissioners) even pass statutes (edicts under martial law) for it.

"In all matters in which there is any conflict or variance between the rules of equity and common law with reference to the same matter, the rules of equity prevail" (Alberta Judicature Act Section 15). This creates more opportunities for corruption by the Roman Cult BAR member/BAAL priests (bought-and-paid-for) clerks masquerading as judges (military commissioners) whores selling their "justus."

"The more corrupt the state, the more numerous the laws," said Cornelius Tacitus.

Because at common law you don't need statutes "every citizen & freeman is endowed with certain rights & privileges to enjoy *which no written law or statute is required.* These are the fundamental or natural rights, recognized among all free people" (U.S. v. Morris, 125 F 322, 325 [emphasis added]).

In support of their military dictatorship, the Roman Cult BAR member/BAAL priests (bought-and-paid-for) clerks masquerading as judges (military commissioners) created the so-called Fourteenth Amendment to criminally convert citizenship into the opposite of what the founders intended:

"And while the Fourteenth Amendment does not create a national citizenship, it has the effect of making that citizenship "paramount and dominant" instead of "derivative and dependent" upon state citizenship." (Colgate v Harvey 296 US 404 at p 427)

"The amendment (fourteenth) reversed and annulled the original policy of the constitution." (United States v. Rhodes, 27 Federal Cases, 785, 794)

As part of their slavery agenda, and in support of their military dictatorship:

"The thirteenth, fourteenth, and fifteenth amendments were designed mainly for the protection of the newly emancipated negroes." (United States v. Anthony, 24 Fed. Cas. 829, Case No. 14,459)

"*Slavery*, complicating and confounding the ideas of property, (that is of a thing,) and of personality, (that is of humanity,) *exists according to municipal or local law only. The law of nature and nations has never acknowledged it.* The digest of the Roman law enacts the early dictum of the pagan jurist, that "so far as the law of nature is concerned, all men are equal." Fugitives escaping from a country in which they were slaves, villains, or serfs, into another country, have, for centuries past, been held free and acknowledged free by judicial decisions of European countries, even though the municipal law of the country in which the slave had taken refuge acknowledged slavery within its own dominions." (Article 42, General Orders 100 (The Lieber Code) [emphasis added])

"Section 1. Neither slavery nor involuntary servitude, *except as a punishment for crime whereof the party shall have been duly convicted*, shall exist within the United States, or any place subject to their jurisdiction.

"Section 2. Congress shall have power to enforce this article by appropriate legislation." ([current] Article Thirteen in Amendment [emphasis added])

"He [the prisoner] has as a consequence of his crime, not only forfeited his liberty but all his personal rights except those which the law in its humanity affords him. *He is for the time being a slave of the state*." (62 Va. (21 Gratt.) 790, 796 (1871) [emphasis added])

All of this demonstrates that anyone who is a slave, volunteered into it under the Roman Cults municipal law with their criminally converted US citizen / slave / cestui que trust (JOHN HENRY SMITH), which was created by the Roman Cult, and their Roman Cult BAR member/BAAL priests (bought and paid for) Clerks masquerading as Judges (Military Commissioners) assault you (presume) with their cestui que trust (JOHN HENRY SMITH) and then use that as justification for the theft of property with taxes (warfare), and because of the Roman Cult's martial law dictatorship.

Cestui que Trust = US Citizen

A *cestui que use* is a shortened version of *cestui a que use le feoffment fuit fait*, literally, "The person for whose benefit the feoffment was made." It is one way to gain freedom with a petition for a writ of habeas corpus, which essentially means to bring the body ("corpus" that is being held ransom for the Roman Cult *cestui que* trust) before a judge to review the cause for the imprisonment, and the Roman Cult *cestui que* trust was affirmed by the Congress in their Code of law for the District of Columbia that is now called United States Code:

"Chap. 854. – An Act to establish a code of law for the District of Columbia." Approved on March 3, 1901, by the Fifty-Sixth Congress, Session II, at 31 Stat. 1189, and at 2, where it says:

"And be it further enacted, That in the interpretation and construction of said code the following rules shall be observed namely:

"Third. *The word "person" shall be held to apply to partnerships and corporations*" [emphasis added]

"The Legal Estate to be in Cestui Que Use" (Chapter Fifty-Six in Sec. 1617, at 31 Stat. 1432)

They even presume you are dead at Chapter three: *Absence for Seven Years*, in Sec. 252, at 31 Stat. 1230, where it says:
"SEC. 252. PRESUMPTION OF DEATH. .... he shall be presumed to be dead, in any case wherein his death shall come in question, unless proof be made that he was alive within that time.,

"(2) the term "individual" means a citizen of the United States or an alien lawfully admitted for permanent residence;"
5 USC § 552a.(a)(2)

. . . (E)very taxpayer is a cestui qui trust having sufficient interest in the preventing abuse of the trust to be recognized in the field of this court's prerogative jurisdiction . . In Re Bolens (1912), 135 N.W. 164

A *"citizen of the United States"* is a civilly dead entity operating as a co-trustee and co-beneficiary of the *PCT (Public Charitable Trust)*, the constructive, *cestui que trust* of US Inc. under the *14th Amendment*, which upholds the debt of the USA and US Inc. Congressional Record, June 13 1967, pp. 15641-15646

"Slater's protestations to the effect that he derives no benefit from the United States government have no bearing on his legal obligation to pay income taxes. *Cook v. Tait*, 265 U.S. 47, 44 S.Ct. 444, 68 L.Ed. 895 (1924); *Benitez Rexach v. United States*, 390 F.2d 631, (1st Circ.), cert. *denied* 393 U.S. 833, 89 S.Ct. 103, 21 L.Ed.2d 103 (1968). *Unless the defendant can establish that he is not a citizen of the United States, the IRS possesses authority to attempt to determine his federal tax liability."* (UNITED STATES of America v. William M. SLATER (1982) (D. Delaware) 545 F.Supp 179, 182. [emphasis added])

Their Roman Cult cestui que trust JOHN HENRY SMITH is codified here:

"Corporation" shall be deemed to include any company, trust, so-called Massachusetts trust, or association, incorporated or unincorporated, which is organized to carry on business

for its own profit or that of its members, and has shares of capital or capital stock or certificates of interest, and *any* company, *trust*, so-called Massachusetts trust, or association, incorporated or *unincorporated, without shares of capital or capital stock or certificates of interest*, except partnerships, *which is organized to carry on business for its own profit or that of its members*." (15 USC § 44 Definitions [emphasis added])

Their criminally converted US citizen / *cestui que* trust (JOHN HENRY SMITH) fails to have access to the first eight amendments to the Constitution against the powers of the federal government:
> "...the privileges and immunities of citizens of the United States do not necessarily include all the rights protected by the first eight amendments to the Federal constitution against the powers of the Federal government." Maxwell v Dow, 20 S.C.R. 448, at pg 455

> "The *right of trial by jury* in civil cases, guaranteed by the 7th Amendment (Walker v. Sauvinet, 92 U. S. 90), and the *right to bear arms*, guaranteed by the 2nd Amendment (Presser v. Illinois, 116 U. S. 252), *have been distinctly held not to be privileges and immunities of citizens of the United States* guaranteed by the 14th Amendment against abridgement by the states, and in effect the same decision was made in respect of the guarantee against prosecution, except by indictment of a grand jury, contained in the 5th Amendment (Hurtado v. California, 110 U.S. 516), and in respect of the right to be confronted with witnesses, contained in the 6th Amendment." (West v Louisiana, 194 US 258)

Their criminally converted US citizen / cestui que trust (JOHN HENRY SMITH) has no rights at all, in support of their slavery agenda and their military dictatorship for their Roman Cult handlers, especially since they converted all of the States into territories with their military dictatorship:

"The only absolute and unqualified right of a United States citizen is to residence within the territorial boundaries of the United States." (US vs. Valentine 288 F. Supp. 957)

"Civil rights under the 14th amendment are for Federal citizens and not State Citizens; Federal citizens, as parents, have no right to the custody of their infant children except subject to the paramount right of the State." (Wadleigh v. Newhall, Circuit Court N. Dist. Cal., Mar 13, 1905)

"[I]t is evident that they [U.S. citizens] have not the political rights which are vested in citizens of the States. They are not constituents of any community in which is vested any sovereign power of government. Their position partakes *more of the character of subjects than of citizens.* They are subject to the laws of the United States but have no voice in its management. If they are allowed to make laws, the validity of these laws is derived from the sanction of a Government in which they are not represented. Mere citizenship they may have, but the political rights of citizens they cannot enjoy." (People v. De La Guerra,40 Cal. 311, 342 (AD 1870))

"[T]he term "citizen," in the United States, is analogous to the term "subject" in the common law." (State vs Manual 20 NC 122, 14 C.J.S. 4, p 430)

The unborn children of their criminally converted US citizen /cestui que trust (JOHN HENRY SMITH) have no rights. "The unborn are not included within the definition of 'person' as used in the 14th Amendment" (Roe v. Wade US Supreme Court 410 US 13, 35 L.Ed. 2d 147, 1973) and therefore can be murdered, which is another blood sacrifice to the Roman Cult's satanic god BAAL.

The criminally converted US citizen/cestui que trust/slave (JOHN HENRY SMITH) fails to be entitled to an Article 3 court because the ruling class have stated that "*the District of Columbia is not a state within Article 3 of the Constitution.* In other words cases between citizens of the District and those of the states were not included of the catalogue of controversies over which the Congress could give jurisdiction to the federal courts by virtue of Article 3. In other words *Congress has exclusive legislative jurisdiction over citizens of Washington District of Columbia and through their plenary power nationally covers those citizens even when in one of the several states as though the district expands for the purpose of regulating its citizens wherever they go throughout the states in union*" (National Mutual Insurance Company of the District of Columbia v. Tidewater Transfer Company, 337 U.S. 582, 93 L.Ed. 1556 (1948)).

Quasi Contracts

The reason the Roman Cult's military police needs to fabricate evidence against US citizens/slaves is so they can assault them with one of their quasi contracts.

An assumpsit, or common law actions used to enforce obligations arising in tort were "soon transformed into an action of contract, becoming afterwards a remedy where there was neither tort nor contract. *Based at first only upon an express promise, it was afterwards*

supported upon an implied promise, and even upon a fictitious promise.
Introduced as a special manifestation of the action on the case, it soon
acquired the dignity of a distinct form of action, which superseded
Debt, became concurrent with Account, with Case upon a bailment,
a warranty, and bills of exchange, *and competed with Equity in the
case of the essentially equitable quasi-contracts* growing out of the
principle of unjust enrichment. Surely, it would be hard to find a
better illustration of the flexibility and power of self-development of
the Common Law" (James Barr Ames, "The History of Assumpsit,"
in three Select Essays in Anglo-American Legal History 298 (1909)"
and *Black's Law Dictionary*, 8th Edition, page 379 [emphasis added]).

In Roman and English law there are certain obligations "which
were not in truth contractual, but which the law treats as IF they
were. They are contractual in law, but not in fact, being the subject-
matter of a *fictitious* extension of the sphere of contract to cover
obligations which do not in reality fall within it" (Salmond, Salmond
on Jurisprudence, p. 642 (9th Edition, 1937, Sweet & Maxwell, Ltd.
England) [emphasis added]).

Furthermore, "a quasi contractual action presupposes acceptance
and retention of a benefit by one party with full appreciation of the
facts, under circumstances making it *inequitable* for him to retain the
benefit without payment of its reasonable value" (Major-Blakeney
Co. v. Jenkins (1953), 121 C.A.2d 325, 263 P.2d 655, hear den.;
Townsend Pierson, Inc. v. Holly-Coleman Co. (1960), 178 C.A.2d
373, 2 Cal. Rptr. 812. [emphasis added]). Therefore, it is absolutely
critical to fabricate evidence of their Roman Cult cestui que trust
slave:

"Constructive/quasi contracts are based solely upon a legal
fiction or fiction of law." (Hill v. Waxberg, 237 F.2d 936)

"But individuals, when acting as representatives of a collective group, cannot be said to be exercising their personal rights and duties, nor be entitled to their purely personal privileges. Rather they assume the rights, duties and privileges of the artificial entity or association of which they are agents or officers and they are bound by its obligations." (Brasswell v. United States 487 U.S. 99 (1988) quoting, United States v. White 322 U.S. 694 (1944))

They gather evidence so they can assault you with their UNIDROIT (Roman Cult)-controlled and regulated Uniform Commercial Code, which is found in Texas under the *Texas Business and Commerce Code,* which is also part of the Roman Cult's *Private International Law,* which is also covered by *The Hague Conference on Private International Law,* which says that whenever the uniform commercial code *creates a "presumption"* with respect to a fact, or provides that a fact is "presumed," *the trier of fact must find the existence of the fact unless and until evidence is introduced that supports a finding of its nonexistence"* (Uniform Commercial Code § 1-206 Presumptions [emphasis added]). And then they forge your signature onto their so-called contract to sell you into slavery:

"In an action with respect to an instrument, the authenticity of, and *authority to make, each signature on the instrument are admitted unless specifically denied in the pleadings.* If the validity of a signature is denied in the pleadings, the burden of establishing validity is on the person claiming validity, *but the signature is presumed to be authentic and authorized* unless the action is to enforce the liability of the purported signer and the signer is dead or incompetent at the time of trial of the issue of validity of the signature." (Uniform Commercial Code § 3.308 Proof of Signatures and Status as Holder in Due Course [emphasis added])

"He [the prisoner] has as a consequence of his crime, not only forfeited his liberty but all his personal rights except those which the law in its humanity affords him. *He is for the time being a slave of the state*." (62 Va. (21 Gratt.) 790, 796 (1871) [emphasis added])

"Penitentiary has meant: a penitent, an ordainer of penances, and *a place for penitents*. See Locus, Penitentias." (Andersons Law Dictionary, 1889 Edition, page 764 [emphasis added])

And the Roman Cult's penance is a punishment "imposed for a Crime by the Ecclesiastical Laws. It is an Acknowledgment of the Offence… *Penance may be changed into a Sum of Money* to be applied to pious uses, called Commuting. 3 lnst. 150. 4 Inst. 336" (Jacob A New Law Dictionary, 1750 Edition). Penance, therefore, was always for sale, and then they securitize it and sell it on Wall Street:

> "The following rules apply in an action on a certificated security against the issuer: (1) *Unless specifically denied in the pleadings, each signature on a security certificate or in a necessary indorsement is admitted.* (2) If the effectiveness of a signature is put in issue, the burden of establishing effectiveness is on the party claiming under the signature, *but the signature is presumed to be genuine or authorized.*" (Uniform Commercial Code § 8-114 Evidentiary Rules Concerning Certificated Securities [emphasis added])

Before they can do any of this, they need to get rid of their little common law problem by orchestrating the Roman Cult's martial law. They need to ensure that "statutes have been passed extending the courts of admiralty and vice-admiralty far beyond their ancient limits for depriving us the accustomed and inestimable privilege of trial by jury, in cases affecting both life and property . . . *to supersede the course of common law and instead thereof to publish and order the use and exercise of the law martial*" (Causes and Necessity of Taking Up Arms (1775) [emphasis added]). They do this, because otherwise, at common law they would all be put to death:

> "If a man be found stealing any of his brethren of the children of Israel, and maketh merchandise of him, or selleth him; then that thief shall die; and thou shalt put evil away from among you." (Deuteronomy 24:7)

> "And through covetousness shall they with feigned words make merchandise of you: whose judgment now of a long time lingereth not, and their damnation slumbereth not." (2 Peter 2:3)

> Your life is in danger because you are literally in a contract with the devil, but their Roman Cult slave scam *IS SO GOOD FOR BUSINESS!!!*

> "In doing this, I shall have occasion incidentally to evince, how true it is that States and Governments were made for man, and, at the same time, how true it is that his creatures and servants have first deceived, next vilified, and, at last oppressed their master and maker." (Chisholm v Georgia, 2 Dall 419 at p 455)

"A state like a merchant makes a contract. *A dishonest state, like a dishonest merchant willfully refuses to discharge it.*" (Chisholm v Georgia, 2 Dall 419 at p 456 [emphasis added])

Penal = Breach of Contract

Even in so-called criminal matters the Roman Cult are assaulting you with one of their so-called contracts. The penal action, "an action for recovery of penalty given by statute" (McNeely v. City of Natchez, 114 So. 484, 487; 148 Miss. 268), is an action "founded entirely upon a statue, and the only object of it is to recover a penalty or forfeiture, such action is a 'penal action' " (Gawthrop v. Fairmont Coal Co., 81 S.E. 560, 561; 74 S.Va. 39).

The words *penal* and *penalty* denote a "punishment, *whether corporal or pecuniary*, imposed and enforced by the state for a crime or offense against its laws. *The noun penalty is defined forfeiture or to be forfeited for noncompliance with an agreement.* The words *forfeit* and *penalty* are substantially synonymous" (Missouri, K. & T. Ry. Co. v. Dewey Portland Cement Co., 242 P. 257, 259, 113 Okla. 142 [emphasis added]).

Therefore, a penal action is *only* using edicts under the Roman Cult's martial law:

"A 'penal action' is one founded entirely on statute, and the only object is to recover a penalty or a forfeiture imposed as a punishment for a certain specific offense, while a 'remedial action': is one which is brought to obtain compensation or indemnity." (Cummings v. Board of Education of Okla. City, 125 P2d 989, 994, 190 Okl. 533)

"PECUNIARY CAUSE. Such as arise either from the withholding ecclesiastical dues, or the doing or neglecting some act relating to the church whereby some damage accrues to the plaintiff; towards obtaining satisfaction for which, he is permitted to institute a suit in the spiritual court. Such, for instance, are the subtraction and withholding of tithes from the parson or vicar; the *non-payment of ecclesiastical dues to the clergy*, as pensions, mortuaries, compositions, and the like.-3 BI. 88, 89." (Holthouse A New Law Dictionary, 1850 Edition, page 299)

So we find that a penal action is a civil suit "brought for the recovery of a statutory forfeiture when inflicted as punishment for an offense against the public. Such actions are 'civil actions,' on the one hand closely related to criminal prosecutions and on the other to actions for private injuries in which the party aggrieved may, by statute, recover punitive damages" (State ex rel. McNamee v. Stobie, 92 SW 191, 212, 194 Mo. 14). Therefore, all so-called crimes are commercial, (breach of contract) and fall under the Roman Cult's

Figure 8 – TSA Molestation

UNIDROIT controlled and regulated uniform commercial code under the Roman Cult's Law of Nations and Private International Law

"Any of the following types of crimes (Federal or State); <u>Offenses</u> <u>against the revenue laws</u>; burglary; larceny; robbery; illegal sale or possession or deadly weapons; prostitution (including soliciting, procuring, pandering, white slaving, keeping house of ill fame, and like offenses); extortion; swindling and confidence games; and attempting to commit, or compounding any of the foregoing crimes, <u>addiction to narcotic drugs and use of marijuana</u> <u>will be treated as</u> <u>if such were commercial crime</u>." 27 CFR § 72.11 [emphasis added] which is why they will even torture you to get evidence of their Roman Cult cestui que trust / US citizen / slave (JOHN HENRY SMITH)

US citizen = Enemy of the State

Their criminally converted US citizen is also an enemy of the state "Martial Law extends to property, and to persons, *whether they are subjects of the enemy* or aliens to that government." Article 7, General Orders 100 (The Lieber Code) [emphasis added]

"(a) The President, if he shall find it compatible with the safety

Figure 9 – *War on Terror is War on YOU!*

of the United States and with the successful *Prosecution of the war*, may… "(b)(1) During the time of the war, the President may, through any agency that he may designate, and under such rules and regulations as he may prescribe, by means of instructions, licenses, or otherwise, "(B) …regulate, direct and compel, nullify, void, prevent or prohibit,…or exercising any right, power or privilege with respect to…*any property…by any person*…subject to the jurisdiction of the United States:…and upon the terms, directed by the President, in such agency or person… and such designated agency or person may perform any and all acts incident to the accomplishment or furtherance of these purposes…" 50 U.S.C. Appendix 5 Trading with the Enemy Act

Which is the same thing that precipitated the War of Independence "He has abdicated Government here, by declaring us out of his protection, and *waging War against us.*" Declaration of Independence, 1776 [emphasis added];

With their so-called War on Terror that is really a war on you!

United Nations

The Roman Cult's owned and operated Crown and their owned-and-operated bankster thieves, and their owned-and-operated news media were behind the creation of their United Nations municipal corporation.

"Mr. Speaker, the information contained in this booklet is important at this time, particularly in

Figure 10 – If we can't rape you the Terrorists Win!

view of the fact that the pro-English groups in the United States are now working in close cooperation with world internationalist organizations.

"Before 1917, foreign influence came mainly from Anglo-American groups. *Since the World War, these groups have been fortified by the international financiers and the internationalists, or the so-called minority group.* The pressure is therefore more than double, for combined, *these groups control all avenues of communication and are now using them to further their plan of British domination to establish a world federation of states.*

Figure 11 – You think this is for your protection

"Let me call your attention to the fact that *on the reverse of the great seal of the United States, which appears on our dollar bills, you will find the exact symbol of the British Israel world federation movement.*

This symbol is also carried on literature of other organizations promoting a world government and a world religion. *At the bottom of the circle surrounding the pyramid, you will find the wording:* "Novus Ordo Seclorum." *It was this new order that was advocated by Clinton Roosevelt several hundred years ago*; recently in Philip Dru, and now followed by the Executive.

Figure 12 – Say No to Globalism

"Do you not think, as good American people. that the administration has gone far from constitutional government, when there is inscribed a symbol on the reverse of our great seal, that advocates a new order? *Yes, an order which means the destruction of our Republic as formulated in the Constitution of the United States.*

"It may also interest you to know that this contemplated "Union Now," as advocated by Clarence Streit, will be under the control of Great Britain, *and is a movement to return the United States as a colony in the British Empire. Should we become a part of this union, our traditional rights and liberties will be lost, and we will have no greater status than an English possession.* This was the dream of Cecil Rhodes and Andrew Carnegie, when the latter wrote his book, Triumphant Democracy, in 1893. Steps Toward British Union, a World State, and Internal Strife-Part V." (J Thorkelson of Montana, Congressional Record, Monday, August 19, 1940, [emphasis added])

The Roman Cult's BAR member / BAAL priests in the US Congress ratified the United Nations Charter on behalf of their unconstitutional municipal corporation called UNITED STATES OF AMERICA as an edict under the Roman Cult's martial law.

The Roman Cult's BAR member / BAAL priests in the US Congress acceded to Hague Convention IV which is the Law of War on Land, on behalf of their unconstitutional municipal corporation called UNITED STATES OF AMERICA as an edict under the Roman Cult's martial law.

Figure 13 – The United Nations is Satanic

The Roman Cult's BAR member / BAAL priests in the US Congress acceded to the Geneva Convention relative to the Protection of Civilian Persons in a Time of War_of 1949, on behalf of their unconstitutional municipal corporation called UNITED STATES OF AMERICA as an edict under the Roman Cult's martial law.

The Roman Cult's BAR member / BAAL priests in the US Congress acceded to the International Covenant on Civil and Political Rights, on behalf of their unconstitutional municipal corporation called UNITED STATES OF AMERICA as an edict under the Roman Cult's Martial Law;

The Roman Cult's BAR member / BAAL priests in the US Congress acceded to the Universal Declaration of Human Rights on behalf of their unconstitutional municipal corporation called UNITED STATES OF AMERICA as an edict under the Roman Cult's martial law.

The Roman Cult's BAR member / BAAL priests in the US Congress acceded to the UNIDROIT statute, on behalf of their unconstitutional municipal corporation called UNITED STATES OF AMERICA as an edict under the Roman Cult's martial law.

The Roman Cult's BAR member / BAAL priests in the US Congress acceded to the Concordat of 1933, on behalf of their unconstitutional municipal corporation called UNITED STATES OF AMERICA as an edict under the Roman Cult's martial law.

The Roman Cult's BAR member / BAAL priests in the US Congress acceded to the Lateran Pact, on behalf of their unconstitutional municipal corporation called UNITED STATES OF AMERICA, which guarantees that their unconstitutional municipal corporation called UNITED STATES OF AMERICA will defend the Roman Cult as an edict under the Roman Cult's martial law.

Their Geneva Convention relative to the Protection of Civilians in a Time of War of 1949 applies to any armed conflict, and all military occupations that "*shall apply to all cases* of declared war or *of any other armed conflict* which may arise. . . . *The Convention shall also apply to all cases of partial or total occupation of the territory*" (Article 2, Geneva Convention Relative to the Protection of Civilians in Time of War of 1949 [emphasis added]).

And certain provisions apply for the duration of the occupation:

> "the Occupying Power shall be bound, for the duration of the occupation, to the extent that such Power exercises the functions of government in such territory, by the provisions of the following Articles of the present Convention: 1 to 12, 27, 29 to 34, 47, 49, 51, 52, 53, 59, 61 to 77, 143." (Article 6, Geneva Convention Relative to the Protection of Civilians in Time of War of 1949 [emphasis added])

And since ANY interaction with the Roman Cult's military police is warfare and since the military police are armed, it is an armed conflict "A mixed war is one which is made on one side by public authority, and the other by mere *private* persons" (*Black's Law Dictionary*, 5th Edition, page 1420). And there is a right to political opinions, and a right *not* to participate in satanic religious ceremony/court case/kangaroo court under their Article 27:

> "Protected persons are entitled, in all circumstances, to respect for their persons, their honour, their family rights, *their religious convictions* and practices, and their manners and customs . . . all protected persons shall be treated with the same consideration by the Party to the conflict in whose power they are, without any adverse distinction based, in particular, on race, *religion or political opinion*" (Article 27, Geneva Convention Relative to the Protection of Civilians in a Time of War of 1949 [emphasis added]).

> And under their Universal Declaration of Human Rights "everyone has the right to freedom of thought, conscience and religion; this right includes freedom to change his religion or belief, and freedom, either alone or in community with others and in public or private, to manifest his religion or belief in teaching, practice, worship and observance" (Article 18, Universal Declaration of Human Rights).

Taking reprisals for political opinions, is a war crime, and terrorism, pillaging, and reprisals, as well as punishing for crimes not personally committed under their Article 33, are all war crimes:

"No protected person may be punished for an offence he or she has not personally committed. *Collective penalties and likewise all measures of intimidation or of terrorism are prohibited.* . . . Pillage is prohibited. Reprisals against protected persons and their property are prohibited." (Article 33, Geneva Convention Relative to the Protection of Civilian Persons in Time of War of 1949 [emphasis added]).

Military uniforms and the colors and paint scheme of the Roman Cult's military police vehicles, and military police emergency lights are all designed to be threatening and intimidating. Therefore the Roman Cult's military police are the terrorists, (war crimes).

There is a right *not* to be punished for the offenses of their Roman Cult cestui que trust and seizing property is pillaging, under Article 33, and nobody may be compelled to work for the occupying power under their Article 52, and by coercing someone to produce a

Figure 14 – Can you Spot the Terrorists

government issued identification card, which is for government employees *only*, or a social security number, which is a number for "Federal Personnel", or even a date of birth (that can be used to retrieve a social security number) the Roman Cult's military police are compelling them to work for the occupying power, which is another war crime.

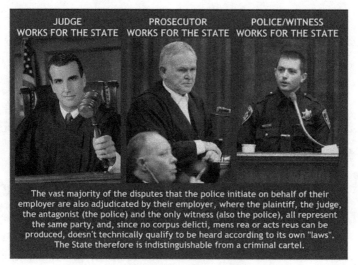

Figure 15 – Kangaroo Court

"*All measures aiming at creating unemployment or at restricting the opportunities offered to workers in an occupied territory, in order to induce them to work for the Occupying Power, are prohibited.*" Article 52, Geneva Convention Relative to the Protection of Civilians in Time of War of 1949 [emphasis added]

This means anybody with a social security number is "federal personnel, *or "individuals entitled to receive immediate or deferred retirement benefits under any retirement program of the Government of the United States (including survivor benefits)*" (5 USC § 552a. (a)(13) [emphasis added]). And the Roman Cult's military police coercing information from anyone or from third parties, like the Texas Department of Public Safety hearsay database, is a violation of their Article 31: "No physical or moral coercion shall be exercised against protected persons, in particular to obtain information from them or from third parties" (Article 31, Geneva Convention Relative to the Protection of Civilians in a Time of War of 1949).

There is a right to a neutral and unbiased judge in any proceedings under their International Covenant on Civil and Political Rights, Article 14, Clause 1:

> "All persons shall be equal before the courts and tribunals. *In the determination of any criminal charge against him, or of his rights and obligations in a suit at law, everyone shall be entitled to a fair and public hearing by a competent, independent and impartial tribunal established by law.*" (International Covenant on Civil and Political Rights, Article 14, Clause 1)

> "It is a fundamental right of a party to have a neutral and detached judge preside over the judicial proceedings." (Ward v Village of Monroeville, 409 U.S. 57, 61-62, 93 S.Ct 80, 83, 34 L.Ed. 2d 267 (1972); Tumey v Ohio, 273 U.S. 510, 5209, 47 S. Ct. 437, 440, 71 L.Ed. 749 (1927))

And no government employee is qualified to sit on a jury for "An employee of United States is not qualified to serve as member of grand jury in any District" (UNITED STATES v. GRIFFITH et al., 2 F.2d 925, (Court of Appeals of District of Columbia. Submitted October 9, 1924. Decided December 1, 1924.), No. 4114). This means they cannot have a social security number.

"No one shall be subjected to arbitrary arrest, detention or exile" (Article 9, Universal Declaration of Human Rights) and government employees on a jury is also another War Crime under their Article 71:

> "No sentence shall be pronounced by the competent courts of the Occupying Power except after a regular trial." (Article

71 Geneva Convention Relative to the Protection of Civilians in a Time of War of 1949)

This is also found in General Orders 100, which says that "*All wanton violence committed against persons in the invaded country, all destruction of property not commanded by the authorized officer,* all robbery, *all pillage* or sacking, even after taking a place by main force, all rape, wounding, maiming, or killing of such inhabitants, are prohibited under the penalty of death, or such other severe punishment as may seem adequate for the gravity of the offense. A soldier, officer or private, in the act of committing such violence, and disobeying a superior ordering him to abstain from it, may be lawfully killed on the spot by such superior" (Article 44, General Orders 100 (The Lieber Code) [emphasis added]). And anyone who is neither a subject, nor an alien, has a right *not* to be subjected to a military commission, or a courts-martial "because it brings into action, and enforces this great and glorious principle, that the people are the sovereign of this country, and consequently that fellow citizens and joint sovereigns *cannot be degraded by appearing with each other in their own courts to have their controversies determined*" (Chisholm v Georgia, 2 Dall 419, at p 479, [Emphasis added]).

Government Shields State Citizens from Law of Nations

It is the duty of the government to protect its citizens from the Roman Cult's Law of Nations. When we think about this we "must be borne in mind that *there is no law of nations standing between the people of the United States and their Government,* and interfering with their relation to each other. The powers of the Government, and the rights of the citizens under it, are positive and practical regulations plainly written down. The people of the United States *have delegated to it certain enumerated powers, and forbidden it to exercise others*" (Dred Scott v. Sandford, 19 How (60 U.S.) 393, 452, 15 L.Ed. 691 (A.D. 1856-1857) [emphasis added]).

Madison insisted that just "because this power is given to Congress," it did not follow that the treaty power was "absolute and unlimited." The President and the Senate lacked the power "to dismember the empire," for example, because "[t]he exercise of the power must be consistent with the object of the delegation. . . . The object of treaties," in Madison's oft-repeated formulation, "is the regulation of intercourse with foreign nations, *and is external.* . . . Today, it is enough to highlight some of the structural and historical evidence suggesting that the Treaty Power can be used to arrange intercourse with other nations, *but not to regulate purely domestic affairs*" (Bond v United States 572 US _____ (2014) case number 12-158 [emphasis added]).

"The government of the United States . . . is one of limited powers. *It can exercise authority over no subjects, except those which have been delegated to it.* Congress cannot, by legislation, enlarge the federal jurisdiction, *nor can it be enlarged under the treaty-making power*" (Mayor of New Orleans v. United States, 10 Pet. 662, 736 [emphasis added]). This is also why the *only* lawful court for state citizens is a common law jury of their peers. Otherwise they are degraded by appearing in their own courts to have their controversies determined:

> "It is a general rule that the sovereign cannot be sued in his own court without his consent; and hence no direct judgement can be rendered against him therein for costs, except in the manner and on the condition he has prescribed;

40 La. Ann. 856." (*Bouviers Law Dictionary*, 1897 Edition,
Vol. 1)

"No action can be taken against a sovereign in the non-
constitutional courts of either the United States or the state
courts & any such action is considered the crime of Barratry.
Barratry is an offense at common law." (State vs. Batson, 17
S.E. 2d 511, 512, 513)

"[I]t brings into action, and enforces this great and glorious
principle, that the people are the sovereign of this country,
*and consequently that fellow citizens and joint sovereigns cannot
be degraded by appearing with each other in their own courts
to have their controversies determined.*" (Chisolm v Georgia 2
Dall. 419)

No Nations on Earth

There are no nations on the planet, all of which have been
replaced by Roman Cult municipal corporations, except the United
States of America, the Republic of Texas, and maybe Russia and
Ukraine.

"The question to be determined is, whether this State, so
respectable, and whose claim soars so high, is amenable to the
jurisdiction of the Supreme Court of the United States? This
question, important in itself, will depend on others, more
important still; and may perhaps, be ultimately resolved into
one, no less radical than this- "do the people of the United
States form a NATION?" By that law the several States

and Governments spread over our globe, are considered as forming a society, not a NATION." (Chisholm v. Georgia, 2 Dall 419, at p 453, (1794))

The United States of America was the last bastions of true freedom on this planet in 1794, the Republic of Texas in 1836, and now possibly Russia and Ukraine are the holdouts for freedom, and the forces of hell have been arrayed against the United States of America from the beginning, which is why the forces of hell are working so hard to remove Donald J Trump.

Summary

The Law of Nations (International Law) is a branch of the Roman Cult's Roman Law and Canon Law. The Law of War is a branch of the Law of Nations. The UNIDROIT statute controls and governs the Uniform Commercial Code, which is a branch of the Roman Cult's Private International Law, which is a branch of the Roman Cult's International Law.

There are no Article 3 Courts, and all so-called judges are actually military commissioners, (bought-and-paid-for) clerks masquerading as judges, foreign agents of the Roman Cult, British Accredited Regency (BAR) Members, whores selling their "justus." All so-called courts are United Nations courts operating under the Roman Cult's Uniform Commercial Code, selling their "justus" for a profit.

9

THE ROMAN CULT AND COMMON LAW

Common Law can mean a lot of different things because common law is really the rulings of courts. There is a common law of the federal courts in the USA, which are all under martial law. Therefore, the technical meaning of the phrase "common law" is determined by how it is used and the context in which it is used. Generally, when people speak of common law, they are talking about the common law of England, which is eight hundred years of jury trial decisions.

Law of the Land = Natural Law

Common law is called the unwritten law, or natural law, which says that you can do anything you want as long as you don't damage somebody else or their property:

> "As general rule men have natural right to do anything which their inclinations may suggest, if it be not evil in itself, and in no way impairs the rights of others." (In Re Newman (1858), 9 C. 502)

"Every citizen & freeman is endowed with certain rights & privileges to enjoy *which no written law or statute is required.* These are the fundamental or natural rights, recognized among all free people." (U.S. v. Morris, 125 F 322, 325 [emphasis added])

"*This law of nature, being coeval with mankind and dictated by God himself, is of course superior in obligation to any other. It is binding over all the globe in all countries, and at all times: no human laws are of any validity, if contrary to this*; and such of them as are valid derive all their force, and all their authority, mediately or immediately, from this original." (*Blackstone's Commentaries on the Laws of England* (1765-1769) at number 41)

Sir William Blackstone was an English jurist (judge) who fell out of favor with the king (got *fired!*) and went into politics. He wrote a set of books called *Blackstone's Commentaries on the Laws of England.* Jefferson used phrases from Blackstone's books in the Declaration of Independence:

"When in the Course of human events, it becomes necessary for one people to dissolve the political bands which have connected them with another, and to assume among the powers of the earth, the separate and equal station to which the *Laws of Nature and of Nature's God* entitle them, a decent respect to the opinions of mankind requires that they should declare the causes which impel them to the separation."

Common Law Is the Most Ancient Law

Common Law appears in England with the Magna Carta and other ancient statutes and existed before the Magna Carta:

"The law of England is divided into three parts:

1.   The common law, which is the most general and ancient law of the realm...

2.   Statutes or Acts of Parliament, and

3.   Particular Customs

The Common Law appeareth in the statute of Magna Carta and other ancient statutes (which for the most part are affirmations of the common law)" (Sir Edward Coke, 1552-1634, The First Part of the Institutes of the Laws of England)

Common Law Comes from the Bible

"This has given manifold occasion for the benign interposition of divine Providence, which, in compassion to the frailty, the imperfection, and the blindness of human reason, hath been pleased, at sundry times and in divers manners, to discover and enforce its laws by an immediate and *direct revelation. . . . The doctrines thus delivered we call the revealed or divine law, and they are to be found only in the holy scriptures.* These precepts, when revealed, are found upon comparison to be really a part of the original law of nature, as they tend in all their consequences to man's felicity." (*Blackstone's Commentaries on the Laws of England,* (1765-1769) Section 2, Page 41 [emphasis added]

"Upon these two foundations, the *law of nature and the law of revelation,* depend all human laws; that is to say, *no human laws should be suffered to contradict these.*" (Blackstone's Commentaries on the Law of England, (1765-1769) Sect 2, Page 42 [emphasis added])

Common Law = God's Law

John Adams declared that the Constitution was "made only for a moral and religious people. It is wholly inadequate to the government of any other." And all acts of the legislature apparently contrary to "natural *rights* and justice are, in our law and must be in the nature of things, considered as void. *The laws of nature are the laws of God,* whose authority can be superseded by no power on earth. A legislature must not obstruct our obedience to him from whose punishments they cannot protect us. All human constitutions which contradict his (God's) laws, we are in conscience *bound to disobey*" (1772, Robin v. Hardaway, 1 Jefferson 109).

Common Law = Law of the Land

The words "by the law of the land" do not always mean a statute passed for the purpose of working the wrong. In the twenty-ninth chapter of the Magna Carta, which provided that no freeman should be taken or imprisoned or be "disseized of his freehold etc., but by the lawful judgment of his peers or by the law of the land, [Sir Edward] Coke in his commentary upon this statute says that these words 'by the law of the land' mean 'by the due course and process of law,' which he afterwards explains to be, 'by indictment and presentment of good and lawful men where such deeds are done in due manner or by writ original of the common law' " (2 Inst. 45,50" Tayler v

Porter, 4 Hill 773 (1843) New York Supreme Court). Furthermore, we see that

> "To be that *statutes* which would deprive a citizen of the *rights* of person or property without a regular trial, according to the course and usage of *common law*, would not be the law of the land." ((Jury) Hoke vs Henderson, 15, N.C. 15, 25 AN Dec 677)

> "History is clear that the first ten amendments to the *Constitution* were adopted to secure certain *common law rights* of the people, against invasion by the Federal Government." (Bell v. Hood, 71 F.Supp., 813, 816 (1947) U.S.D.C. -- So. Dist. CA.)

The principle that no person should be deprived of life, liberty, or property except by *due process of law* did not originate in the American system of *constitutional* law, but was contained in the Magna Carta, which declared:
"No freeman shall be taken, or imprisoned, or disseised, or outlawed, or exiled, or anywise destroyed; nor shall we go upon him, nor send upon him, but by lawful judgement of his peers or by the law of the land." (Magna Carta, chapter 29, June 19, 1215)

It has even been said that the principle was known before Magna Carta and that it was originally designed to secure the subject against arbitrary action of the crown—and to place him under the protection of the law. It is settled beyond question that this principle came from England to America as part of the common law and has been a fundamental rule in common law. When first adopted in Magna Carta, the phrase, "law of the land," referenced the common law and has been a fundamental rule in common law. (16 Am. Jur. 2d, Constitutional Law, Section 543)

Law of the Land Was Before any Government

Individuals stand on their constitutional rights as citizens. They are entitled to carry on private business and their power to contract is unlimited. An individual "owes no duty to the state or to his neighbors to divulge his business, or to open his doors to an investigation, so far as it may tend to incriminate him. *He owes no such duty to the state, since he receives nothing therefrom*, beyond the protection of his life, liberty, and property. *His rights are such as existed by the law of the land long antecedent to the organization of the state, and can only be taken from him by due process of law*, and in accordance with the Constitution. Among his rights are a refusal to incriminate himself, and the immunity of himself and his property from arrest or seizure except under (a judicial power warrant) a warrant of the law. He owes nothing to the public so long as he does not trespass upon their rights." (Hale v. Henkel, 201 U.S. 43 [emphasis added])

The War of Independence was precipitated by the military dictatorship that was imposed by the tyrant King George. We see that in the language of the Declaration of Independence:

"*We hold these truths to be self-evident*, that all men are created equal, that they are *endowed by their Creator with certain unalienable Rights*, that among these are *Life, Liberty and the pursuit of Happiness*.--That to secure these rights,

Governments are instituted among Men, *deriving their just powers from the consent of the governed*, --That whenever any Form of Government becomes destructive of these ends, it is the Right of the People to alter or to abolish it . . . But when a long train of abuses and usurpations, pursuing invariably the same Object evinces a design to reduce them under absolute Despotism, it is their right, it is their duty, to throw off such Government, and to provide new Guards for their future security." [emphasis added]

All acts of the legislature, contrary to natural justice and common law are void (Robin v. Hardaway, 1 Jefferson 109 (1772)) but it was just business for the tyrant and his Roman Cult handlers:

"Whereas *taxation by the parliament of Great Britain*, for the purpose of raising a revenue in his Majesty's colonies, provinces, and plantations, in North America, *has been found by experience to occasion great uneasiness and disorders...*That from and after the passing of this act the *King and Parliament of Great Britain will not impose any duty, tax, or assessment whatever*, payable in any of the colonies, provinces, or plantations, in North America or the West Indies; *except only such duties as it may be expedient to impose for the regulation of commerce.*" (George III, CAP XII 1778 [emphasis added])

And, among other things, they were routinely selling people into slavery under the Roman Cult's ecclesiastical law (or canon law). The law said if a prisoner "has as a consequence of his crime, [he] not only forfeited his liberty but all his personal rights except those which the law in its humanity affords him. *He is for the time being a slave of*

THE ROMAN CULT AND COMMON LAW

the state" (62 Va. (21 Gratt.) 790, 796 (1871)). *Penitentiary* came to mean "a penitent, an ordainer of penances, and *a place for penitents. See Locus, Penitentias*" (Andersons Law Dictionary, 1889 Edition, page 764 [emphasis added]). And the Roman Cult's penance was always for sale:

> "Penance, (Paenitentia) Is a Punishment imposed for a Crime by the Ecclesiastical Laws. It is an Acknowledgment of the Offence… *Penance may be changed into a Sum of Money* to be applied to pious Uses, called Commuting. 3 Inst. 150. 4 Inst. 336." (Jacob A New Law Dictionary, 1750 Edition)

The Roman Cult's BAR members are creating more business for their BAR member buddies by selling people into slavery

Roman Cult Replaces God's Law with Satanic Roman Law

No action can be brought against the people in any court without their permission. It is a general rule that a sovereign "cannot be sued in his own court without his consent; and hence no direct judgement can be rendered against him therein for costs, except in the manner and on the condition he has prescribed; 40 La. Ann. 856" (*Bouviers Law Dictionary*, 1897 Edition, Vol. 1). Therefore

> "No action can be taken against a sovereign in the non-constitutional courts of either the United States or the state courts & any such action is considered the crime of Barratry. Barratry is an offense at common law." (State vs. Batson, 17 S.E. 2d 511, 512, 513)

> "[A]nd because it brings into action, and enforces this great and glorious principle, that the people are the sovereign of

this country, *and consequently that fellow citizens and joint sovereigns cannot be degraded by appearing with each other in their own courts to have their controversies determined."* (Chisolm v Georgia 2 Dall. 419 [emphasis added])

This is why they have to get rid of their common law problem with martial law, because at common law they would all be put to death as we see in the Bible:

> "If a man be found stealing any of his brethren of the children of Israel, and maketh merchandise of him, or selleth him; then that thief shall die; and thou shalt put evil away from among you." (Deuteronomy 24:7)

> "And through covetousness shall they with feigned words make merchandise of you: whose judgment now of a long time lingereth not, and their damnation slumbereth not." (2 Peter 2:3)

Summary

It is absolutely critical for the Roman Cult to impose martial law through warfare, or a bankruptcy so they can get rid of their little common law problem, and thereby replace God's law with their satanic law.

Once they impose martial law, they can bring in their Roman Cult BAR members for their kangaroo courts, they can eliminate lawful money with their "forced loans," and they can plunder as much as they desire. And they think they don't have to worry about getting their necks stretched!

— *War is important in many ways for establishing the New World Order.*

— *War creates a constant flow of profits to our Military Industrial Complex.*

— *War rids the world of a large number of useless eaters,*

— *War keeps people hating each other rather than focusing their attention on us, the people who create the conflicts,*

— *War establishes legitimate grounds for occupation and control of regimes resistant to full domination by the elites,*

— *Wars are enjoyable and amusing when you think about the dumb stupid animal canon fodder people that enlist to fight them,*

— *War creates the chaos out of which the New World Order will be established,*

— *But you must understand; war is not the ultimate goal,*

— *Power is the ultimate aphrodisiac, Power over the remaining few, that is our ultimate goal,*

— *Slavery is even more fun and satisfying than the mass murder of war.*

—Henry Kissinger, former secretary of state, Nixon Administration

10

CITIZENSHIP

The People Are Sovereign

A sovereign doesn't need to tell another sovereign that he is sovereign. The sovereign is "merely sovereign by his very existence. The rule in America is that the American people are the sovereigns" (Kemper v. State, 138 Southwest 1025 (1911), page 1043). People are not bound by general words in statutes. They are not bound by "restrictive of prerogative right, title or interest, unless expressly named. Acts of limitation do not bind the King or the people. The people have been ceded all the rights of the King, the former sovereign" (People v Herkimer, 4 Cowen (NY) 345, 348 (1825)). And "in the United States, sovereignty resides in people" (Perry v. U.S. (294 US 330)).

> "A Sovereign is exempt from suit, not because of any formal conception or obsolete theory, but on the logical and practical ground that there can be no legal Right as against the authority that makes the law on which the Right depends." (Kawananakoa v. Polyblank, 205 U.S. 349, 353, 27 S. Ct. 526, 527, 51 L. Ed. 834 (1907))

"[A]t the revolution the Sovereignty devolved on the people; and they are truly the sovereigns of the country, but they are sovereigns without subjects ......and have none to govern but themselves; the citizens of America are equal as fellow citizens, and as joint tenants in the sovereignty." (Chisholm v Georgia, 2 Dall. 419, at p 471)

"The words 'people of the United States' and 'citizens' are synonymous terms. They both describe the political body who, according to our republican institutions, form the sovereignty, and who hold the power and conduct the Government through their representatives. They are what we familiarly call the "sovereign people," and every citizen is one of this people, and a constituent member of the sovereignty." (Dred Scott v Sandford, 60 US 393, pg 404)

"People of a state are entitled to all rights, which formerly belong to the King by his prerogative." (Lansing v Smith, (1829) 4 Wendell 9,20 (NY))

"It will be admitted on all hands that with the exception of the powers granted to the states and the federal government, through the Constitutions, the people of the several states are unconditionally sovereign within their respective states." (Ohio L. Ins. & T. Co. v. Debolt, 16 How. 416, 14 L.Ed. 997)

Two Classes of Citizens

According to the US Constitution citizens of each "State shall be entitled to all Privileges and Immunities of Citizens in the several

States" (Article 4, Section 2, Clause 1). "There is a clear distinction between national citizenship and state citizenship" (256 P. 545, affirmed 278 US 123, Tashiro vs. Jordan).

This means that someone "may be a citizen of a State and yet not a citizen of the United States" (Thomasson v State, 15 Ind. 449; Cory v Carter, 48 Ind. 327 (17 Am. R. 738); McCarthy v. Froelke, 63 Ind. 507; In Re Wehlitz, 16 Wis. 443. Mc Donel v State, 90 Ind. Rep. 320, pg 323). Citizenship of the United States does not entitle citizens to privileges and immunities of "Citizens of the State, since privileges of one are not the same as the other . . . that there was a citizenship of the United States and a citizenship of the states, which were distinct from each other, depending upon different characteristics and circumstances in the individual; that it was only privileges and immunities of the citizens of the United States that were placed by the [Fourteenth] amendment under the protection of the Federal Constitution, and that the privileges and immunities of a citizen of a state, whatever they might be, were not intended to have any additional protection by the paragraph in question, but they must rest for their security and protection where they have heretofore rested" (Maxwell v Dow, 20 S.C.R. 448, at pg 451)

A US Citizen Doesn't Exist

It might be correctly said that "there is no such thing as a citizen of the United States. . . . A citizen of any one of the States of the Union, is held to be, and called a citizen of the United States, although technically and abstractly there is no such thing" (Ex Parte Frank Knowles, 5 Cal. Rep. 300)

The martial law and the so-called Fourteenth Amendment failed to affect the original state citizens: "The rights of (original judicial)

Citizens of the States, as such, are not under consideration in the fourteenth amendment. They stand as they did before the fourteenth amendment and are fully guaranteed under other provisions" (United States v. Anthony, 24 Fed. Cas. 829, 930 (1873)).

And it is always about divide and conquer, which has been the Roman Cult's strategy from the beginning, to divide and conquer by race:

> "No white person born within the limits of the United States and subject to their jurisdiction, or born without those limits and subsequently naturalized under their laws, owes his status of citizenship to the recent amendments to the Federal Constitution." (Van Valkenburg v. Brown, 43 Cal 43)

But the truth is that anybody of any race can be a state citizen, as a man or (wo)man because a US citizen is a *cestui que trust*, and treated as a corporation, and no corporation has any rights because they are considered property, and it really comes down to what you tell them—what evidence you give against yourself.

US Citizens Have no Rights

The Fourteenth Amendment referred to slavery. "Consequently, the only persons embraced by its provisions, and for which Congress was authorized to legislate in the manner were those then in slavery" (Bowling v. Commonwealth, (1867), 65 Kent. Rep. 5, 29). That there was a citizenship of the United States and "a citizenship of

Figure 16 – Divide and Conquer

the states, which were distinct from each other, depending upon different characteristics and circumstances in the individual; that it was only privileges and immunities of the citizens of the United States that were placed by the [Fourteenth] amendment under the protection of the Federal Constitution, and that the privileges and immunities of a citizen of a state, whatever they might be, were not intended to have any additional protection by the paragraph in question, but they must rest for their security and protection where they have heretofore rested" (Maxwell v Dow, 20 S.C.R. 448, pg 451; [emphasis added])

The term "citizen," in the United States, is analogous to the term "subject" in the common law" (State vs Manual 20 NC 122, 14 C.J.S. 4, p 430) and furthermore:

> "Civil rights under the 14th amendment are for Federal citizens and not State Citizens; Federal citizens, as parents, have no right to the custody of their infant children except subject to the paramount right of the State." (Wadleigh v. Newhall, Circuit Court N. Dist. Cal., Mar 13, 1905)

> "[I]t is evident that they [U.S. citizens] have not the political rights which are vested in citizens of the States. They are not constituents of any community in which is vested any sovereign power of government. Their position partakes *more of the character of subjects than of citizens.* They are subject to the laws of the United States, but have no voice in its management. If they are allowed to make laws, the validity of these laws is derived from the sanction of a Government in which they are not represented. Mere citizenship they may have, but the political rights of citizens they cannot enjoy." (People v. De La Guerra, 40 Cal. 311, 342 (AD 1870))

"The only absolute and unqualified right of a United States citizen is to residence within the territorial boundaries of the United States." (US vs. Valentine 288 F. Supp. 957)

And the unborn children of their criminally converted US citizen have no rights and can be murdered: "The unborn are not included within the definition of "person" as used in the 14th Amendment" (Roe v. Wade US Supreme Court 410 US 13, 35 L.Ed. 2d 147, 1973).

One can be a State citizen without being a US citizen

There is in our political system, "a government of each of the several states and a government of the United States. Each is distinct from the other and has citizens of its own" (U.S. vs. Cruikshank, 92 US 542). There is "a clear distinction between national citizenship and state citizenship" (256 P. 545, affirmed 278 US 123, Tashiro vs. Jordan).

Instead this provision protects "only those rights peculiar to being a citizen of the federal government; it does not protect those rights which relate to state citizenship" (Jones v. Temmer, 89 F. Supp 1226 (1993)). "Such construction *ignores the rights of a state in virtue of its sovereignty to confer citizenship within its own limits*, where the rights incident to such a status are not of the citizenship mentioned in the federal Constitution. *It does not follow that, because one has all the rights and privileges of a citizen of a state, he must be a citizen of the United States.* Such a distinction has long been recognized in this County. See Scott v. Sandford, 19 How. (U.S.) 393, 15 L.Ed. 691" (Mitchell v. Wells, 37 Miss. 235).

Merely being native born within the territorial boundaries of the United States of America "*does not make* such an *inhabitant* a Citizen of the United States subject to the jurisdiction of the Fourteenth Amendment" (Elk v. Wilkins, Neb (1884), 5s.ct.41, 112 U.S. 99, 28 L. Ed. 643).

State Citizens = *Only* Ones Living Under Free Government

The state citizen is *"immune from any and all government attacks and procedure,* absent contract." (See Dred Scott vs. Sandford, 60 U.S.) Or as the Supreme Court has stated clearly: "[E]very man is independent of all laws, except those prescribed by nature. He is not bound by any institutions formed by his fellowmen without his consent" (CRUDEN vs. NEALE, 2 N.C. 338 2 S.E. 70, [emphasis added]).

Other rulings that prove the superiority of state citizenship:

"The rights of the individuals are restricted only to the extent that they have been voluntarily surrendered by the citizenship to the agencies of government." (City of Dallas v Mitchell, 245 S.W. 944)

"State citizens are the only ones living under free government, *whose rights are incapable of impairment by legislation or judicial decision."* (Twining v. New Jersey, 211 U.S. 97, 1908 [emphasis added])

"State Citizenship is a vested substantial property right, and the State has no power to divest or impair these rights." (Favot v. Kingsbury, (1929) 98 Cal. App. 284, 276 P. 1083)

"Taxpayers are not [de jure] State Citizens." (Belmont v. Town of Gulfport, 122 So. 10)

"Every citizen & freeman is endowed with certain rights & privileges to enjoy which no written law or statute is required. These are the fundamental or natural rights, recognized among all free people." (U.S. v. Morris, 125 F 322, 325)

"The sovereignty of a state does not reside in the persons who fill the different departments of its government, but in the People, from whom the government emanated; and they may change it at their discretion. Sovereignty, then in this country, abides with the constituency, and not with the agent; and this remark is true, both in reference to the federal and state government." (Spooner v. McConnell, 22 F 939 @ 943)

State Citizens Are "We the People"

We see that even his Brittanic Majesty acknowledged that the "United States, viz., New Hampshire, Massachusetts Bay, Rhode Island and Providence Plantations, Connecticut, New York, New Jersey, Pennsylvania, Maryland, Virginia, North Carolina, South Carolina and Georgia," were *free sovereign and independent states*, that he treats with them as such, and for himself, his heirs, and successors, relinquishes all claims to the government, propriety, and territorial rights of the same and every part thereof" (Article I, Definitive Treaty of Peace of 1783 [emphasis added]).

Furthermore, we see that

"the revolution the Sovereignty devolved on the people; and they are truly the sovereigns of the country, but they are sovereigns without subjects ......and have none to govern but themselves; the citizens of America are equal as fellow citizens, and as joint tenants in the sovereignty." (Chisholm v Georgia, 2 Dall. 419, pg 471)

"The words "people of the United States" and "citizens" are synonymous terms, and mean the same thing. They both describe the political body who, according to our republican institutions, form the sovereignty, and who hold the power and conduct the Government through their representatives. They are what we familiarly call the "sovereign people," and every citizen is one of this people, and a constituent member of the sovereignty." (Dred Scott v Sandford, 60 US 393, pg 404)

"People of a state are entitled to all rights, which formerly belong to the King by his prerogative." (Lansing v Smith, (1829) 4 Wendell 9,20 (NY))

"It will be admitted on all hands that with the exception of the powers granted to the states and the federal government, through the Constitutions, the people of the several states are unconditionally sovereign within their respective states." (Ohio L. Ins. & T. Co. v. Debolt, 16 How. 416, 14 L.Ed. 997)

State Citizens Are also Judicial Power Citizens

The judicial power is the power to "hear those matters which affect life, liberty or property of the Citizens of the State" (Sapulpa v Land, 101 Okla. 22, 223 Pac. 640, 35 A.L.R. 872). The very meaning of *sovereignty* "is that the decree of the sovereign makes law" (American Banana Co. v. United Fruit Co., 29 S.Ct. 511, 513, 213 U.S. 347, 53 L.Ed. 826, 19 Ann.Cas. 1047).

Sovereignty itself is, of course, "not subject to law, for it is the author and source of law; but in our system, while sovereign powers are delegated to the agencies of government, sovereignty itself remains with the people, by whom and for whom all government exists and acts" (Yick Wo v Hopkins, 118 US 356, pg 370). For there is no such thing as "power of inherent Sovereignty in the government of the United States. It is a government of delegated powers, supreme within its prescribed sphere but powerless outside of it. In this country sovereignty resides in the People, and Congress can exercise no power which they have not, *by their Constitution entrusted to it*; All else is withheld" (Julliard v Greenman 110 U.S. 421, p 467).

> "A Sovereign is exempt from suit, not because of any formal conception or obsolete theory, but on the logical and practical ground that there can be no legal Right as against the authority that makes the law on which the Right depends." (Kawananakoa v. Polyblank, 205 U.S. 349, 353, 27 S. Ct. 526, 527, 51 L. Ed. 834 (1907))

> "[T]he power which is derived cannot be greater than that from which it is derived" (Deritiva potestas non potest esse major primitiva. – *Bouvier's Law Dictionary*, 1856 Edition)

The two classes of citizens continue to this day as found in their own District of Columbia codes (edicts under the Roman Cult's martial law) with more of the Roman Cult's divide and conquer strategy:

"All citizens of the United States shall have the same right, in every State and Territory, as is enjoyed by white citizens thereof to inherit, purchase, lease, sell, hold, and convey real and personal property." (42 USC § 1982)

The two classes of citizens are talked about in the Constitution for the United States of America: "The Citizens of each State shall be entitled to all Privileges and Immunities of Citizens in the several States" (Article 4, Section 2, Clause 1, US Constitution).

The Judiciary Act of 1911 talks about the two classes of citizens under the heading; CHAPTER Two. DISTRICT COURTS - JURISDICTION:

"The district courts shall have original jurisdiction as follows: First. Of all suits of a civil nature, *at common law* or in equity, ..., or between citizens of the same State claiming lands under grants from different States; or, where the matter in controversy exceeds, exclusive of interest and costs, the sum or value of three thousand dollars, and (a) arises under the Constitution or laws of the United States, or treaties made, or which shall be made, under their authority, or *(b) is between Citizens of different States,* or (c) *is between citizens of a State and foreign States citizens, or subjects.* . . .

"Second. Of all crimes and offenses cognizable under the authority of the United States. Third. Of all civil causes of admiralty and maritime jurisdiction, saving to suitors in all cases the right of a common-law remedy where the common law is competent to give it; of all seizures on land or waters not within admiralty and maritime jurisdiction; of all prizes brought into the United States; and of all proceedings for the condemnation of property taken as prize." (Judiciary Act of 1911, at 36 Stat. 1087, 36 Stat. 1091 [emphasis added])

The two classes of citizens are even found in the Bible where a stranger is the equivalent to the US citizen or resident alien today, which is also how the children of Israel were enslaved:

"But the *stranger* that dwelleth among you shall be unto you as one born among you, and thou shalt love him as thyself; for ye were *strangers* in the land of Egypt." (Leviticus 19:34)

"Love ye therefore the stranger; for ye were *strangers* in the land of Egypt." (Deuteronomy 10:19)

The banksters will not provide any of their fake loans to anyone who fails to provide a social security number, which means that a social security number is for strangers, and is a privilege:

"Thou shalt not lend upon usury to thy brother; usury of money, usury of victuals, usury of any thing that is lent upon usury: Unto a *stranger* thou mayest lend upon usury; but unto thy brother thou shalt not lend upon usury:" (Deuteronomy 23:19-20)

"And as they bound him with thongs, Paul said unto the centurion that stood by, Is it lawful for you to scourge a man that is a Roman and uncondemned? When the centurion heard that he went and told the chief Captain; saying, Take heed what thou doest: for this man is a Roman. Then the chief captain came, and said unto him, Tell me, art thou a

Roman? He said, yea. And the chief captain answered, With a great sum obtained I this freedom. And Paul said, but I was free born. Then straightway they departed from him which should have examined him; and the chief captain was also afraid, after he knew that he was a Roman, and because he had bound him." (Acts 22:25-29)

And the courts sometimes even use the same words:
"*The rights of sovereignty extend to all persons and things, not privileged that are within the territory.* They extend to all *strangers resident* therein; not only to those who are naturalized, and to those who are domiciled therein, having taken up their abode with the intention of permanent residence, but also to those whose residence is transitory. All *strangers* are under the protection of the sovereign while they are within his territory and owe a temporary allegiance in return for that protection." (Carlisle v United States 83 U.S. 147, 154 (1873))

Illegal Aliens

There is no such thing as an "illegal alien." I sent registered letters to every member of Judiciary Committee in the House (about thirty-five congressmen) and also every member of the Judiciary Committee in the Senate (about seventeen senators). I told them there is no such thing as an illegal alien because once they set foot on America soil, they become state citizens. They have more rights than anyone who thinks they are a US citizen, and they came out on national television calling them "undocumented workers." This is because of common law, and it is *only* because of common law that we are free. *We all need to understand that when the rights of the least of us are violated, we are all diminished!*

All People Are Sovereign

"The rights of sovereignty extend to all persons and things, not privileged that are within the territory." (Carlisle v United States 83 U.S. 147, 154 (1873)).

Amistadt

A group of black slaves from Africa were able to get control of a ship, and they killed everybody (their captors) except one man because they didn't know how to sail. They told him to take them back to Africa. He sailed in circles off the coast of Virginia until the US Navy captured the ship and brought them to the US and put them on trial for murder. The case went all the way to the US Supreme Court (United States v Amistadt 40 US 518 (1841)). Their defense arguments were twofold. Either they were property like a dog or a cat, and a dog or a cat can't murder anyone, or they were free men and had every right to do what they did. The court ruled that they were free men and had every right to do what they did, and they sent them back to Africa. This case is proof that everybody of all races are free, and slavery is all about dividing and conquering. The Roman Cult promotes the satanic agenda, which is why it was introduced into America in colonial days.

Trump Is Right!

Slavery is exactly the reason that trump is 100 percent correct in building the wall. The Central and South Americans *must not* be allowed to set foot on American soil. Foreign people have no rights against the government on foreign soil. That is also why the communists in Congress are so adamant about all sorts of freebies for the so-called illegal aliens that are here, because they *must* get them into a contract to enslave them. When they become "privileged," they are no longer sovereign.

Early in the Trump administration, there was an article about a lady who was deported to Mexico. Immigration authorities had to go and bring her back because I think she was married to an American and all common-law countries hold "that the wife and minor children take the nationality of the husband and father. That is common-law doctrine" (In Re Page 12 F (2d) 135).

Green Card

My wife is Canadian. When we first got married, I got her a green card. We ended up moving to Canada for a while, and she gave it back. After learning of this, I told her I was *not* getting her another one.

One time she got stopped by a peace officer in Arizona, and she gave him her Canadian driver's license. He asked her whose minivan she was driving. She said it belongs to her husband. He asked why I had not gotten her a green card. She said, "He thinks to do so would mean giving up his rights." The Peace Officer said; "He is probably right."

Another time my wife travelled from Canada to Arizona, and the Border gustapo gave her a visa (permission to enter the country) and told her she had to go back to Canada within six months. She called up the Immigration Service, and they told her she did *not* have to go back to Canada because she is married to an American. They said she could just throw the visa in the garbage.

Good Faith

Because of martial law, and because so many people are so clueless about the two classes of citizens, our public servants can presume we are one of their US citizen slaves and claim good faith:

"All wanton violence committed against persons in the invaded country, all destruction of property not commanded by the authorized officer, all robbery, all *pillage* or sacking, even after taking a place by main force, all rape, wounding, maiming, or killing of such inhabitants, are prohibited under the penalty of death, or such other severe punishment as may seem adequate for the gravity of the offense. . . . A soldier, officer or private in the act of committing such violence, and disobeying a superior ordering him to abstain from it, may be lawfully killed on the spot by such superior." (Article 44, General Orders 100 (The Lieber Code) [emphasis added])

This is codified in their statutes (edicts under martial law): "(a) No evidence obtained by an officer or other person in violation of any provisions of the Constitution or laws of the State of Texas, or of the Constitution or laws of the United States of America, shall be admitted in evidence against the accused on the trial of any criminal case.

(b) *It is an exception to the provisions of Subsection (a) of this Article that the evidence was obtained by a law enforcement officer acting in objective good faith reliance upon a warrant issued by a neutral magistrate based on probable cause."* (Texas Code of Criminal Procedure, Article 38.23 Evidence Not to Be Used [emphasis added])

And it's codified in their federal statutes (edicts under martial law):

"(e)DEFENSE.—A good faith reliance on—

(1) a court warrant or order, a grand jury subpoena, a legislative authorization, or a statutory authorization (including a request of a governmental entity under section 2703(f) of this title);

(2) a request of an investigative or law enforcement officer under section 2518(7) of this title; or

(3) a good faith determination that section 2511(3) of this title permitted the conduct complained of; *is a complete defense to any civil or criminal action brought under this chapter or any other law.*" (18 US Code § 2707 Civil Action)

This may be so, except when they can be put in the position of honoring their oath by explaining to them that you fail to be one of their slaves in a way that can be proven. This puts them into estoppel, which is a "bar that prevents one from asserting a claim or right that contradicts what one has said or done before or what has been legally established as true" (*Black's Law Dictionary*, 8th Edition, page 1662). Another type of estoppel is "estoppel by silence," also called "estoppel by standing" or "estoppel by inaction" and "arises when a party is under a duty to speak but fails to do so" (*Black's Law Dictionary*, 8th Edition, page 1664 [emphasis added]). "The principles of estoppel apply against the state as well as individuals" (Cal. v. Sims, 32 C3d 468).

Summary

There have always been two classes of citizens. Under the Constitution, US citizens are derivative and dependent upon being a state citizen, and the so-called Fourteenth Amendment converted citizenship into the opposite of what the founders intended. While the Fourteenth Amendment does not "create a national citizenship, it has the effect of making that citizenship 'paramount and dominant' instead of 'derivative and dependent' upon state citizenship" (Colgate v Harvey 296 US 404 at p 427).

The Fourteenth Amendment "reversed and annulled the original policy of the constitution" (United States v. Rhodes, 27 Federal Cases, 785, 794). State Citizens are the equivalent of the king, and federal citizens (US citizens) are subjects (slaves). US citizens are 15 USC § 44 unincorporated corporation, and no government official has any duty to a corporation:

> *'Corporation' shall be deemed to include* any company, trust, so-called Massachusetts trust, or association, incorporated or unincorporated, which is organized to carry on business for its own profit or that of its members, and has shares of capital or capital stock or certificates of interest, and *any* company, *trust,* so-called Massachusetts trust, or association, incorporated or *unincorporated, without shares of capital or capital stock or certificates of interest,* except partnerships, *which is organized to carry on business for its own profit or that of its members."* (15 USC § 44 Definitions [emphasis added])

Because most people have become involved in what is viewed as a contract to be a slave for the Roman Cult, our public servants can presume we are one of the slaves until we take away their presumption and put them in the position of being required to honor their oath. Satanists throughout history have used privileges:

> "*The rights of sovereignty extend to all persons and things, not privileged that are within the territory.* They extend to all *strangers resident* therein; not only to those who are naturalized, and to those who are domiciled therein, having taken up their abode with the intention of permanent residence, but also to those whose residence is transitory. All *strangers* are under the protection of the sovereign while they are within his territory and owe a temporary allegiance in return for that protection." (Carlisle v United States 83 U.S. 147, 154 (1873))

And strangers:

> "But the *stranger* that dwelleth among you shall be unto you as one born among you, and thou shalt love him as thyself; for ye were *strangers* in the land of Egypt." (Leviticus 19:34)

> "Love ye therefore the stranger; for ye were *strangers* in the land of Egypt." (Deuteronomy 10:19)

As a mechanism for us to volunteer into slavery, the Roman Cult uses a maxim of equity, which says that *equity will not help a volunteer.* Therefore, we need to be very careful because when the rights of the least of us are violated, we are all diminished!

11

THE ROMAN CULT

Goal of the
New World Order
One World Leader
REVELATIONS 13:7

One World Government
REVELATIONS 13:2 & DANIEL 7:4

One World Religion
REVELATIONS 13:8

One World Currency
REVELATIONS 13:16-18

Roman Cult Atrocities

The Roman Cult is responsible for some of the worst atrocities in history and an account of only one of many atrocities is found in The Vatican's Holocaust by Avro Manhattan

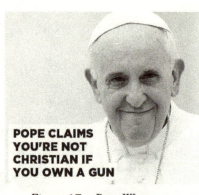

POPE CLAIMS YOU'RE NOT CHRISTIAN IF YOU OWN A GUN

Figure 17 – Pope Wants you unarmed

"The sensational account of the most horrifying religious massacre of the 20th century by Avro Manhattan (1914-1990) Knight of Malta

About the author: Avro Manhattan is the world's foremost authority on Roman Catholicism in politics. A resident of London during WWII he operated a radio station called "Radio Freedom" broadcasting to occupied Europe. He was the author of over 20 books including the best-seller *The Vatican in World Politics*, twice Book-of-the-Month and going through 57 editions. He was a Great Briton who risked his life daily to expose the darkest secrets of the Papacy. His books were #1 on *The Forbidden Index* for the past 50 years!! Ed. Note: This issue from 1986 – in 2006 the record is now 70 years on the forbidden book list!!

PREFACE TO THE AMERICAN EDITION

THE VATICAN'S HOLOCAUST is not a misnomer, an accusation, and even less a speculation. It is an historical fact. Rabid nationalism and religious dogmatism were the two main ingredients. During the existence of Croatia as an independent Catholic State, over 700,000 men, woman, and children perished. Many were executed, tortured, died of starvation, buried alive, or were burned to death. Hundreds were forced to become Catholic. Catholic padres ran concentration camps; Catholic priests were officers of the military corps which committed such atrocities. 700,000 in a total population of a few million proportionally, would be as if one-third of the USA population had been exterminated by a Catholic militia. What has been gathered in this book will vindicate veracity of these facts. Dates, names, and places, as well as photos are there to prove them. They should become known to the American people, not to foster vindictiveness, but to warn them of the danger, which racialism and sectarianism when allied with religious intolerance can bring to any contemporary nation, whether in Europe or in the New World. This book should be assessed without prejudice and as a lesson, but even more vital, as a warning for the future of the Americans, beginning with that of the USA. Avro Manhattan 1986

Editor's Note

An armed Serbia could have easily prevented this holocaust

Thanks God for the 2nd Amendment to the Constitution which guarantees the right to bear arms. Freedom of religion and an armed citizenry go hand in hand and is the only guarantee that this won't happen in the U.S.

Ed. Note: It is the Vatican One World government that doesn't want you to have the right to own arms or to use any means to defend yourself." The Vatican's Holocaust by Avro Manhattan, [emphasis added]

KNOW YOUR POPES

POPE JOHN XXIII

Thirty-seven of his own clergy members witnessed and professed against John XXIII (1410-1415) on charges of: fornication, adultery, incest, sodomy, simony, theft, and murder. He also had a harem of mistresses in Boulogne numbering two hundred consisting mostly of nuns

---

KNOW YOUR POPES

POPE BONIFACE VIII

After massacring the entire population in the Italian town of Palestrina, Boniface VIII (1294-1303) indulged in menages with a married woman and her daughter and became renowned through Rome as a shameless pedophile. He famously declared that having sex with young boys was no more a sin than rubbing one hand against the other. The poet Dante reserved a place for him in the eighth circle of Hell.

The "Vatican One World government" talked about in the preface to Avro Manhattan's book, The Vatican's Holocaust, sounds very similar to the New World Order that George H.W. Bush talked about, and the New World Order looks a lot like the United Nations as described herein.

Of course the Roman Cult would want to make sure you are unable to defend yourself against their New World Order, as if they are experts in what it means to be Christian.

"Pope Francis and the United Religions Initiative – Pope Francis Encourages One World Church…" Catholic Family News – Daily Blog – 2016 Family News

Georgetown University, in the District of Columbia, is owned by the Roman Cult and run by Jesuits, which would explain why many government employees behave the way they do, by assaulting state citizens, kidnapping state citizens, and falsely imprisoning state citizens, and then claiming "good faith" under their BAR member controlled and governed statutes, codes, rules and regulations.

Jesuit Oath

Superior speaks:

"My son, heretofore you have been taught to act the dissembler: among Roman Catholics to be a Roman Catholic, and to be a spy even among your own brethren; to believe no man, to trust no man. Among the Reformers, to be a reformer; among the Huguenots, to be a Huguenot; among the Calvinists, to be a Calvinist; among other Protestants, generally to be a Protestant, and obtaining their confidence, to seek even to preach from their pulpits, and to *denounce with all the vehemence in your nature our Holy Religion and the Pope*; and even to descend so low as to become a Jew among Jews, that you might be enabled to gather together all information for the benefit of your Order as a faithful soldier of the Pope.

You have been taught to insidiously *plant the seeds of jealousy and hatred between communities, provinces, states that*

*were at peace, and incite them to deeds of blood, involving them
in war with each other, and to create revolutions and civil wars in
countries* that were independent and prosperous, cultivating
the arts and the sciences and enjoying the blessings of peace.
To take sides with the combatants and to act secretly with
your brother Jesuit, who might be engaged on the other
side, but openly opposed to that with which you might be
connected, only that the Church might be the gainer in the
end, in the conditions fixed in the treaties for peace and that
the end justifies the means [satanism].

You have received all your instructions heretofore as a
novice, a neophyte, and have served as co-adjurer, confessor
and priest, but you have not yet been invested with all that is
necessary to command in the Army of Loyola in the service of
the Pope. You must serve the proper time as the instrument
and executioner as directed by your superiors; <u>for none can
command here who has not consecrated his labors with the
blood of the heretic; for "without the shedding of blood no
man can be saved."</u> Therefore, to fit yourself for your work
and make your own salvation sure, you will, in addition to
your former oath of obedience to your order and allegiance
to the Pope, repeat after me---"

The Extreme Oath of the Jesuits:
   "I, now, in the presence of Almighty God, the Blessed
Virgin Mary, the blessed Michael the Archangel, the blessed
St. John the Baptist, the holy Apostles St. Peter and St. Paul
and all the saints and sacred hosts of heaven, and to you, my

ghostly father, the Superior General of the Society of Jesus, founded by St. Ignatius Loyola in the Pontificate of Paul the Third, and continued to the present, do by the womb of the virgin, the matrix of God, and the rod of Jesus Christ, declare and swear, that his holiness the Pope is Christ's Vice-regent and is the true and only head of the Catholic or Universal Church throughout the earth; and that by virtue of the keys of binding and loosing, given to his Holiness by my Savior, Jesus Christ, he hath power to depose heretical kings, princes, states, commonwealths and governments, all being illegal without his sacred confirmation and that they may safely be destroyed.

Therefore, to the utmost of my power I shall and will defend this doctrine of his Holiness' right and custom against all usurpers of the heretical or Protestant authority whatever, especially the Lutheran of Germany, Holland, Denmark, Sweden, Norway, and the now pretended authority and churches of England and Scotland, and branches of the same now established in Ireland and on the Continent of America and elsewhere; and all adherents in regard that they be usurped and heretical, opposing the sacred Mother Church of Rome. I do now renounce and disown any allegiance as due to any heretical king, prince or state named Protestants or Liberals, or obedience to any of the laws, magistrates or officers.

I do further declare, that I will help, assist, and advise all or any of his Holiness' agents in any place wherever I shall be, in

Switzerland, Germany, Holland, Denmark, Sweden, Norway, England, Ireland or America, or in any other Kingdom or territory I shall come to, and do my uttermost to extirpate the heretical Protestants or Liberals' doctrines and to destroy all their pretended powers, regal or otherwise.

I do further promise and declare, that I will have no opinion or will of my own, or any mental reservation whatever, even as a corpse or cadaver (perinde ac cadaver), but will unhesitatingly obey each and every command that I may receive from my superiors [order follower] in the Militia of the Pope and of Jesus Christ.

I furthermore promise and declare that I will, when opportunity present, make and wage relentless war, secretly or openly, against all heretics, Protestants and Liberals, as I am directed to do, *to extirpate and exterminate them from the face of the whole earth*; and that I will spare neither age, sex or condition; and that *I will hang, waste, boil, flay, strangle and bury alive these infamous heretics, rip up the stomachs and wombs of their women and crush their infants' heads against the walls, in order to annihilate forever their execrable race.* That when the same cannot be done openly, I will secretly use the poisoned cup, the strangulating cord, the steel of the poniard or the leaden bullet, regardless of the honor, rank, dignity, or authority of the person or persons, whatever may be their condition in life, either public or private, as I at any time may be directed so to do by any agent of the Pope or Superior of the Brotherhood of the Holy Faith, of the Society of Jesus.

Figure 18 – The Jesuits Rule

In confirmation of which, I hereby dedicate my life, my soul and all my corporal powers, and with this dagger which I now receive, I will subscribe my name written in my own blood, in testimony thereof; and should I prove false or weaken in my determination, may my brethren and fellow soldiers of the Militia of the Pope cut off my hands and my feet, and my throat from ear to ear, my belly opened and sulphur burned therein, with all the punishment that can be inflicted upon me on earth and my soul be tortured by demons in an eternal hell forever!

"All of which, I, do swear by the Blessed Trinity and blessed Sacraments, which I am now to receive, to perform and on my part to keep inviolable; and do call all the heavenly and glorious host of heaven to witness the blessed Sacrament of the Eucharist, and witness the same further with my name written and with the point of this dagger dipped in my own blood and sealed in the face of this holy covenant." (Taken from the book Subterranean Rome by Charles Didier, translated from the French and published in New York in 1843. Dr. Alberto Rivera escaped from the Jesuit Order in 1967, and he describes his Jesuit oath in exactly the same way as it appears in this book. The Jesuit Oath of Induction is also recorded in the Congressional Record of the U.S.A. (House Bill 1523, Contested election case of Eugene C. Bonniwell, against Thos. S. Butler, Feb. 15, 1913, pp. 3215-3216) [emphasis added])

Figure 19 – The Jesuits = Roman Emperor Families

John Adams, second President of the United States was familiar with the Jesuits:

"My history of the Jesuits is not eloquently written, but it is supported by unquestionable authorities, [and] is very particular and very horrible. Their [the Jesuit Order's] restoration [in 1814 by Pope Pius VII] is indeed a step toward darkness, cruelty, despotism [and] death,....I do not like the appearance of the Jesuits. If ever there was a body of men who merited eternal damnation on earth and in hell, it is this Society of [Ignatius de] Loyola."

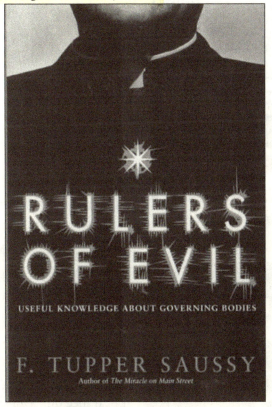

Figure 20 – Rulers of Evil

According to Napoleon Bonaparte, the Jesuits are a "military organization, not a religious order. Their chief is a general of an army, not a mere father abbot of a monastery."

Jesuits = Roman Emperor Families

The Jesuit assistancies are run by the Venetian Black Nobility (or Papal Occult Noble Council), which are from the same families

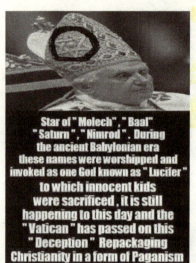

Figure 21 – Star of Molech

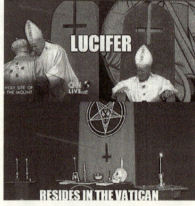

Figure 22 – Lucifer Resides in the Vatican

as the Roman emperors' families. A couple of Professors from the University of California at Davis exposed these families as being from what is now modern-day Iran. American composer Frederick Tupper Saussy wrote *Rulers of Evil: Useful Knowledge about Governing Bodies,* a 2001 book about the Jesuits and their influence on the Colonial days.

Father Malachi Martin

A Catholic monk by the name of Father Malachi Martin was on a talk radio program called *Coast to Coast AM* in the 1990s. He explained how Satan had gained control of the Vatican in 1955. Father Malachi Martin died mysteriously shortly after his appearance on *Coast to Coast AM*. Obviously, the Catholic church does not approve of people exposing the satanic activities of the Vatican.

Catholic Bishops in Chile are in open revolt against the Vatican, and many of the Catholic priests in Ireland have formed an organization to discuss leaving the Catholic church , which also means that many people in the Catholic church do not approve of the satanic activities of the Vatican.

The Roman Cult *loves* to shed innocent blood, the more innocent the better as evidenced by the convictions of Popes Ratzinger and Bergolio, and Queen Elizabeth and others, by the International Common Law Court of Justice with over forty-eight eye-witnesses for participating in a Ninth Circle satanic cult blood sacrifice of a child by slitting its throat and drinking its blood (after terrorizing it because the adrenaline gives a rush).

Vatican Is Practicing Child Sacrifice

According to a recent book the Vatican performed a ceremony in which they "sacrificed a little boy. After that the man dressed in scarlet went to the side of the room, and I had to kneel before him and kiss his ring and swear my undying loyalty to the New World Order" (Svali, Svali Speaks: Breaking Free of Cult Programming (Omnia Veritas Ltd, 2016)

Satanic Courts

A citation is a process in the Roman Cult's ecclesiastical courts. As we have seen before a citation is a summons to appear. It is also the name of the process used " *the English ecclesiastical, probate, and divorce courts* to call the defendant or respondent before them" (3 Bl. Comm. 100. 3 Steph. Comm. 720." Blacks Law Dictionary, 2nd Edition, at page 202). A citation is a way to subject you to their satanic religious ceremony:

"COURTS ECCLESIASTICAL, Curia Ecclesiasticae, Spiritual Courts.] Are those courts which are held by the king's authority as supreme governor of the church, for matters which chiefly concern religion. 4 Inst. 321. And the *laws and constitutions whereby the church of England is governed*, are, *1. Divers immemorial customs. 2.* Our own provincial constitutions; and the *canons made in convocations,* especially those in the year 1603. ....Much oppression having been exercised through the channel of these courts, on persons charged with trifling offences within their spiritual jurisdiction" (Tomlins Law Dictionary, 1835 Edition, Volume 1, [emphasis added])

COURTS ECCLESIASTICAL ... The proceedings in the Ecclesiastical Courts are, *according to the civil and canon law* by *citation, libel,* answer upon oath, *proof by* witnesses, and *presumptions,* &c., and after sentence, for contempt, by excommunication: and *if the sentence is disliked, by appeal.* (Tomlins Law Dictionary, 1835 Edition, Volume 1, [emphasis added])

NINTH CIRCLE EXPOSED

THE NINTH CIRCLE SECRET SOCIETY EXPOSED

JESUIT POPE FRANCIS BERGOLIO, WAS FOUND GUILTY OF CHILD TRAFFICING, RAPE AND MURDER

Defendants Pope Francis Bergolio, Catholic Jesuit Superior General Adolpho Pachon and Archbiship of Canterbury Justin Welby were found guilty of rape, torture, murder and trafficking of children. Five judges of the International Common Law Court of Justice in Brussels determined that the crimes occurred as recently as 2010. Since last March over 48 eyewitnesses have come forward to testify before this ICLCJ Court about the Defendants' activities as members of the Ninth Circle Satanic Child Sacrifice Cult.

Sold into Slavery

A citation is a way for the so-called holy elites to sell you into slavery:

> "He [the prisoner] has as a consequence of his crime, not only forfeited his liberty but all his personal rights except those which the law in its humanity affords him. *He is for the time being a slave of the state.*" 62 Va. (21 Gratt.) 790, 796 (1871) [emphasis added]

> "Penitentiary has meant: a penitent, an ordainer of penances, and *a place for penitents*. See Locus, Penitentias." Andersons Law Dictionary, 1889 Edition, page 764 [emphasis added]

And if one fails to appear, they are excommunicated and imprisoned as an ecclesiastical censure. They will be excommunicated and an excommunicated person had no rights:

"An excommunicated person was disabled to do any act required to be done by one that that is *probus* and *legalis homo.* *He could not serve upon juries, nor be a witness in any court, nor bring an action, either real or personal, to recover lands or money due to him. Litt. § 201."* (Tomlins Law Dictionary, 1835 Edition, Volume 1 [emphasis added])

Then they were put in jail until they submitted to the Roman Cult as an ecclesiastical censure, which is why they MUST get rid of their common law problem because at common law they would all be put to death.

"If a man be found stealing any of his brethren of the children of Israel, and maketh merchandise of him, or selleth him; then that thief shall die; and thou shalt put evil away from among you." (Deuteronomy 24:7)

"And through covetousness shall they with feigned words make merchandise of you: whose judgment now of a long time lingereth not, and their damnation slumbereth not." (2 Peter 2:3)

"And it shall come to pass in that day, that the LORD shall punish the host of the high ones that are on high, and the *kings of the earth* upon the earth. And they shall be gathered together, *as prisoners* are gathered in the pit, and shall be shut up in the prison, and after many days shall they be visited." (Isaiah 24: 21-22 [emphasis added])

"And the kings of the earth, and the great men, and the rich men, and the chief captains, and the mighty men, and every bondman, and every free man, hid themselves in the dens and in the rocks of the mountains; And said to the mountains and rocks, Fall on us, and hide us from the face of him that sitteth on the throne, and from the wrath of the Lamb: For the great day of his wrath is come; and who shall be able to stand?" (Revelation 6: 15-17)

The Roman Cult's penance was always for sale. It is a punishment imposed for a crime by the Ecclesiastical Laws. "It is an Acknowledgment of the Offence... *Penance may be changed into a Sum of Money* to be applied to pious Uses, called Commuting" (Jacob A New Law Dictionary, 1750 Edition, [emphasis added]).

People were so eager to leave England for the new world to get away from the Roman Cult, because all inquisitions originated with the Roman Cult:

> "Inquisition, Ex Officio Mero, Is one Way of proceeding in Ecclesiastical Court. Wood's Inst. 596." (Jacob A New Law Dictionary, 1750 Edition)

"Ye are of your father the devil, and the lusts of your father ye will do. He was a murderer from the beginning, and abode not in the truth, because there is no truth in him. When he

speaketh a lie, *he speaketh of his own: for he is a liar, and the father of it.*" (John 8:44)

Roman Cult Administration

An administrator is a "person authorized to manage and distribute the estate *of* an intestate, or of a testator who has no executor. In English law, administrators are the officers of the Ordinary appointed by him in pursuance of the statute, and their title and authority are derived exclusively from the ecclesiastical judge, by grants called letters of administration" (*Bouviers Law Dictionary*, 1883 Edition, page 119). Donald J Trump is the Administrator of the estates (cestui que trust) of the American people in what is commonly called the Trump administration. And Trump is an officer of the ordinary, or a court "*which has jurisdiction of the probate of wills and the regulation of the management of decedents' estates.* Such courts exist in Georgia, New Jersey, South Carolina, and *Texas.* See 2 Kent, Comm. 409 ; *Ordinary*" (Bouviers Law Dictionary, 1856 Edition, page 383).

Figure 23 – Inquisition Torture Tools

Donald Trump's title and authority are derived exclusively from an ecclesiastical judge. We see that a civil law term for any judge who hath authority to take cognizance of causes in his own right, and not by deputation: "*by the common law it is taken for him who hath ordinary or exempt and immediate jurisdiction in causes ecclesiastical*" (*Co. Litt. 344; Stat. Westm. 2. 13 Edw. 1. st. 1. c. 19*).

This name is applied to a bishop who hath original jurisdiction; and "an archbishop is the ordinary of the whole province, to visit and receive appeals from inferior jurisdictions, &c. *2 Inst. 398; 9 Rep. 41; Wood's Inst. 25.* The word *ordinary* is also used for every commissary or official of the bishop, or other ecclesiastical judge having judicial power: an archdeacon is an ordinary; and ordinaries may grant administration of intestates' estates, &c. *31 Edw. 3. c. 11; 9 Rep. 36.* But the bishop of the diocese is the true and only ordinary to certify excommunications, lawfulness of marriage, and such ecclesiastical and spiritual acts, to the judges of the common law, for he is the person to whom the court is to write in such things. *2 Shep. Abr. 472*" (Tomlins Law Dictionary, 1835 Edition, Volume 2).

This is why the First Amendment prohibits Congress from making any laws about religion.

Constitution = Christian Government

We are intended to be a Christian nation, just not associated with any particular denomination. We read that no one who denies the being of a God, or a future state of rewards and punishments, "shall hold any office in the civil department of this state. . . . Religious morality, and knowledge being necessary to good government, the preservation of liberty, and the happiness of mankind, schools, and the means of education, shall forever be encouraged in this state" (Sections 4 & 14, Article 7, Constitution of Mississippi 1832).

Many other rulings affirm the Christian nature of our country and Constitution:

"This is a religious people. This is historically true. From the discovery of this continent to the present hour, there is a single voice making this affirmation....these are not individual sayings, declarations of private persons: they are organic utterances; they speak the voice of the entire people...these and many other matters which might be noticed, add a volume of unofficial declarations to the mass of organic utterances that this is a Christian nation." (U.S. Supreme Court, Church of the Holy Trinity v. U.S., 143 US 457 (1892))

"I, A. B., do profess faith in God the Father, and in Jesus Christ His only Son, and in the Holy Ghost, one God, blessed for evermore, and I do acknowledge the Holy Scriptures of the Old and New Testament to be given by divine inspiration." (Article 22 Constitution of Delaware 1776)

"Christianity, general Christianity, is, and always has been, a part of the common law of Pennsylvania; . . . not Christianity with an established church and tithes and spiritual courts, but Christianity with liberty of conscience to all men." (Updegraph v Commonwealth 11 S. & R. 394, 400)

Figure 24 – One World Religion

"It is also said, and truly, that the Christian religion is a part of the common law of Pennsylvania." (Vidal v. Girard's Executors, 2 How. 127, 43 U. S. 198)

"We, the people of the State of Illinois, grateful to Almighty God for the civil, political, and religious liberty which He hath so long permitted us to enjoy, and looking to Him for a blessing upon our endeavors to secure and transmit the same unimpaired to succeeding generations," (Constitution of Illinois, 1870)

"The rights of sovereignty extend to all persons and things, not privileged that are within the territory. They extend to all *strangers resident* therein; not only to those who are naturalized, and to those who are domiciled therein, having taken up their abode with the intention of permanent residence, but also to those whose residence is transitory. All strangers are under the protection of the sovereign while they are within his territory and owe a temporary allegiance in return for that protection." (Carlisle v United States 83 U.S. 147, 154 (1873))

The Founders did *not* want the government to be associated with any particular religion, which is what happened in Europe with the Roman Cult.

HOW YOU GOT YOUR BIBLE

Constantine and his bishops VOTED a bunch of books as the WORD OF GOD (AD 325)

They picked and chose what they wanted, and they burnt all other pre-Christian documents that conflicted with their "approved" party line (AD 391)
In order to make their religion popular they killed everyone who failed to agree with the new religion. It was illegal (heresy) to disagree with the church (AD 380 to AD 1800s) as evidenced by the Spanish Inquisition and by the fact that is was illegal to be in possession of the Bible in many European countries up to the 1800s.

By 1794 all of the nations on this planet had been replaced by Roman Cult municipal corporations, except the United States of America:

"The question to be determined is, whether this State, so respectable, and whose claim soars so high, is amenable to the jurisdiction of the Supreme Court of the United States? This question, important in itself, will depend on others, more important still; and may perhaps, be ultimately resolved into one, no less radical than this- "do the people of the United States form a NATION? "By that law the several States and Governments spread over our globe, are considered as forming a society, not a NATION." (Chisholm v. Georgia, 2 Dall. 419, at p 453, 1 L.Ed. 440 (1794) [caps in the original])

Churchianity

The Roman Cult is busy with its "one world religion" agenda to combine all churches into a single religion.

This idea of a one world religion is nothing new. When the Roman Emperor Constantine brought all of the Christian

Figure 25 – Holy Roman Empire

churches together in his day, they proposed a standard of doctrine and a certain set of books for the Holy Bible. Some objected, and they were murdered on the spot.

The Roman Cult has always intended that the Catholic church be the universal church and their Holy Roman Empire the ruling authority.

Summary

The Roman Cult is Satanic, and was responsible for slavery in America. It was responsible for people fleeing their tyranny

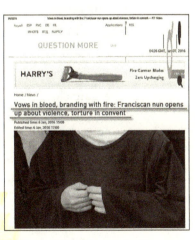

Figure 26 – Torture in Convent

in Europe. It was responsible for some of the worst atrocities in history.

The United States of America was the last bastion of freedom on this planet in 1794, and the forces of hell have been arrayed against The United States of America from the beginning.

There are three major stages for the New World Order to be fully implemented:

1. One world government
2. One world currency
3. One world religion

The first two components are already documented, admitted, and in the final stages. The one world religion is slightly more complicated to understand for most, but part of the preparation for this stage is the preparation and conditioning of the mind, through the news media, Hollywood, and the music industry.

Through symbols, subliminal messages, themes, are all setting the stage for our minds to accept the great deception of their false messiah or anti-Christ who will usher in the new age one world religion.

This is why the symbolism has become more and more frequent and blatant. We are close.

The Constitution was intended to establish a Christian government in America, but it was intended to be Christian government without the government being associated with any particular Christian church.

12

ORDER FOLLOWERS – A PILLAR OF SATANISM

Radio talk show host Mark Passio says "order followers are the ones keeping the system of slavery in place. Is it any wonder that in the century that the Roman Cult rules the world :

> "Within twenty years this country is going to rule the world. Kings and Emperors will soon pass away and the democracy of the United States will take their place....When the United States rules the world, *the Catholic Church will rule the world. . . .* Nothing can stand against the church" (Roman Catholic Archbishop James E. Quigley (October 15, 1854 – July 10, 1915) Chicago Daily Tribune May 5, 1903 [emphasis added])

Rules, murder, and warfare and atrocities are taken to a previously unheard of levels?

> "You assist an evil system most effectively by obeying its orders and decrees. An evil system never deserves such allegiance. Allegiance to it means partaking of the evil. A good person will resist an evil system with his or her whole soul."
>
> – *Mahatma Gandhi*

Mark Passio

Mark Passio is a former Priest of the Church of Satan turned whistleblower and has a YouTube channel called "What on Earth Is Happening."

He has video lectures about natural law, mind control and eugenics. He discusses the highest tenet of Satanism as being "order following" (i.e., how people become willing slaves, following unlawful commands). Order followers are responsible for all of the atrocities in history.

> "Just Following Orders" is never a valid excuse or "justification" for immoral, criminal behavior, and this lame attempt to abdicate personal responsibility never should be accepted as a valid excuse for such behavior!

Mark Passio talks about Pillars of Satanism which are forms of mind control.

Pillars of Satanism

Figure 27 – Order Followers

1. Survival

Self-preservation is the highest law of Satanism.

2. Social Darwinism

Certain classes of society think they are most fit to rule. This thinking postulates the survival of the most socially ruthless.

3. Eugenics

This is the idea that the elite get to determine who lives or dies

4. Moral Relativism

There is no absolute right or wrong—truth is relative. We just make up what is right or wrong. What is right or wrong is what we decide today, and tomorrow it will be something else. (All court cases fall within this category.) Two-thirds of the American people believe in moral relativism = practicing Satanists.

The people will believe what the media tells them they believe.

—*George Orwell*

Soviet Union Collapse

The final nail in the coffin of the former Soviet Union, if anyone remembers, was in Berlin, when people would run across the no-man's-land between East Berlin and West Berlin. The East German Police, being good order followers, gunned down the people fleeing the communist tyranny in East Germany. But one day the order

Figure 28 – Government = Mass Murder

followers refused to follow orders and then a lone freedom seeker became tens, then hundreds, then thousands, then tens of thousands, and then millions of people came out and started to tear down the wall brick by brick.

Every Great injustice has been at the hands of somebody
"just following orders"

World War II War Crimes Tribunals

All of the Nazi leaders were put on trial in Nuremburg, Germany, for war crimes, and they all said they were just following orders. That failed to be a good excuse because almost all of them were sentenced to death by hanging. The ones who escaped the gallows spent the rest of their lives in jail. Some of them are still hunted to this day.

Summary

Most so-called Christians aren't Christians at all! We all need to take a hard look at our behavior. Mark Passio says that two-thirds of the American people are practicing Satanists, and he may be right!

Figure 29 – Just Following Orders

13

LAW ENFORCEMENT OFFICERS AND THE ROMAN CULT

Martial Law is warfare. "Under International Law of Warfare, all parties to a cause must appear by <u>nom de guerre</u>, because an "alien enemy cannot maintain an action <u>during the war</u> in his own name". Merriam-Webster Dictionary, pg. 1534 "**A mixed war is one which is made on one side by public authority, and the other by mere <u>private</u> persons.**" Blacks Law Dictionary, 5th Edition, page 1420 Martial law affects chiefly the police and collection of public revenue and taxes, whether "imposed by the expelled government or by the invader, and refers mainly to the support and efficiency of the army, its safety, and the safety of its operations" (Article 10, General Orders 100 (The Lieber Code)).

Martial Law affects subjects of the enemy and aliens and extends to property, and to persons, "whether they are subjects of the enemy or aliens to that government" (Article 7, General Orders 100 (The Lieber Code)).

A subject is something created by the government. All subjects over which the sovereign power of the state extends are "objects of taxation, but those over which it does not extend are exempt from taxation. This proposition may also be pronounced as self-evident. The sovereignty of the state extends to everything which exists by its authority or its permission" (McCullough v Maryland, 17 U.S. [4 Wheat] 316 (1819)). [emphasis added]

Law Enforcement Officer = Enforcing Martial Law

The Roman Cult's military police hire screened for low intelligence They give the thugs guns and tell them to go out and assault people because it makes so much business for their so-called court, as evidenced in the case Jordan v City of New London where Robert Jordan had a master's degree and scored too high on their intelligence test to get the job. This is also one of the pillars of Satanism: order followers, according to a man called Mark Passio, a former Priest of the Church of Satan turned whistleblower, are not of high intelligence. I have friends who have been turned down for jobs with police because they scored too high on the intelligence test.

Law Enforcement Officer = Privateer

A privateer is a vessel owned and operated by private individual and are authorized by a nation on certain conditions to damage the commerce of the enemy by acts of piracy. It is the *"practice of arming privately owned merchant ships for the purpose of attacking enemy trading ships.* Before the practice was outlawed, governments commissioned privateers by issuing letters of marque to their merchant fleets. Privateering was prohibited by the Declaration of Paris Concerning Naval Warfare of 1856, which has been observed by nearly all nations since that time" (*Black's Law Dictionary*, 8th Edition, page 3785 [emphasis added]).

Because Law enforcement Officers are all US citizens in interstate commerce "We therefore decline to overrule the opinion of Chief Justice Marshall: We hold that *the District of Columbia is not a state within Article 3 of the Constitution.* In other words cases between citizens of the District and those of the states were not included of the catalogue of controversies over which the Congress could give jurisdiction to the federal courts by virtue of Article 3. In other words *Congress has exclusive legislative jurisdiction over citizens of Washington District of Columbia and through their plenary power nationally covers those citizens even when in one of the several states as though the district expands for the purpose of regulating its citizens wherever they go throughout the states in union"* National Mutual Insurance Company of the District of Columbia v. Tidewater Transfer Company, 337 U.S. 582, 93 L.Ed. 1556 (1948)

Under international law rule both statutory and common laws are federalized. "*The civil laws effective in an area of exclusive Federal jurisdiction are Federal law, notwithstanding their derivation from State laws,* and a cause arising under such laws may be brought in or removed to a Federal district court under sections 24 or 28 of the former Judicial Code (now sections 1331 and 1441 of title 28, United States Code), giving jurisdiction to such courts of civil actions arising under the laws of the United States Jurisdiction over Federal Areas Within the States – Report of the Interdepartmental Committee for the Study of Jurisdiction over Federal Areas Within the States, Part II, A Text of the Law of Legislative Jurisdiction Submitted to the Attorney General and Transmitted to the President June 1957, page 158-165 operating under the Admiralty Jurisdiction.

"The term "special maritime and territorial jurisdiction of the United States", as used in this title, includes:

(1) The high seas, any other waters within the admiralty and maritime jurisdiction of the United States and out of the jurisdiction of any particular State, and *any vessel belonging in whole or in part to the United States or any citizen thereof, or to any corporation created by or under the laws of the United States, or of any State, Territory, District, or possession thereof, when such vessel is within the admiralty and maritime jurisdiction of the United States* and out of the jurisdiction of any particular State." (18 USC § 7 Special maritime and territorial jurisdiction of the United States defined (edict under martial law))

"And it may embrace also the vehicles and persons engaged in carrying it on. It would be in the power of Congress to confer admiralty jurisdiction upon its courts, over the cars engaged in transporting passengers or merchandise from one State to another, and over the persons engaged in conducting them, and deny to the parties the trial by jury." (Propeller Genessee Chief et al. v. Fitzhugh et al. 12 How. 443 (U.S. 1851))

"This power [of admiralty jurisdiction] is as extensive upon land as upon water. The Constitution makes no distinction in that respect. And if the admiralty jurisdiction, in matters of contract and tort which the courts of the United States may lawfully exercise on the high seas, can be extended to the lakes under the power to regulate commerce, it can with the same propriety and upon the same construction, be extended to contracts and torts on land when the commerce is between different States. " Propeller Genessee Chief et al. v. Fitzhugh et al. 12 Hw. 443 (U.S. 1851)

Operating under the Federal Tax Lien Act of 1966, and their District of Columbia codes 18 USC § 31, and their full military dictatorship, and their Roman Cult UNIDROIT statute and their Uniform Commercial Code making war on anyone they can victimize by engaging commercial warfare on them

Same Strategies as Old England

The privateers would issue a citation to subject you to their satanic religious ceremony and hold an Inquisition and they would forge your signature onto a contract—except in Texas it is called *a capias pro fine,* but it is still a debt instrument:

"Capias" means a writ that is:

(A) issued by a court having jurisdiction of a case after judgment and sentence; and (B) directed "To any peace officer of the State of Texas" and commanding the officer to arrest a person convicted of an offense and bring the arrested person before that court immediately or on a day or at a term stated in the writ.

(2) "Capias pro fine" means a writ that is:

(A) issued by a court having jurisdiction of a case after judgment and sentence for unpaid fines and costs; and

(B) directed "To any peace officer of the State of Texas" and commanding the officer to arrest a person convicted of an offense and bring the arrested person before that court immediately." (Texas Code of Criminal Procedure Article 43.015 Definitions)

But a capias fails to be a warrant but is a debt instrument where they forge your signature onto their quasi contract (Knox v State, 586 S.W. 2d 504, 506 (Tex.Crim.App. 1979)).

Traffic Offenses

An offense is an offense against the martial law. All traffic offenses are based on presumptions. Before we go further, let's look at some definitions:

"(1) <u>SECURITY INTEREST</u>.-The term 'security interest' means any interest in property acquired by contract for the purpose of securing payment or performance of an obligation or indemnifying against loss or liability. A security interest exists at any time

"(3) MOTOR VEHICLE.-The term 'motor vehicle' means a self-propelled vehicle *which is registered* for highway use under the laws of any State or foreign country.

"<u>(4) SECURITY</u>.-*The term 'security' means any bond, debenture, note, or certificate or other evidence of indebtedness, issued by a corporation or a government or political subdivision thereof,* with interest coupons or in registered form, share of stock, voting trust certificate, or any certificate of interest or participation in, certificate of deposit or receipt for, temporary or interim certificate for, or warrant or right to subscribe to or purchase any of the foregoing: *negotiable instrument: or money.*" (Federal Tax Lien Act of 1966 at Public Law 89-719 at 80 Stat. 1130-1131 [emphasis added])

A motor vehicle is commercial. The term *motor vehicle* means every description of carriage or other contrivance propelled or drawn by mechanical power and *"used for commercial purposes on the highways in the transportation of passengers, passengers and property, or property or cargo. The term "used for commercial purposes" means the carriage of persons or property for any fare, fee, rate, charge or other consideration, or directly or indirectly in connection with any business, or other undertaking intended for profit"* (18 USC § 31 [emphasis added]).

But the same vehicle used for a purpose other than to carry passengers or property for hire is "consumer goods" and is not subject to taxation:

> "Goods are; (1) "consumer goods" if they are used or bought for use primarily for personal, family or household purposes; (2) "equipment" if they are used or bought for use primarily in business (including farming or a profession) or by a debtor who is a non-profit organization or a governmental subdivision or agency or if the goods are not included in the definitions of inventory, farm products or consumer goods." (Uniform Commercial Code 9-109 Classification of Goods: "Consumer Goods"; "Equipment"; "Farm Products"; "Inventory")

> "Under UCC §9-109 there is a real distinction between goods purchased for personal use and those purchased for business use. The two are mutually exclusive and the principal use to which the property is put should be considered as determinative." (James Talcott, Inc. v Gee, 5 UCC Rep Serv 1028; 266 Cal.App.2d 384, 72 Cal.Rptr. 168 (1968))

"The classification of goods in UCC §9-109 are mutually exclusive." (McFadden v Mercantile-Safe Deposit & Trust Co., 8 UCC Rep Serv 766; 260 Md 601, 273 A.2d 198 (1971))

"Automobile purchased for the purpose of transporting buyer to and from his place of employment was ``consumer goods" as defined in UCC §9-109." (Mallicoat v Volunteer Finance & Loan Corp., 3 UCC Rep Serv 1035; 415 S.W.2d 347 (Tenn. App., 1966))

"The provisions of UCC §2-316 of the Maryland UCC do not apply to sales of consumer goods (a term which includes automobiles, whether new or used, that are bought primarily for personal, family, or household use)." (Maryland Independent Automobile Dealers Assoc., Inc. v Administrator, Motor Vehicle Admin., 25 UCC Rep Serv 699; 394 A.2d 820, 41 Md App 7 (1978))

"A vehicle not used for commercial activity is a 'consumer goods,' . . . it is NOT a type of vehicle required to be registered and "use tax" paid of which the tab is evidence of receipt of the tax." (Bank of Boston v. Jones, 4 UCC Rep. Serv. 1021, 236 A2d 484, UCC PP 9-109.14)

"Thus self-driven vehicles are classified according to the use to which they are put rather than according to the means by which they are propelled." (Ex Parte Hoffert, 148 NW 20)

"The Supreme Court, in Arthur v. Morgan, 112 U.S. 495, 5 S.Ct. 241, 28 L.Ed. 825, held that carriages were properly classified as household effects, and we see no reason that automobiles should not be similarly disposed of." (Hillhouse v United States, 152 F. 163, 164 (2nd Cir. 1907))

"A soldier's personal automobile is part of his "household goods[.]" U.S. v Bomar, C.A.5(Tex.), 8 F.3d 226, 235" (19A Words and Phrases - Permanent Edition (West) pocket part 94)

"[T]he exemptions provided for in section 1 of the Motor Vehicle Transportation License Act of 1925 (Stats. 1925, p. 833) in favor of those who solely transport their own property or employees, or both, and of those who transport no persons or property for hire or compensation, by motor vehicle, have been determined in the Bacon Service Corporation case to be lawful exemptions." (In re Schmolke (1926) 199 Cal. 42, 46)

"Consumer goods – automobile for transportation to and from work. The use of a vehicle by its owner for purposes of travelling to and from his employment is a personal, as opposed to a business use, as that term is used in UCC 9-109(1) and the vehicle will be classified as consumer goods rather than equipment." (In Re Barnes, 11 UCC Reporting Service 670)

"In view of this rule a statutory provision that the supervising officials "may" exempt such persons when the transportation

is not on a commercial basis means that they "must" exempt
them." (State v. Johnson, 243 P. 1073; 60 C.J.S. section 94,
page 581)

And under the Texas constitution, consumer goods (household
goods), like my private conveyance, are *"exempt from ad valorem
taxation household goods not held or used for the production of income
and personal effects not held or used for the production of income"*
(Article 8, Sec. 1 (d) Texas Constitution [emphasis added]). And
traffic offenses are a Class C Misdemeanor in Texas:

"(e) An offense under this section is a Class "C" misdemeanor
if the offense for which the actor's appearance is required is
punishable by fine only." (Texas Penal Code § 38.10 Bail
Jumping and Failure to Appear)

"(c) Conviction of a Class C misdemeanor does not impose
any legal disability or disadvantage." (Texas Penal Code §
12.03 Classification of Misdemeanor)

"An individual adjudged guilty of a Class "C" misdemeanor
shall be punished by fine only, not to exceed $500." (Texas
Penal Code § 12.23 Class (C) Misdemeanors)

And a class C Misdemeanor in Texas is not a crime in Texas
because it is punishable by fine *only* (and probably everywhere else).
And if it fails to be a crime, then it is a civil matter. Take speed
signs as an example. The government shall erect and maintain on
the highways and roads of the state "appropriate signs that show
the maximum lawful speed for commercial vehicles, truck tractors,

truck trailers, truck semitrailers, and motor vehicles engaged in the business of transporting passengers for compensation for hire" (Texas Transportation Code § 201.904 Speed Signs). Yet "at Common Law there is no precise limit of speed. A traveler by automobile must adopt a reasonable speed" (Gallagher v. Montplier, 52 ALR 744; 5 Am Jur. page 645). And we see that "the reason for the initial detention, speeding & running a red light are not a breach of the peace" (Perkins v Texas, 812 S.W. 2d 326).

And there is no probable cause for an arrest, and they are operating in their private capacity as a revenue officer, a privateer. We see that "an officer who acts in violation of the Constitution ceases to represent the government" (Brookfield Const. Co. v. Stewart, 284 F. Supp. 94).

> "OATH....All oaths must be lawful, allowed by the common law, or some statute; *if they are administered by persons in a private capacity, or not duly authorized, they are coram non judice, and void."* (Tomlins Law Dictionary, 1835 Edition, Volume 2 [emphasis added])

The test for police officer's sufficient basis for probable cause— did the officer have a sufficient basis to make a *practical, common sense"* decision that a *"fair probability of crime existed."* Once the officer's actions fail to satisfy this test, it may appear that *no reasonably objective officer could have believed that probable cause existed* to make an arrest (Allen v. City of Portland, 73 F.3d 232 (9th Cir. 1995)). The Ninth Circuit Court of Appeals (citing cases from the U.S. Supreme Court, Fifth, Seventh, Eighth and Ninth Circuits) held that "by definition, probable cause to arrest can only exist in relation

to criminal conduct; civil disputes cannot give rise to probable cause"
(Paff v. Kaltenbach, 204 F.3d 425, 435 (3rd Cir. 2000)):

> "The people shall be secure in their persons, houses, papers
> and possessions, from all unreasonable seizures or searches,
> and no warrant to search any place, or to seize any person
> or thing, shall issue without describing them as near as
> may be, nor without probable cause, supported by oath or
> affirmation." (Article 1, Section 9 Searches and Seizures,
> Texas Constitution)

Article Four in Amendment prohibits law enforcement
officers from arresting citizens without probable cause (citations
omitted). In Santiago v. City of Vineland and Hill v. Algor arrests
made without probable cause violated the Fourth Amendment
(Santiago v. City of Vineland, 107 F.Supp.2d 512, 561-62, 564
(D.N.J. 2000); Hill v. Algor, 85 F.Supp.2d 391, 397-98 (D.N.J.
2000)). In Rzayeva v. Foster holding involuntary civil confinement
is a "massive curtailment of liberty" and is tantamount to the
infringement of being arrested and can be made only upon probable
cause (Rzayeva v. Foster, 134 F.Supp.2d 239, 248-49 (D.Conn.
2001) citing Vitek v. Jones, 445 U.S. 480, 491, 100 S.Ct. 1254,
63 L.Ed.2d 552 (1980); Schneider v. Simonini, 749 A.2d 336, 163
N.J. 336, 361-65 (2000)).

When there is no Probable Cause for an arrest, then it is a
malicious prosecution. "Although probable cause may not be inferred
from malice, malice may be inferred from lack of probable cause"
(Pauley v. Hall, 335 N. W. 2d 197, 124 Mich App 255). And false
arrest: "The only thing the plaintiff needs to do is to allege a false arrest,
is either (1) that the defendant made an arrest or imprisonment, or

(2) that the defendant affirmatively instigated, encouraged, incited, or caused the arrest or imprisonment" (Burlington v. Josephson, 153 Fed.2d 372,276 (1946)).

Furthermore we see restrictions:

"As in the case of illegal arrests, the officer... must keep within the law at his peril." (Thiede v. Scandia, 217 Minn. 231, 14 N.W.2d 400 (1944))

"When the plaintiff has shown that he was arrested, imprisoned or restrained of his liberty by the defendant, "the law presumes it to be unlawful." (People v. McGrew, 20 Pac. 92 (1888); Knight v. Baker, 133 P. 544 (1926))

"The burden is upon the defendant (cop) to show that the arrest was by authority of law." (McAleer v. Good, 65 Atl. 934, 935 (1907); Mackie v. Ambassador, 11 P.2d 6 (1932))

"ANY ARREST, made without a PROPER warrant, Signed by a judge and backed up by an affidavit from two persons that states, under penalty of perjury, you have broken a contract or hurt somebody, if challenged by the defendant (person), is presumptively invalid...the burden is upon the state" to justify it as authorized by statute, and does not violate the constitutional provisions and/or human rights. (State v. Mastrian, 171 N.W.2d 695 (1969); Butler v. State, 212 So.2d 577 (Miss 1968))

Figure 30 – Constituional Sheriffs and Peace Officers Association (cspoa)

Peace Officers

Police officers wear two hats: as a law enforcement officers enforcing the martial saw and also as peace officers keeping the peace. In spite of their training, many officers learn about their duty to keep the peace as evidenced by Sheriff Richard Mack's Constitutional Sheriffs and Peace Officers Association (CSPOA.org). They are *posse comitatus:*

> "Posse comitatus. Latin. The power or force of the county. The entire population of a county above the age of fifteen, which a sheriff may summon to his assistance in certain cases, as to aid him in keeping the peace, in pursuing and arresting felons, etc. Williams v. State, 253 Ark. 973, 490 S.W.2d 117, 121." (*Black's Law Dictionary*, 6th Edition, page 1990)

They can be a peace officer or a LEO (law enforcement officer), depending on their understanding of the law.

Good Faith

Because of the martial law, and because so many people are so clueless about the two classes of citizens, our public servants can presume we are one of their US citizen slaves and claim good faith:

"All wanton violence committed against persons in the invaded country, all destruction of property not commanded by the authorized officer, all robbery, *all pillage* or sacking, even after taking a place by main force, all rape, wounding, maiming, or killing of such inhabitants, are prohibited under the penalty of death, or such other severe punishment as may seem adequate for the gravity of the offense.

A soldier, officer or private, in the act of committing such violence, and disobeying a superior ordering him to abstain from it, may be lawfully killed on the spot by such superior." (Article 44, General Orders 100 (The Lieber Code) [emphasis added])

Which is codified in their statutes (edicts under martial law): "(a) No evidence obtained by an officer or other person in violation of any provisions of the Constitution or laws of the State of Texas, or of the Constitution or laws of the United States of America, shall be admitted in evidence against the accused on the trial of any criminal case.

(b) It is an exception to the provisions of Subsection (a) of this Article that the evidence was obtained by a law enforcement officer acting in objective good faith reliance upon a warrant issued by a neutral magistrate based on probable cause." (Texas Code of Criminal Procedure, Article 38.23 Evidence Not to Be Used [emphasis added])

And their federal statutes (edicts under martial law):
"(e) DEFENSE.—A good faith reliance on—

1. a court warrant or order, a grand jury subpoena, a legislative authorization, or a statutory authorization (including a request of a governmental entity under section 2703(f) of this title);

2. a request of an investigative or law enforcement officer under section 2518(7) of this title; or

3. a good faith determination that section 2511(3) of this title permitted the conduct complained of; *is a complete defense to any civil or criminal action brought under this chapter or any other law."* (18 US Code § 2707 Civil Action)

Except that they can be put in the position of honoring their oath by explaining to them that you fail to be one of their slaves, in a way that can be proven, thereby putting them into estoppel.

Summary

They can be a peace officer at common law, or they can be a law enforcement officer under martial law for those who are in a contract with the government by way of a privilege:

"The rights of sovereignty extend to all persons and things, not privileged that are within the territory. They extend to all *strangers resident* therein; not only to those who are naturalized, and to those who are domiciled therein, having taken up their abode with the intention of permanent residence, but also to those whose residence is transitory. All *strangers* are under the protection of the sovereign while they are within his territory and owe a temporary allegiance in return for that protection." (Carlisle v United States 83 U.S. 147, 154 (1873))

Figure 31 – Murdered by Police

Their Roman Cult handlers want to make sure they get away with their assaults and kidnappings and murders because they bring in so much business, and if a lawsuit is filed, the Roman Cult's BAR members will sit there and play stupid and get their (screened for low intelligence) military police out of being responsible. The fact that the rights under the Geneva Convention Relative to the Protection of Civilians in a Time of War of 1949 may not be given up:

"Protected persons may in no circumstances renounce in part or in entirety the rights secured to them by the present Convention." (Article 8, Geneva Convention Relative to the Treatment of Civilians in a Time of War of 1949)

Their criminal corporation is responsible, even if they let their gustapo thugs off the hook because the party to the conflict in whose hands protected persons may be, "is responsible for the treatment accorded to them by its agents, irrespective of any individual responsibility which may be incurred." (Article 29, Geneva Convention Relative to the Treatment of Civilians in a Time of War of 1949).

And if you fail to bring up those issues the Roman Cult BAR member, (bought-and-paid-for) clerk masquerading as a judge will sit there and play stupid, and you will get nothing!

14

THE ROMAN CULT AND COLOR OF LAW

Pretend Legislation

One of the issues in the Declaration of Independence was "pretend legislation." He has combined with others to subject us to a "jurisdiction foreign to our constitution, and unacknowledged by our laws; *giving his Assent to their Acts of pretended Legislation*: For transporting us beyond Seas to be tried for *pretended offences*" (Declaration of Independence, 1776 [emphasis added]).

And the English tyrants were busy passing all sorts of pretended legislation on behalf of their Roman Cult handlers:

"Fornication, Fornicatio, 1 H. 7. 4. Whoredom, the Aft of incontinency between single persons; for if either Party be married, it is Adultery: The first offense herein was punished with Three Months Imprisonment; the second was made Felony in the late Times of Usurpation, *by a pretended Act made 1650*. Cap. 10. *Scobells* Collection." (Cowells Law Dictionary, 1708 Edition)

"Judicial Proceedings. No Judicial Proceedings commenced or prosecuted in the Stile of Oliver Lord Protector, &c. were abateable by his Majesty King Charles the second'. re-assuming the Government; And *a pretended Act of Parliament*, for turning the Books of the Law, and Proceedings of Courts of Justice, into English, was declared to be in Force, by Stat. 12 Car. z. c. 3. See process." (Jacob A New Law Dictionary, 1750 Edition)

"Statute, *(Statutum)* Has divers Significations: *First,* It signifies an Act of Parliament made by the King, and the three Estates of the Realm; and *Secondly,* it is a short Writing called a *Statute-Merchant,* or *Statute-Staple,* which are in the Nature of Bonds, *etc.* and called *Statutes,* as they are made according to the Form expressly provided in certain *Statutes.* 5 *H.* 4. c. 12. *To Statutes enacted in Parliament, there must be the Assent of the King, Lords, and Commons, without which there can be no good Act of Parliament*; but there are many Acts in Force, though these three Assents are not mentioned therein, as *Dominus Rex* statuit *in Parliamento,* and *Diminus Rex in Parliamento suo* Statuta edit, and *de Communi Concilio* Statuit, *etc. Plowd.* 79. 2 *Bulst.* 186. And Sir *Edw. Coke* says, that several *Statutes* are penned like Charters in the King's Name only; though they were made by lawful Authority. 4 *Inst.* 25....A *Statute* which concerns the King is a public Act and yet the *Stat.* 23 *Hen.* 8. *concerning Sheriffs, etc., is a Private Act. Plowd.* 38. *Dyer 119,* 'Tis a Rule *in* Law, that the Courts at *Westminster* ought to take Notice of a General *Statute,* without Pleading it; but they are not bound to take Notice of

particular or private *Statutes* unless they are pleaded. 1 *Inst.*
98." (Jacob A New Law Dictionary, 1750 Edition [emphasis
added])

Color of Law

This is another way of saying that it is color of law. "Color"
means "An appearance, semblance, or simulacrum, as distinguished
from that which is real. A *prima facia* or *apparent* right. Hence, a
deceptive *appearance*, a plausible, assumed exterior, concealing a
lack of reality; a disguise or pretext. See also colorable" (*Black's Law
Dictionary*, 5th Edition, on page 240 [emphasis added]).

Other definitions:

"Colorable" means "That which is in appearance only, and
not in reality, what it purports to be, hence counterfeit
feigned, having the appearance of truth." (Windle v. Flinn,
196 Or. 654, 251 P.2d 136, 146)

"Colourable - Presenting an appearance that does not
correspond with reality, or an appearance intended to conceal
or deceive. Etherington v Wilson (1875), 1 Ch.D. 160"
(Barrons Dictionary of Canadian Law, Sixth Edition, page 51)

"Color of Law" means "The appearance or semblance, without
the substance, of legal right. Misuse of power, possessed by
virtue of state law and made possible only because wrongdoer
is clothed with authority of state is action taken under 'color
of law.'" (Atkins v. Lanning. D.C.Okl., 415 F. Supp. 186,
188.)

"Colour of Law – Mere semblance of a legal right. An action done under colour of law is one done with the apparent authority of law but actually in contravention of law." (Barrons Dictionary of Canadian Law, Sixth Edition, page 51)

Color of Office

And they were doing the same thing that happens today with their low intelligence thugs operating under color of office:

"Color of office. *An act which is done by an officer under the pretence or semblance that it is within his authority*, when in truth it is not, is said to be done by color of office, or, in the Latin form, *colore officii.* The phrase implies, we think, some official power vested in the actor, - he must be at least officer *de facto;* we do not understand that an act of a *mere pretender to* an office, or false personator of an officer, is said to be done by color of office. And it implies an illegal claim of authority, by virtue of the office, to do the act or thing in question. Burrall 11. Acker, 23 *Wend.* 606; Winter *v.* Kinney, 1 *N. Y.* 365; Decker *v.* Judson, 16 *ld.* 439, 442; Griffiths *v.* Hardenbergh, 41 *!d.* 464. It imports a design to do an act in excess of authority, Kelly *v.* McCormick, 28 *N. Y.318.* but not necessarily an evil or corrupt intent on the officer's part, Richardson *v.* Crandall, 48 ld. 348." (Abbotts Law Dictionary, Volume 1, 1879 Edition, page 242)

"COLOUR OF OFFICE, color officii.] Is when an act is evilly done by the countenance of an office; and always taken in the worst sense, being grounded upon corruption, to which the office is as a shadow and colour. *Plowd. Comment. 64.* See as to the distinction between acts done *colore officii* and *virtute officii, 9 East, 364: 2 Barn. & Cres. 729. See Bribery; Extortion."* (Tomlins Law Dictionary, 1835 Edition, Volume 1)

And it is like a feeding frenzy by the Roman Cult's BAR members and their military police, with their exactions:

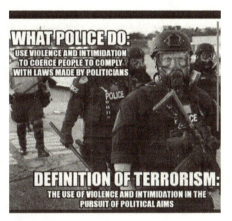

Figure 32 – Terrorists

"Exaction. Is a Wrong done by an Officer, or one *pretending to have Authority*, in taking a Reward or Fee for that which the Law allows not. The Difference between Exaction and Extortion is this, Extortion is, where an Officer extorts more than his due. Exaction is, where he wrests a Fee or Reward, where none is due. See Extortion." (Cowells Law Dictionary 1727 Edition)

"Exaction, Is. defined to be a Wrong done by an Officer, *or one in pretended Authority*, by taking a Reward or Fee for that which the Law allows not, And the Difference between Exaction and Extortion, is this: Extortion is where an Officer extorts more than his Due, when something is due to him; and Exaction is when he wrests a Fee or Reward, where none is due, for which the Offender is to be fined and imprisoned, and render to the Party twice as much as the Money he so takes. Co. Lit. 368. 10 rep. 100." (Jacob A New Law Dictionary, 1750 Edition)

"EXACTION, is a wrong done by an officer, *or one in pretended authority,* by taking a reward or fee for that which the law allows not. And the difference between exaction and extortion, is this: Extortion is, where an officer extorts more than his due, when something is due to him: Exaction is, when he wrests a fee or reward where none is due. For which the offender may be indicted, fined, and imprisoned." (Burn A New Law Dictionary, 1792 Edition, page 273)

And the Roman Cult has been mixed up in it from the beginning: "Jesuits &c. Born in the Kings Dominions and ordained by the *pretended Jurisdiction of Rome* remaining in *England* or coming from beyond Sea into this Kingdom, and not submitting to some Bishop or Justice of Peace within three Days, and taking the Oaths, are guilty of High Treason; and Receivers, Aiders and Harbourers of them, are guilty of Felony. *Stat.* 27 *Eliz. c.* 2. Persons knowing Priests, *Jesuits,* &c. and not discovering them co a Justice of Peace, shall be fined and imprisoned. 22 *Car.* 22." (Jacob A New Law Dictionary, 1750 Edition)

Roman Cult Imposters

The Roman Cult is full of imposters, but something tells me that statutes like those described below were probably used against somebody else:

"IMPOSTORS, religious. Those who falsely pretend an extraordinary commission from heaven; or terrify and *abuse the people with false denunciations of judgments*. They are punishable by the temporal courts with fine, imprisonment, and infamous corporal punishment. 1 *Hawk. P. C. c. 5.*" (Tomlins Law Dictionary, 1835 Edition, Volume 1, [emphasis added])

"IMPOSTORS, religious. Those who falsely pretend an extraordinary commission from heaven; or terrify and *abuse the people with false denunciations of judgments*, are punishable by the temporal courts with fine, imprisonment, and infamous corporal punishment. 1 *Hawk. P. C. c. 7. 4 Black 62*" (Williams Law Dictionary, 1816 Edition, [emphasis added])

"IMPOSTORS in religion, are such as falsely pretend an extraordinary commission from heaven, or terrify and *abuse the people with false denunciations of judgments*. They are punishable by fine, imprisonment, and infamous corporal punishment. 1 *Haw.* 7. And by the statute 9 G.*2.c.5.* all persons who pretend to use any kind of witchcraft, forcery, inchantment, or conjuration; or undertake to tell fortunes; or pretend, from their skill in the occult sciences, to find out, goods that have been stolen; shall be imprisoned for a year, and once in every quarter of that year be set on the pillory." (Burn A New Law Dictionary, 1792 edition, page 376)

Today they use words like "prima facia," "color of law," "appearance," and "presume," all of which are used together, and in

The Matrix:

"[1] It is well settled that "the Code cannot prevail over the Statutes at Large, when the two are inconsistent." Stephan v. United States, 319 U.S. 423, 63 S.Ct. 1135, 1137, 80 L.Ed. 1490; Royer's Inc. v. United States, 3 Cir., 265 F.2d 615. The provisions of the Code are merely prima facie evidence of the law. 1 U.S.C. § 204 (a)." (American Export Lines Inc. v. United States, 290 F.2d 925, at 929 (July 19, 1961))

"But the legislature specifically disclaimed any intention to change the meaning of any statute. The compilers of the code were not empowered by congress to amend existing law, and doubtless had no thought of doing so ..." ...the act before us does not purport to amend a section of an act, but only a section of a compilation entitled "REVISED CODE OF WASHINGTON," WHICH IS NOT THE LAW. Such an act purporting to amend only a section of the prima facie compilation leaves the law unchanged. En Banc." (PAROSA v. TACOMA, 57 Wn.(2d) 409 (Dec.22, 1960))

" 'Prima facia": At first sight; *on the first appearance*; on the face of it; so far as can be judged from the first disclosure; *presumably*; a fact *presumed* to be true unless disproved by some evidence to the contrary." State ex rel. Herbert v. Whims, 68 Ohio App. 39, 38 N.E.2d 596, 599, 22 O.O. 110. (*Black's Law Dictionary*, 5th Edition page 1071 [emphasis added])
"Because of their respect for what appears to be a law many people are cunningly coerced into waiving their rights due to ignorance." (US v Minker, 350 US 179 (1956))

Emergency Is Justification for Nothing

They even insert emergency clauses as an excuse for failing to follow their own procedures, which is further that all statutes are edicts under martial law for subjects *only:*

> "The fact that the laws relating to criminal procedure *in this state* have not been completely revised and re-codified in more than a century past and the further fact that the administration of justice, in the field of criminal law." (Texas Code of Criminal Procedure Article 54.03 Emergency Clause [emphasis added])

Any society that would give up a little liberty to gain a little security will deserve neither and lose both.

— *Benjamin Franklin*

They know that emergency is justification for nothing. Emergency does not create power. Emergency does not increase granted power or remove or diminish the restrictions imposed upon power granted or reserved. "The Constitution was adopted in a period of grave emergency. Its grants of power to the Federal Government and its limitations of the power of the States were determined in the light of emergency, and they are not altered by emergency" (Home Building and Loan Association v Blaisdel, 290 US 398 (1934))

Roman Cult BAR Members Blame the People

The Roman Cult's BAR member BAAL priests like to blame it on the people:

"Persons dealing with government are charged with knowing government statutes and regulations, and they assume the risk that government agents may exceed their authority and provide misinformation" (Lavin v. Marsh, 644 F.2nd 1378, 9th Cir., (1981))

"All persons in the United States are chargeable with knowledge of the Statutes-at-Large. It is well established that anyone who deals with the government assumes the risk that the agent acting in the government's behalf has exceeded the bounds of his authority" (Bollow v. Federal Reserve Bank of San Francisco, 650 F.2d 1093, 9th Cir., (1981))

"Persons who are not taxpayers are not within the system and can obtain no benefit by following the procedures prescribed for taxpayers, such as the filing of claims for refunds." (Economy Plumbing and Heating v. U.S., 470 F.2d 585 (Ct. Cl. 1972))

"The revenue laws are a code or a system in regulation of tax assessment and collection. They relate to taxpayers, and not to non-taxpayers. The latter are without their scope. No procedures are prescribed for non-taxpayers, and no attempt is made to annul any of their rights and remedies in due course of law. With them Congress does not assume to deal, and they are neither the subject nor the object of the revenue laws." (Long v. Rasmussen, 281 F. 236, at 238)

But the fact is that they are criminals:

Figure 33 – Tyranny

"In doing this, I shall have occasion incidentally to evince, how true it is that States and Governments were made for man, and, at the same time, how true it is that his creatures and servants have first deceived, next vilified, and, at last oppressed their master and maker." (Chisholm v Georgia, 2 Dall 419 at p 455)

"A state like a merchant makes a contract. A dishonest state, like a dishonest merchant willfully refuses to discharge it." (Chisholm v Georgia, 2 Dall 419 at p 456)

And their judgment day is coming:
"And through covetousness shall they with feigned words make merchandise of you: whose judgment now of a long time lingereth not, and their damnation slumbereth not." (2 Peter 2:3)

"And it shall come to pass in that day, that the LORD shall punish the host of the high ones that are on high, and the *kings of the earth* upon the earth. And they shall be gathered together, *as prisoners* are gathered in the pit, and shall be shut up in the prison, and after many days shall they be visited." (Isaiah 24: 21-22 [emphasis added])

"And the kings of the earth, and the great men, and the rich men, and the chief captains, and the mighty men, and every bondman, and every free man, hid themselves in the dens and in the rocks of the mountains; And said to the mountains and rocks, Fall on us, and hide us from the face of him that sitteth on the throne, and from the wrath of the Lamb: For the great day of his wrath is come; and who shall be able to stand?" (Revelations 6: 15-17)

Everything Is a Fraud

It is all a fraud:

"Once a fraud, always a fraud." (13 Vin. Abr. 539.)

"Things invalid from the beginning cannot be made valid by subsequent act." (Trayner, Max. 482. Maxims of Law, *Black's Law Dictionary*, 9th Edition, page 1862)

"A thing void in the beginning does not become valid by lapse of time." (1 S. & R. 58. Maxims of Law, *Black's Law Dictionary*, 9th Edition, page 1866)

"Time cannot render valid an act void in its origin." (Dig. 50, 17, 29; Broom, Max. 178, Maxims of Law, *Black's Law Dictionary*, 9th Edition, page 1862)

"Ex dolo malo non oritur action. Out of fraud no action arises. Cowper, 343; Broom's Max. 349." (Bouviers Maxims of Law, 1856 Edition)

And any act by any government official to conceal the fraud becomes an act of fraud:"fraus est celare fraudem. It is a fraud to conceal a fraud. 1 Vern. 270" (Bouviers Maxims of Law, 1856 Edition). And fraud is inexcusable and unpardonable: "Fraus et dolus nemini patrocianari debent. Fraud and deceit should excuse no man. 3 Co. 78" (Bouviers Maxims of Law, 1856 Edition). And any fraud amounts to injustice:

"Fraus et jus nunquam cohabitant. Fraud and justice never dwell together." (Maxims of Law, *Black's Law Dictionary*, 9th Edition, page 1832)

"Quod alias bonum et justum est, si per vim vei fraudem petatur, malum et injustum efficitur. What is otherwise good and just, if sought by force or fraud, becomes bad and unjust. 3 Co. 78." (Bouviers Maxims of Law, 1856 Edition)

And the Roman Cult's BAR members get people to participate in the fraud with their color of law and confession and avoidance, thereby arguing the terms of the contract, and thereby giving them the contract:

"*[G]ive color*, vb. Hist. To admit, either expressly or impliedly by silence, that an opponent's allegations appear to be meritorious. • In common-law pleading, a defendant's plea of *confession and avoidance had to give color* to the plaintiff's allegations in the complaint or the plea would be fatally defective." (*Black's Law Dictionary*, 8th Edition, page 2031 [emphasis added])

Because when you participate in the fraud, you may *not* claim fraud.

The Matrix Is Real

Under the Roman Cult's satanic system, you have:

Color of money – Federal Reserve Notes – Bank Notes

Color of Title – fake title

Color of Law – Fake law

Color of Justice – Fake Justice – "Justus"

Colorable Judges – fake Judges – BAR members - Fake courts

Everything is a fraud. The Matrix is real. It is here all day every day, and most people are completely oblivious to it.

Even the attorney with the rank of general is the highest law enforcement officer in the state or Federal government, which means he is enforcing the martial law instead of protecting the people, which is what he is supposed to be doing:

> "It is true that at common law the duty of the Attorney General is to represent the King, he being the embodiment of the state. But under the democratic form of government now prevailing the People are King so the Attorney General's duties are to that Sovereign rather than to the machinery of government." (Hancock V. Terry Elkhorn Mining Co., Inc., KY., 503 S.W. 2D 710 KY Const. §4, Commonwealth Ex Rel. Hancock V. Paxton, KY, 516 S. W. 2D. PG 867)

Summary

Everything is an illusion.

Things are *not* what they appear.

The Matrix is real, and it is all voluntary.

Do you know who you are?

15

THE ROMAN CULT
AND THE COURTS

UNIDROIT

All Courts fall under the UNIDROIT (Unification of Private Law) statute and have been for more than thirty years. UNIDROIT covers negotiable instruments, civil procedure, transnational civil procedure, transportation, secured transactions, legal status of women, maintenance obligations, contracts, banking law, franchises, leasing, capital markets, hotels, insurance, intellectual property, and more.

The last time I checked, there were 63 countries around the world that had become members of the UNIDROIT Statute, including Canada, the United States, most of Europe, South America, Australia, China, and more.

UNIDROIT governs the Uniform Commercial Code, and changes incorporated into the Uniform Commercial Code are automatically effective in all of the member states. The UNIDROIT (Roman Cult) controlled and regulated Uniform Commercial Code, which is found in Texas under the Texas Business and Commerce

Code, is also part of the Roman Cult's Private International Law, which is also covered by The Hague Conference on Private International Law as described herein.

UNIDROIT also covers children which is also covered by the Hague Conference on Private International Law and also the International Covenant on Civil and Political Rights.

UNIDROIT = Uniform Commercial Code

Whenever the Uniform Commercial Code *creates a presumption* with respect to a fact, or provides that a fact is presumed, "*the trier of fact must find the existence of the fact unless and until evidence is introduced that supports a finding of its nonexistence*" (Uniform Commercial Code § 1-206 Presumptions [emphasis added]). In the sense of a judicial proceeding, the Uniform Commercial Code "includes recoupment, counterclaim, set-off, suit in equity, and any other proceeding in which rights are determined" (Uniform Commercial Code Sec. 1-201. General Definitions (b) (1)). This is when they forge your signature onto their so-called contracts to sell you into slavery:

> "(a) In an action with respect to an instrument, the authenticity of, and *authority to make, each signature on the instrument are admitted unless specifically denied in the pleadings.* If the validity of a signature is denied in the pleadings, the burden of establishing validity is on the person claiming validity, *but the signature is presumed to be authentic and authorized* unless the action is to enforce the liability of the purported signer and the signer is dead or incompetent at the time of trial of the issue of validity of the signature." (Uniform Commercial

Code § 3-308 Proof of Signatures and Status as Holder in Due Course [emphasis added])

"The following rules apply in an action on a certificated security against the issuer:
(1) *Unless specifically denied in the pleadings, each signature on a security certificate or in a necessary indorsement is admitted.*
(2) If the effectiveness of a signature is put in issue, the burden of establishing effectiveness is on the party claiming under the signature, *but the signature is presumed to be genuine or authorized.*" (Uniform Commercial Code § 8-114 Evidentiary Rules Concerning Certificated Securities [emphasis added])

All presumptions are taken in Roman Cult so-called courts by Roman Cult BAR Member BAAL Priests:
COURTS ECCLESIASTICAL …The proceedings in the Ecclesiastical Courts are, *according to the civil and canon law by citation, libel,* answer upon oath, *proof by* witnesses, and *presumptions,* &c., and after sentence, for contempt, by excommunication: and *if the sentence is disliked, by appeal.* (Tomlins Law Dictionary, 1835 Edition, Volume 1, [emphasis added])

"IN PROPRIA PERSONA. In one's own proper person. It is a rule in pleading that pleas to the jurisdiction of the court must be plead *in propria persona, because if pleaded by attorney they admit the jurisdiction, as an attorney is an officer of the court, and he is presumed to plead after having obtained leave, which admits the jurisdiction.* Lawes, Pl. 91." (*Black's Law Dictionary,* 4th Edition, page 899-900)

Unconstitutional Municipal Corporation ONLY

The UNIDROIT website says nothing about Texas or Arizona, or any of the states. Therefore, it is for federal areas *only* and to US citizens *only* in the "territories":

> "We therefore decline to overrule the opinion of Chief Justice Marshall: We hold that *the District of Columbia is not a state within Article 3 of the Constitution.* In other words cases between citizens of the District and those of the states were not included of the catalogue of controversies over which the Congress could give jurisdiction to the federal courts by virtue of Article 3. In other words *Congress has exclusive legislative jurisdiction over citizens of Washington District of Columbia and through their plenary power nationally covers those citizens even when in one of the several states as though the district expands for the purpose of regulating its citizens wherever they go throughout the states in union*" (National Mutual Insurance Company of the District of Columbia v. Tidewater Transfer Company, 337 U.S. 582, 93 L.Ed. 1556 (1948))

International Law Rule

The International Law Rule was *adopted for areas under Federal legislative jurisdiction.* It *federalizes "State civil law, including common law.--*The rule serves to federalize not only the statutory but the common law of a State. ...STATE AND FEDERAL VENUE DISCUSSED: *The civil laws effective in an area of exclusive Federal jurisdiction are Federal law, notwithstanding their derivation from State laws,* and a cause arising under such laws may be brought in or removed to a Federal district court under sections 24 or 28 of the former Judicial Code (now sections 1331 and 1441 of title

28, United States Code), giving jurisdiction to such courts of civil actions arising under the laws of the United States")Jurisdiction over Federal Areas Within the States – Report of the Interdepartmental Committee for the Study of Jurisdiction over Federal Areas Within the States, Part II, A Text of the Law of Legislative Jurisdiction Submitted to the attorney general and transmitted to the President June 1957, page 158-165).

Congress may *not* exercise jurisdiction in the states unless it is under the commerce clause:

> "To exercise exclusive legislation, in all cases whatsoever, over such district (not exceeding ten miles square) as may by cession of particular States, and the acceptance of Congress, become the seat of the government of the United States, and to exercise like authority over all places purchased by the consent of the legislature of the State in which the same shall be, for the erection of forts, magazines, arsenals, dock-yards, and other needful buildings." (Article I, Section 8, Clause 17, US Constitution)

> "The law of Congress… do not extend into the territorial limits of the states, but have force only in the District of Columbia, and other places that are within the exclusive jurisdiction of the national government." (Caha v. United States, 152 U.S. 211 (1894))

> "The exclusive jurisdiction which the United States have in forts and dock-yards ceded to them, is derived from the express assent of the states by whom the cessions are made. It could be derived in no other manner; because without it,

the authority of the state would be supreme and exclusive therein." (U.S. v. Bevans, 16 U.S. 336, 3 Wheat, at 350, 351 (1818)).

Fees = Revenue Officers = Private Capacity

Under the Code of Law for the District of Columbia, which is now called United States Code, District Attorneys get a fee for

-attending court at 31 Stat. 1363

-conviction of indictable offense at 31 Stat. 1363

-counsel fee in proportion to the importance of the cause at 31 Stat. 1363

-judgment without jury at 31 Stat. 1363

-when a case is discontinued at 31 Stat. 1363

-depositions at 31 Stat 1363

-removals at 31 Stat. 1363

-examination of person charged with crime before commissioner at 31 Stat. 1363

-for each day attendance in court at 31 Stat 1363

-for appearing on behalf of any officer of revenue at 31 Stat. 1363

Commissioners (Clerks masquerading as Judges) get fees for

-drawing a complaint at 31 Stat. 1366

-issuing a warrant of arrest at 31 Stat. 1366

-issuing a commitment at 31 Stat. 1366

-entering a return at 31 Stat 1366

-Issuing a subpoena at 31 Stat. 1366

-drawing a bond at 31 Stat 1366

-Administering an oath at 31 Stat 1366

-Recognizance of witnesses at 31 Stat. 1366

-transcripts at 31 Stat 1366

-certifying depositions at 31 Stat 1366

There is no justice that goes on in these so-called courts. It is nothing more than another commercial transaction. All Courts in the District of Columbia are ecclesiastical courts because under Marshall's Fees at 31 Stat. 1365 it says:

"For holding an inquisition or other proceeding before a jury."

Summary

There are no state or federal Article 3 courts. They are all corporations in business to make a profit for their Roman Cult handlers being run by the Roman Cult's BAR Members under private international law, and the UNIDROIT controlled and regulated Uniform Commercial Code.

This is the same in any of the sixty-three countries that have acceded to the UNIDROIT statute.

They are all Roman Cult kangaroo courts:

"and because it brings into action, and enforces this great and glorious principle, that the people are the sovereign of this country, *and consequently that fellow citizens and joint sovereigns cannot be degraded by appearing with each other in their own courts to have their controversies determined.*" (Chisolm v Georgia 2 Dall. 419)

16

THE ROMAN CULT AND LAND

Do you think you own your land? Do you pay a yearly rent in the form of Property taxes?

> RYOT-TENURE. A system of land-tenure, where the government takes the place of landowners and collects the rent by means of tax gatherers. The farming is done by poor peasants, (ryots,) who find the capital, so far as there is any, and also do the work. The system exists in Turkey, Egypt, Persia, and other Eastern countries, and in a modified form in British India. After Slavery, it is accounted the worst of all systems, because the government can fix the rent at what it pleases, and it is difficult to distinguish between rent and taxes. (*Black's Law Dictionary*, 3rd Edition, page 1572)

Unlawful Detainer = Renter

What happens when you fail to pay the yearly rent? They sell your land and then do an unlawful detainer action, which is used to evict renters.

Joint Tenants or Tenants in Common

Why do you think they want to know whether you want your home vested as *joint tenants* with your wife, or *tenants in common*? A tenant is a renter.

Is your land "paid" for?

What did you use to pay for it? All mortgages fall under Roman Law, and negotiable instrument law is a branch of Roman Law. If you used Federal Reserve Notes, then it is *not* paid for because all "legal tender" is forced loans and military script:

> "*The forced loans of 1862 and 1863, in the form of legal tender notes,* were vital forces in the struggle for national supremacy. They formed a part of the public debt of the United States, the validity of which is *solemnly established by the Fourteenth Amendment to the Constitution.*" (Julliard v. Greenman, 110 US 432 [emphasis added])

> "This rule does not interfere with the right of the victorious invader to tax the people or their property, *to levy forced loans*, to billet soldiers, or to appropriate property, especially houses, lands, boats or ships, and churches, for temporary and military uses." (Article 37, General Orders 100 (The Lieber Code) [emphasis added])

At common law *only* gold or silver coin are legal tender to pay a debt:

> "At common law only gold and silver were a legal tender. (2 Inst. 577.)" (McClarin v. Nesbit, 2 Nott & McC. (11 S.C.L.) 519 (1820))

Money "In the absence of qualifying words, *it cannot mean promissory notes, bonds, or other evidences of debt.*" (36 AM Juris. 1st Money § 8)

And Federal Reserve Notes are military script because they are in support of the military occupation, and mere IOU's because there is no promise to pay anything:

> "PROMISSORY NOTE, contracts. A written promise to pay a certain sum of money, at a future time, unconditionally. 7 Watts & S. 264; 2 Humph. R. 143; 10 Wend. 675; Minor, R. 263; 7 Misso. 42; 2 Cowen, 536; 6 N. H. Rep. 364; 7 Vern. 22. *A promissory note differs from a mere acknowledgment of debt, without any promise to pay, as when the debtor gives his creditor an I 0 U.* (q. v.) See 2 Yerg. 50; 15 M. & W. 23. But see 2 Humph. 143; 6 Alab. R. 373." (Bouviers Law Dictionary, 1856 Edition)

> "The term 'dollars' likewise is incorrect, which, according to constitutional definition, are monetary units, used in exchange, backed by gold and silver. Our present day fiat issues are supported by more printed paper of the same; therefore, they are correctly termed Federal Reserve Notes (FRN), not dollars." (Robert P. Vichas, Handbook of Financial Mathematics, Formulas, and Tables (1979), p. 420)

And nobody is required to accept federal reserve notes:

> "Federal Reserve Bank notes, and other notes constituting a part of common currency of country, are recognized as good tender for money, unless specially objected to." (MacLeod v. Hoover (1925), 159 La. 244, 105 S. 305)

"Bank notes constitute a large and convenient part of the currency of our country, and by *common consent*, serve to a great extent all the purposes of coin. In themselves they are not money, for they are not a legal tender; and yet they are a good tender, unless specifically objected to as being notes merely, and not money. Miller v. Race, 1 Burr. 457; Bank of United States v. Bank of Georgia, 10 Wheat 333; Handy v. Dobbin, 12 Johns. 220; Wright v. Reed, 3 Term R. 554. They sub serve the purposes of money in the ordinary business of life, by the *mutual consent* (express or implied) of the parties to a contract, and not by the binding force of any common usage; for the party to whom they may be tendered *has an undoubted right to refuse accepting them as money*." (Vick v. Howard, 136 S.E. 101; 116 S.E. 465, 468 (March 15, 1923) [emphasis added]

Discharge Debt with Limited Liability

Which also means that Federal Reserve Notes *cannot* be used to pay a debt, but instead discharge a debt with limited liability:

"There is a distinction between a debt discharged and one paid. When discharged, the debt still exists, though divested of its character as a legal obligation during the operation of the discharge." (Stanek v. White (1927), 172 Minn. 390, 215 N.W. 781)

And federal reserve notes are also bills of credit:

"The term "obligation or other security of the United States" includes all bonds, certificates of indebtedness, national bank currency, Federal Reserve notes, Federal Reserve bank notes, coupons, United States notes, Treasury notes, gold certificates, silver certificates, fractional notes, certificates of deposit, bills, checks, or drafts for money, drawn by or upon authorized officers of the United States, stamps and other representatives of value, of whatever denomination, issued under any Act of Congress, and canceled United States stamps." (18 U.S. Code § 8.Obligation or other security of the United States defined)

"Federal reserve notes, to be issued at the discretion of the Board of Governors of the Federal Reserve System for the purpose of making advances to Federal Reserve banks through the Federal Reserve agents as hereinafter set forth *and for no other purpose, are authorized.* The said notes *shall be obligations of the United States* and shall be receivable by all national and member banks and Federal reserve banks and for all taxes, customs, and other public dues." (12 USC § 411 [emphasis added]

Therefore, anything purchased with federal reserve notes are purchased with United States credit, and anything purchased with United States credit is the property of the United States because federal reserve notes are for internal use of the government *only:*
"Sec. 15. As used in this Act the term *"United States"* means the Government of the United States...the term *"currency of the United States"* means currency which is legal tender in the United States, and includes United States notes . . . Federal Reserve Notes..."

"Sec. 17. All Acts and parts of Acts inconsistent with any of the provisions of this Act are hereby repealed." (Gold Reserve Act of 1934, 48 Stat. 337 [emphasis added])

Unless your deed specifically says gold or silver coin was used to pay for the land, the Roman Cult's BAR member BAAL priests will presume that federal reserve notes were used which means that you bought the land for the United States, which is also why you have to pay an annual rent in the form of taxes.

Color of Title

These deeds include the ones as follows: "warranty deed, quit claim deed, sheriff's deed, trustee's deed, judicial deed, tax deed, will, or any other instrument that purportedly conveys the title. Each of these documents state that it conveys the ownership to the land. Each of these, however, is actually a color of title." (G. Thompson, Title to Real Property, Preparation and Examination of Abstracts, Ch. 3, Section 73, p. 93 (1919))

The word *color* means "An appearance, semblance, or simulacrum, as distinguished from that which is real. A prima facia or apparent right. Hence, a deceptive appearance, a plausible, assumed exterior, concealing a lack of reality; a disguise or pretext. See also colorable" (*Black's Law Dictionary*, 5th Edition, on page 240).

The word *colorable* means "That which is in appearance only, and not in reality, what it purports to be, hence counterfeit feigned, having the appearance of truth" (Windle v. Flinn, 196 Or. 654, 251 P.2d 136, 146).

The phrase *color of law* means "The appearance or semblance, without the substance, of legal right. Misuse of power, possessed by virtue of state law and made possible only because wrongdoer is clothed with authority of state is action taken under 'color of law' " (Atkins v. Lanning. D.C.Okl., 415 F. Supp. 186, 188).

And so when we say a person has a color of title, whatever may be the meaning of the phrase, we express the idea, at least, "that act has been previously done . . . by which some title, good or bad, to a parcel of land of definite extent has been conveyed to him" (St. Louis v Gorman, 29 Mo. 593 (1860)).

Land Patents

Land patents are an act of "making further provision for the sale of the public lands." They were approved on April 24, 1820 in Volume 3, Sixteenth Congress, Session I, under Sec. 2, at 3 Stat 566. Later in section 2 we see that " *credit shall not be allowed* for the purchase money on the sale of any of the public lands which shall be sold" (Volume 3, Sixteenth Congress, Session I, under Sec. 2, at 3 Stat 566) [emphasis added].

Land patents were "were calculated to plant in the new country a population of *independent unembarrassed freeholder* . . . that it would place, in every man, the Power to Purchase a freehold, the price of which could be cleared in 3 years . . . that it would cut up speculation and monopoly . . . that *it would prevent the accumulation of alarming debt, which experience proved never would and never could be paid*" (emphasis added) Senator King of New York, in March 1820 during the passage of the Act for the sale of public lands.

After the American Revolution, lands in Maryland became "allodial, subject to no tenure nor to any services incident thereto" (in re Waltz et al., Burlow v Security Trust and Savings Bank, 240 P. 19 (1925), quoting Matthews v Ward, 10 Gill & Johnson (Md.) 443 (1839)):

"From what source does the title to the land derived from a government spring? In arbitrary governments, from the supreme head - be he the emperor, king or potentate; or by whatever name he is known. In a republic, from the law making or authorizing to be made the grant or sale. In the first case, the party looks alone to his letters patent; in the second, to the law and the evidence of the acts necessary to be done under the law,...to a perfection of his grant, donation or purchase ... The law alone must be the fountain from whence the authority is drawn; and there can be no other source." (McConnell v Wilcox, 1 Scammon ILL. 344 (1837))

"We are then to regard the Revolution and these Acts of Assembly as emancipating every acre of the soil of Pennsylvania from the grand characteristic of the feudal system. Even as to the lands held by the proprietaries themselves, they held them as other citizens held, under the Commonwealth, and that by a title purely allodial. All our lands are held mediately or immediately of the state, by the titles purged of all the rubbish of the dark ages, excepting only the feudal names of things not any longer feudal.

"Under the Acts of Assembly I have alluded to, the state became the proprietor of all lands, but instead of giving them like a feudal lord to an enslaved tenantry, she has sold them for the best price, she could get, *and conferred on the purchaser the same absolute estate she held herself*, . . . and these have been reserved, as everything else has been granted, by contract." (Wallace v Harmstad, S Ct 492 (1863) [emphasis added])

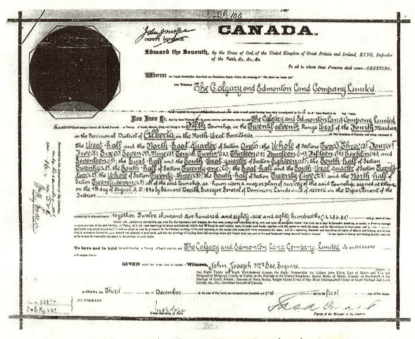

Figure 34 – Crown Patent (inside a box)

The land patent is the muniment of title, such title being absolute in its nature, *making the sovereigns absolute freeholders on their lands*. Finally, the patent is the only evidence of the legal fee simple title. (McConnell v Wilcox, 1 Scammon (ILL.) 381 (1837)).

"A patent to land, issued by the United States under authority of law, is the highest evidence of title, something upon which its holder can rely for peace and security in his possession. *It is conclusive evidence of title against the United States and all the world*." (2 The American Law of Mining, § 1.29 at 357. Nichols v. Rysavy, (S.D. 1985) 610 F. Supp. 1245)

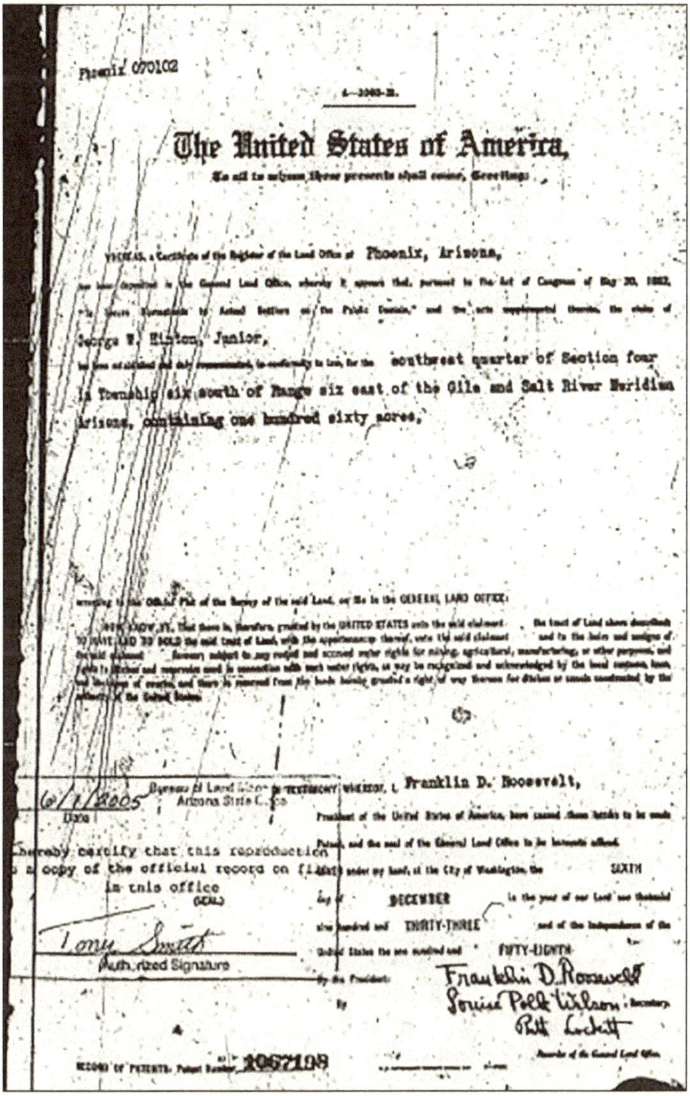
Phoenix 070102

The United States of America,

To all to whom these presents shall come, Greeting:

WHEREAS, a Certificate of the Register of the Land Office at Phoenix, Arizona,

George W. Hinton, Junior,

southwest quarter of Section four in Township six south of Range six east of the Gila and Salt River Meridian Arizona, containing one hundred sixty acres,

IN TESTIMONY WHEREOF, I, Franklin D. Roosevelt,

President of the United States of America, have caused these letters to be made Patent, and the seal of the General Land Office to be hereunto affixed.

GIVEN under my hand, at the City of Washington, the SIXTH day of DECEMBER in the year of our Lord one thousand nine hundred and THIRTY-THREE and of the Independence of the United States the one hundred and FIFTY-EIGHTH.

By the President: Franklin D. Roosevelt

By Louise Polk Wilson, Secretary.

Paul Lockett

Recorder of the General Land Office.

RECORD OF PATENTS: Patent Number 1067108

6/1/2005 Date

Bureau of Land Management Arizona State Office

I hereby certify that this reproduction is a copy of the official record on file in this office

(SEAL)

Tony Smith

Authorized Signature

Figure 35 – Arizona Land Patent (NOT inside a box)

Vol. 41-B   No. 333

In The Name of   the State of Texas

To All to Whom These Presents Shall Come, Know Ye:

I,   DOLPH BRISCOE   , Governor of the State aforesaid, by virtue of the power vested in me by

law and in accordance with the laws of said State in such case made and provided, do by these presents Grant to

M. B. CARROLL, Assignee   his

heirs and assigns forever,   Six Hundred Forty (640)   acres of land situated and described

as follows in   Hudspeth   County, known as Section No. 26,
Block No. 73, Township No. 7, T. & P. Ry. Company, Certificate No. 6599, located
about 16 miles N.74°W. from Sierra Blanca, Texas.

Bought and fully paid for on the application of   L. V. Carroll   filed in the

General Land Office   May 13, 1926   under the laws regulating the sale of Public Free School land.

   BEGINNING at a stake and mound set for Southwest corner of Survey No. 24,
Southeast corner of Survey No. 23 and Northwest corner of Survey No. 25;

   THENCE South with West line of Survey No. 25 at 1900 varas a stake and mound
set for Southwest corner of Survey No. 25;

   THENCE West 1900 varas to a stake and mound set for Southwest corner;

   THENCE North 1900 varas to a stake and mound set for Southwest corner of
Survey No. 23 and Southeast corner of Survey No. 22;

   THENCE East with South line of Survey No. 23 at 1900 varas the place of
beginning.

   Said lands having been originally sold to L. V. Carroll on application filed
September 2, 1924, forfeited for non-payment of interest; and repurchased by said
L. V. Carroll under the provisions of Chapter 94, Acts of 1925.

   All of the oil, gas and other minerals in the above described lands are reserved to the State.

Hereby relinquishing to   Him   the said   M. B. Carroll

said   His   heirs or assigns forever all the right and title in and to said land heretofore held and possessed by

the said State, and I do hereby issue this Letter Patent for the same.

                     IN TESTIMONY WHEREOF, I have caused the Seal of the State to be affixed,

File: 143724   as well as the Seal of the General Land Office. Done at the City of Austin on

              the   Twelfth   day of   March   in the year

              of Our Lord One Thousand Nine Hundred and   Seventy-Four.

Bob Armstrong   *Dolph Briscoe*
Commissioner of the General Land Office.   Governor.

Figure 36 – Recent Texas Pand Patent (Inside a Box)

Figure 37 – Republic of Texas Land Patent
(NOT inside a box)

Under the law of Four Cornering, anything inside a box is removed from the page. When anything is inside a box, the government is essentially saying it is a fraud. If you build a really strong case exposing the fraud, the judge will simply say: "there is nothing on this page."

If you read the land patent, it says that the land is granted to John Smith, his heirs and/or assigned forever and most of them say nothing about any reservations at all. Some of the more recent land patents from the early 1900s may reserve mineral rights, and I have seen land patents in Arizona reserve water rights but none of them say anything about easements or zoning regulations or city ordinances or taxes, and things like that. There are Spanish land grants in Arizona that are hundreds of years old, when Spain granted huge tracts of land.

Property Taxes

All property taxes originated with an Act of Congress at 12 Stat. 296, Chap XLV, August 5, 1861:

"An Act to provide increased Revenue from imports, to pay Interest on the Public Debt, and for other purposes;

Be at enacted by the Senate and House of Representatives of the United States of America in Congress assembled"

"Sec. 9 . And be it further enacted, That, for the purpose of assessing the above tax and collecting the same, the President of the United States be, and he is hereby authorized, to divide, respectively, the States and Territories of the United States and the District of Columbia into convenient collection districts, and to nominate and, by and with the advice of the Senate, *to appoint an assessor and a collector* for each such district, who shall be freeholders and resident within the same:"

"Sec. 10. And be it further enacted, That before any such collector shall enter upon the duties of his office *he shall execute a bond ...*"

"SEC. 13 . And be it further, enacted, *That the said direct tax laid by this act shall be assessed and laid on the value of all lands and lots of ground, with their improvements and dwelling-houses, ...*"

"SEC. 14. And be it further enacted, That the respective assistant assessors shall, immediately after being required as aforesaid by the assessors, proceed through every part of their respective districts, and *shall require all persons owning, possessing, or having the care or management of any lands, lots of ground, buildings, or dwellinghouses,* lying and being within the collection district where they reside, and liable to a direct tax as aforesaid, to deliver written lists of the same; …"

"Sec. 48. And be it further enacted, That there shall be allowed to the collectors appointed under this act, in full compensation for their services and that of their deputies in carrying this act into effect, *a commission of four per centum upon the first hundred thousand dollars, one per centum upon the second one hundred thousand dollars, and one-half of one per centum upon all sums above two hundred thousand dollars;* such commissions to be computed upon the amounts by them respectively paid…"

You are liable for property taxes, if you are a commercial entity. If you have a mortgage, then technically the bank owns it until the mortgage is paid off. My first house was in St. George, Utah, and I remember signing a document that said that I agreed to pay the property taxes.

In the Texas tax code it says that property has to be "rendered" for taxation. There was a lady I met who lived in Flower Mound, an expensive area north of the Dallas-Fort Worth airport, who had gone through a foreclosure ten years prior and was still in the house. She had been out of work and could not afford the eight thousand dollars a year in property taxes and went to the tax assessor's office and read them the riot act: "Who rendered this property for taxation, I am going to sue their ^%$# off!" They immediately said, "Don't worry, we will take it off the tax rolls."

There is a man in Australia who created his own sovereign nation called the Hutt River Province, which is now known as the Principality of Hutt River. It is interesting to note that while Wikipedia says that Australia fails to recognize it as an independent nation, it is still there after almost fifty years, and they leave him alone. If you need to ask for permission, then the answer is always *no*, and if you know who you are, then you don't need their permission.

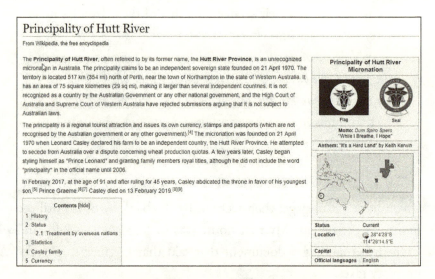

Figure 38 – Principality of Hutt River

Competence and Incompetence

If you don't know what you are doing, then you have to ask for permission. If you don't know what you are doing, then you are incompetent. If you have to ask the bureaucrat for permission, then he knows right away that you are incompetent. Since there is no such thing as an incompetent sovereign, he will correctly tell you that it applies to you.

If you know what you are doing, then you are competent, and you don't need anybody's permission.:

> "One sovereign does not need to tell another sovereign that he/she is sovereign. The sovereign is merely sovereign by his very existence. The rule in America is that the American people are the sovereigns." (Kemper v. State, 138 Southwest 1025 (1911), page 1043)

It is ALWAYS about competence and incompetence. Do you know who you are?

Hope Sanctuary

When I was first learning about this, I met a man in a little town called Littlefield, Arizona, that had set up his own common law town with courts, judiciary, constable, and lots for sale for homes.

Summary

Because of our own ignorance, we work all our lives to pay off a mortgage to end up with the property being owned by the Roman Cult owned and operated municipal corporation called UNITED STATES, and we are paying an annual rent in the form of taxes.

Under the Law of Nations, a nation needs people, land, and resources (gold or silver coin), and you will *never* be truly free if you fail to have absolute ownership in land. You can literally have your own little kingdom.

The Matrix is real because everything is an illusion.

17

THE ROMAN CULT
AND MONEY

The Roman Cult and the Knights Templar

Originally usury was forbidden by the Roman Cult, but because the Knights Templar were pursuing Roman Cult objectives of the Crusades, and also because the Templars came up with creative words, the Roman Cult turned a blind eye. For example instead of calling it "usury," they would call it "rent" and even today they call it "interest."

Negotiable instrument law is Roman law, mortgages and all debts (bonds, stocks, etc.) fall under Roman law and eventually became a mechanism of enslavement with debtors prisons, an ecclesiastical censure.

"I believe that banking institutions are more dangerous to our liberties than standing armies . . . If the American people ever allow private banks to control the issue of their currency, first by inflation, then by deflation, the banks & corporations that will grow up around [the banks] . . . will deprive the people of all property until their children wake-up homeless on the continent their fathers conquered . . . The issuing power should be taken from the banks & restored to the people, to whom it properly belongs". –(Thomas Jefferson in the Debate Over the Recharter of the Bank Bill)

A Federal Reserve Note is no different than money from the monopoly board game. The ONLY difference is that you believe one is worth more than the other.

No Such Thing as a Bank Loan

There is no such thing as a bank loan as found in *Modern Money Mechanics,* which was published by the Chicago Federal Reserve in May 1961:

"The money creation process takes place principally through transaction accounts." (Modern Money Mechanics, page 2)

"Of course, they do not really pay out loans from the money they receive as deposits. If they did this, no additional money would be created. What they do when they make loans is to accept promissory notes in exchange for credits to the borrowers' transaction accounts." (Modern Money Mechanics, page 6)

An unconditional promise to pay is itself money and even though it says it is a promise to pay, the bank is paid with their acceptance of the promissory note:

"What is said to be *an unconditional promise to pay* a sum certain in money *is itself money.* The words on the face of the paper money, "will pay to the bearer on demand", cannot alter its character as money and turn it into a different document which calls for the payment of money." (Bank of Canada v. Bank of Montreal, [1978] 1 S.C.R. 1148 at page 1155 [emphasis added])

"A cashier's check differs in that it is a bill of exchange drawn by the bank upon itself and is accepted by the act of issuance. A cashier's check is the primary obligation of the remitting bank. See RCW 62A.4211(1)(b). ...An ordinary check is considered as merely a promise to pay, but a cashier's check is regarded substantially as money, which it represents. The gift of such a check is completed upon delivery of the check. Pikeville Nat'l Bank & Trust Co. v. Shirley, 281 Ky. 150, 135 S.W.2d 426, 126 A.L.R. 919 (1939). See also Scott v. Seaboard Sec. Co., 143 Wash. 514, 255 P. 660 (1927), which quoted with approval extensively from Drinkall, and then quoted from Hathaway v. Delaware Cy., 185 N.Y. 368, 78 N.E. 153 (1906) as follows: *"That by reason of the peculiar character of cashiers' checks and their general use in the commercial world they were to be regarded substantially as the money which they represented."* (Crunk v State Farm Fire and Casualty 719 P.2d 1338 [emphasis added])

A deposit is made into a bank. The deposit becomes the property of the bank, but the bank has a contract to give it back. And Banks are *not* allowed to loan their own money: "No national bank shall make any loan or discount on the security of the shares of its own capital stock" (12 U.S. Code § 83 - Loans by bank on its own stock).

Forced Loans

Lincoln issued US Treasury notes during the Civil War. US Treasure notes are forced loans, and military script, where government employees, and contractors (subjects of the enemy and aliens) were forced to loan the government money:

> "This rule does not interfere with the right of the victorious invader to tax the people or their property, *to levy forced loans,* to billet soldiers, or to appropriate property, especially houses, lands, boats or ships, and churches, for temporary and military uses." (Article 37, General Orders 100 (The Lieber Code) [emphasis added])

These loans were vital forces in the struggle for national supremacy:

> "The forced loans of 1862 and 1863, in the form of legal tender notes, *were vital forces in the struggle for national supremacy.* They formed a part of the public debt of the United States, *the validity of which is solemnly established by the Fourteenth Amendment to the Constitution."* (Julliard v. Greenman, 110 US 432 [emphasis added])

And Congress was running their owned and operated municipal corporation that they had set up in 1871:

> "Two national governments exist, one to be maintained under the Constitution, with all its restrictions, the other to be maintained by Congress outside and independently of that instrument" (Dissenting opinion of Justice Marshall Harlan. Downes v. Bidwell, 182 U.S. 244 (1901))

Banksters Owned by Roman Cult

The banksters have always been owned and operated by the Roman Cult. "It is a somewhat curious sequel to the attempt to set up a Catholic competitor to the Rothschilds that at the present time the latter are the guardians of the papal treasure" (Jewish Encyclopedia 1901 – 1906, Volume 2, page 497).

"If all bank loans were paid, no one would have a bank deposit and there would not be a dollar of currency or coin in circulation," said Robert H. Hemphill, Credit Manager of the Federal Reserve Bank of Atlanta. "This is a staggering thought. We are completely dependent on the commercial banks. Someone has to borrow every dollar we have into circulation, cash or credit. If the banks create ample synthetic money, we are prosperous; if not, we starve. We are absolutely without a permanent monetary system. When one gets a complete grasp upon the picture, the tragic absurdity of our hopeless position is almost incredible – but there it is. [The banking problem] is the most important subject intelligent persons can investigate and reflect upon. It is so important that our present civilization may collapse unless it is widely understood and the defects remedied very soon."

Furthermore we see as far back as the early twentieth century the prediction that

"[Very] soon every American will be required to register their biological property [babies – birth certificate] in a national system designed to keep track of the people and that will operate under the ancient system of pledging. By such methodology we can compel people to submit to our agenda which will affect our security as a charge-back for our fiat paper currency.

Every American will be forced to register or suffer not being able to work and earn a living. They will be our chattel and we will hold the security interest over them forever by operation of the law merchant under the scheme of secured transactions.

Americans, by unknowingly or unwittingly delivering the bills of lading to us, will be rendered bankrupt and insolvent, forever to remain economic slaves through taxation secured by their pledges.

"They will be stripped of their rights and given a commercial value designed to make us a profit and they will be none the wiser, for not one man in a million could ever figure our plans and, if by accident one or two would figure it out, we have in our arsenal plausible deniability [good faith]. After all this is the only logical way to fund government by floating liens and debt to the registrants in the form of benefits and privileges. This will inevitably reap to us huge profits beyond our wildest expectations and leave every American a contributor to this fraud which we will call "Social Insurance." Without realizing it, every American will insure us for any loss we may incur and in this manner every American will unknowingly be our servant, however begrudgingly. The people will become helpless and without any hope for their redemption and we will employ the high office of the President of our dummy corporation [unconstitutional municipal corporation] to foment this plot against America." (Colonel Edward Mandell House in a private meeting with Woodrow Wilson)

LAWS OF SHIPPING
Born v Birth

"Born" on the land, "birthed" into corporations, once you understand the difference between "Born" and "Birth", you will understand the mistake you made in relation to your "Date of Birth"

Birth is the acknowledgement date of a deed, not the day your body was created

---

"I am a most unhappy man. I have unwittingly ruined my country. A great industrial nation is controlled by its system of credit. . . . The growth of the nation, therefore, and all our activities are in the hands of a few men. We have come to be one of the worst ruled, one of the most completely controlled and dominated governments in the civilized world . . . a government by the opinion and duress of a small group of dominant men." (President Woodrow Wilson after he passed the Federal Reserve Act which instituted the Fractional Reserve System in the United States)

"Capital must protect itself in every possible way, both by [secret] combination and legislation. Debts must be collected, mortgages foreclosed as rapidly as possible. When through process of law, the common people lose their homes, they will become more docile and more easily governed through the strong arm of the government applied by a central power of wealth under leading financiers. These truths are well known among our principal men who are now engaged in forming an imperialism to govern the world. By dividing voters through the political party system, we can get them to expend their energies in fighting for questions of no importance. It is true, by discrete action we can ensure for ourselves that which has been so well planned and so successfully accomplished." (Montague Norman, governor of the Bank of England, addressing the United States Bankers Association, New York, as quoted in the Idaho Leader, 26 August 1924)

Federal Reserve + Twenty Years = Bankruptcy

It took less than twenty years after the Federal Reserve Act in the middle of the night on Christmas eve in 1913 to bankrupt the unconstitutional municipal corporation

"It is an established fact that the United States Federal Government has been dissolved by the *Emergency Banking Act, March 9, 1933, 48 stat. 1, Public Law 89-719*; declared by President Roosevelt, being bankrupt and insolvent, H.J.R. 192, 73rd Congress in session June 5, 1933 - Joint Resolution To Suspend The Gold Standard and Abrogate The Gold Clause dissolved the Sovereign Authority of the United States and the official capacities of all United States Governmental Offices, Officers, and Departments and is further evidence that *the United States Federal Government exists today in name only.*" (United States Congressional Record, March 17, 1993 Vol. 33 [emphasis added])

Bankruptcy = Martial Law

The BAR members imposed Martial Law at the same time they declared their unconstitutional municipal corporation bankrupt:

"*Since March 9, 1933; the United States has been in a state of declared National Emergency* . . . Under the powers delegated by these statutes, the President may: seize property; organize and control the means of production; seize commodities; assign military forces abroad; institute martial law; seize and control all transportation and communication; regulate the operation of private enterprise; restrict travel; and in a plethora of particular ways, control the lives of all American citizens. . . . *A majority of the people of the United States have lived all of their lives under emergency rule.* For 40 years, freedoms and governmental procedures guaranteed by the Constitution have in varying degrees been *abridged by laws brought into force by states of national emergency* . . ." (In Reg: U.S. Senate Report No. 93-549 dated 11/19/73 (73 CIS Serial Set S963-2 - [607 Pages]): [emphasis added])

Lawful Government = Lawful Money

In order to have lawful de jure government, it is mandatory to have just measures: "But thou shalt have a perfect and just weight, a perfect and just measure shalt thou have: that thy days may be lengthened in the land which the LORD thy God giveth thee. For . . . all that do unrighteously, are an abomination unto the LORD thy

God" (Deuteronomy 25: 15-16). This includes lawful money: "At common law only gold and silver were a legal tender (2 Inst. 577)" (McClarin v. Nesbit, 2 Nott & McC. (11 S.C.L.) 519 (1820)).

Money "In the absence of qualifying words, *it cannot mean promissory notes, bonds, or other evidences of debt.*" (36 AM Juris. 1st Money § 8 [emphasis added])

> "Dollar. The unit employed in the United States in calculating money values. It is coined both in gold or silver, and is the value of one hundred cents." (*Black's Law Dictionary*, 2nd Edition. pg 387.)

> "Dollar...each to be of the value of a Spanish milled dollar as the same is now current, and to contain three hundred and seventy-one grains and four sixteenths parts of a grain of pure, or four hundred sixteen grains of standard silver" (Chap. XVI Coinage Act April 2, 1792. Sec 9)

> "The answer to this argument is that the Constitution of the United States is the supreme law, and that no law can be valid which, in violation of that instrument, shall attempt to make anything but gold and silver coin a tender." (Lowry v. McGhee & McDermott, 16 Tenn. 242 (1835))

Bank Notes ≠ Lawful Money

Federal Reserve notes are mere IOUs because there is no promise to pay anything. They are promissory note contracts. "A written promise to pay a certain sum of money, at a future time, unconditionally. 7 Watts & S. 264; 2 Humph. R. 143; 10 Wend.

675; Minor, R. 263; 7 Misso. 42; 2 Cowen, 536; 6 N. H. Rep. 364; 7 Vern. 22. *A promissory note differs from a mere acknowledgment of debt, without any promise to pay, as when the debtor gives his creditor an IOU.* (q. v.) See 2 Yerg. 50; 15 M. & W. 23. But see 2 Humph. 143; 6 Alab. R. 373" (Bouviers Law Dictionary, 1856 Edition).

The term "dollars" likewise is incorrect, which, "according to constitutional definition, are monetary units, used in exchange, backed by gold and silver. Our present day fiat issues are supported by more printed paper of the same; therefore, they are correctly termed Federal Reserve Notes (FRN), not dollars" (Robert P. Vichas, Handbook of Financial Mathematics, Formulas, and Tables (1979), p. 420).

And nobody is required to accept Federal Reserve notes: "Federal Reserve Bank notes, and other notes constituting a part of common currency of country, are recognized as good tender for money, unless specially objected to" (MacLeod v. Hoover (1925), 159 La. 244, 105 S. 305):

> "Bank notes constitute a large and convenient part of the currency of our country, and *by common consent*, serve to a great extent all the purposes of coin. In themselves they are not money, for they are not a legal tender; and yet they are a good tender, unless specifically objected to as being notes merely, and not money. Miller v. Race, 1 Burr. 457; Bank of United States v. Bank of Georgia, 10 Wheat 333; Handy v. Dobbin, 12 Johns. 220; Wright v. Reed, 3 Term R. 554. They sub serve the purposes of money in the ordinary business of life, by the *mutual consent_*(express or implied) of the parties to a contract, and not by the binding force of any common usage; for the party to whom they may be tendered *has an*

undoubted right to refuse accepting them as money." (Vick v. Howard, 136 S.E. 101; 116 S.E. 465, 468 (March 15, 1923) [emphasis added])

This also means they *cannot* pay a debt but instead discharge a debt with limited liability for "There is a distinction between a debt discharged and one paid. When discharged, the debt still exists, though divested of its character as a legal obligation during the operation of the discharge" (Stanek v. White (1927), 172 Minn. 390, 215 N.W. 781). And Federal Reserve notes are also bills of credit:

> "The term "obligation or other security of the United States" includes all bonds, certificates of indebtedness, national bank currency, Federal Reserve notes, Federal Reserve bank notes, coupons, United States notes, Treasury notes, gold certificates, silver certificates, fractional notes, certificates of deposit, bills, checks, or drafts for money, drawn by or upon authorized officers of the United States, stamps and other representatives of value, of whatever denomination, issued under any Act of Congress, and canceled United States stamps." (18 U.S. Code § 8.Obligation or other security of the United States defined)

> "Federal reserve notes, to be issued at the discretion of the Board of Governors of the Federal Reserve System for the purpose of making advances to Federal Reserve banks through the Federal Reserve agents as hereinafter set forth *and for no other purpose, are authorized.* The said notes *shall be obligations of the United States* and shall be receivable by all

national and member banks and Federal reserve banks and
for all taxes, customs, and other public dues." (12 USC § 411
[emphasis added])

Therefore, anything purchased with Federal Reserve notes are
purchased with United States credit, and anything purchased with
United States credit is the property of the United States because
Federal Reserve notes are for internal use of the government *only:*

"Sec. 15. As used in this Act the term 'United States' means
the Government of the United States...the term 'currency of
the United States' means currency which is legal tender in the
United States, and includes United States notes ... Federal
Reserve Notes.

"Sec. 17. All Acts and parts of Acts inconsistent with any of
the provisions of this Act are hereby repealed." (Gold Reserve
Act of 1934, 48 Stat. 337)

If all you have for money are IOUs from a bankrupt corporation,
then technically you too are bankrupt, which is why they want a
pauper's affidavit (Affidavit of Impecuniosity) if you fail to pay their
extortion (filing fee), because at common law, paupers don't have
any rights:

"The better to secure and perpetuate mutual friendship and
intercourse among the people of the different States in this
Union, the free inhabitants of each of these States, *paupers,
vagabonds, and fugitives from justice excepted*, shall be entitled
to all privileges and immunities of free citizens in the several
States; and the people of each State shall have free ingress and

regress to and from any other State, and shall enjoy therein all the privileges." (Article IV, Articles of Confederation (1781))

Bank Notes = Pauper

If all you have for money is Federal Reserve notes, which are meant for internal use of the government *only* and are bills of credit drawn on the privately held Federal Reserve, then you are living at the government's expense, because anything purchased with United States credit belongs to United States, which is also why you are taxed because it is a fee for the privilege of using the private money system:

"Pauper – One so poor he must be supported at the public expense" (Bouviers Law Dictionary, 1856 Edition)

"Pauper: A very poor person, esp. one who receives aid from charity or public funds" (*Black's Law Dictionary*, 8th Edition)

"The money powers prey upon the nation in times of peace and conspire against it in times of adversity. It is more despotic than a monarchy, more insolent than autocracy, and more selfish than bureaucracy. It denounces as public enemies, all who question its methods or throw light upon its crimes. As a result of the war, corporations have been enthroned, an era of corruption in high places will follow, and the money powers of the country will endeavor to prolong it's reign by working upon the prejudices of the people until all wealth is aggregated in a few hands and the Republic is destroyed." (Abraham Lincoln)

Which Symbol Was Used?

The lawful de jure money symbol is $ but how often do you see it? Nothing in the law happens by accident. Everything is voluntary and in order for you to be viewed to have agreed to something, there must be some sort of notice. The $ symbol originated as a U superimposed over a S for US dollar. A dollar is a measurement of weight as found in the Coinage Act of 1792, but they are required to differentiate between lawful money and commercial paper, which gives you notice: "It is one of the fundamental maxims of the common law that ignorance of the law excuses no one" (Daniels v. Dean (1905), 2 C.A. 421, 84 P. 332).

I have seen a lot of tax bills and restaurant bills that have no symbol at all because *only* gold or silver coin are legal tender under the constitution, but they are hoping you will give them commercial paper. They can't ask for commercial paper because that would be a breach of trust, but if you offer it, they can accept it.

Summary

If all you have in your possession is Federal Reserve notes, which are bills of United States credit (a bankrupt corporation) drawn on the privately held Federal Reserve, then you are a pauper and have no rights. You could have billions of Federal Reserve notes, and you would still be a pauper and have no rights, which would give the military authorities, under martial law, the right to abuse you all they want, and sometimes they do!

I know a guy who runs game rooms in several locations in south Texas, and he does not accept Federal Reserve notes. He makes everybody go to a different location to exchange their negotiable instruments into silver coin and his machines accept *only* the silver coin. After they are finished, they go back to the separate location to convert their silver coins into negotiable instruments. The statutes all talk about "cash," which is Federal Reserve notes – negotiable instruments – and since he has no cash and doesn't accept cash, they leave him alone.

18

THE ROMAN CULT
& THE BIRTH CERTIFICATE

The birth certificate falls under private international law and the UNIDROIT Statute and the Uniform Commercial Code:

Birth Certificate = Cestui que trust = Roman Cult

As we saw in chapter 1, the cestui que trust is created by the Roman Cult:

"Yet still it was found difficult to set bounds to ecclesiastical ingenuity; for when they were driven out of all their former holds, they devised a new method of conveyance, by which the lands were granted, not to themselves directly, but to nominal feoffees *to the use* of the religious houses; thus distinguishing between the *possession* and the *use,* and receiving the actual profits, while the seisin of the lands remained in the nominal feoffee, *who was held by the courts of equity (then under the direction of the clergy)* to be bound in conscience to account [taxes] to his *cestui que use* for the rents and emoluments of the estate: *and it is to these inventions that*

our practitioners are indebted for the introduction of uses and trusts, the foundation of modern conveyancing." (Tomlins Law Dictionary, 1835 Edition, Volume 2 under the definition of Mortmain [emphasis added])

US citizen = Cestui que trust = Roman Cult

The cestui que trust is also found in the code of law for the District of Columbia also known as United States Code:

"*The Legal Estate to be in Cestui Que Use*" (Chapter Fifty-Six in Sec. 1617, at 31 Stat. 1432) [emphasis added])

In Chapter three – Absence for Seven Years – of the United States Code they even presume you are dead:

"SEC. 252. PRESUMPTION OF DEATH. - . . . he shall be presumed to be dead, in any case wherein his death shall come in question, unless proof be made that he was alive within that time. . . .

(E)very taxpayer is a cestui qui trust having sufficient interest in the preventing abuse of the trust to be recognized in the field of this court's prerogative jurisdiction . . . In Re Bolens (1912), 135 N.W. 164

A "*citizen of the United States*" is a civilly dead entity operating as a co-trustee and co-beneficiary of the *PCT (Public Charitable Trust)*, the constructive, *cestui que trust* of US Inc. under the 14th Amendment, which upholds the debt of the USA and US Inc. Congressional Record, June 13 1967, pp. 15641-15646

"Slater's protestations to the effect that he derives no benefit from the United States government have no bearing on his legal obligation to pay income taxes. *Cook v. Tait*, 265 U.S. 47, 44 S.Ct. 444, 68 L.Ed. 895 (1924); Benitez Rexach v. United States, 390 F.2d 631, (1st Circ.), *cert. denied* 393 U.S. 833, 89 S.Ct. 103, 21 L.Ed.2d 103 (1968). *Unless the defendant can establish that he is not a citizen of the United States, the IRS possesses authority to attempt to determine his federal tax liability.*" (UNITED STATES of America v. William M. SLATER (1982) (D. Delaware) 545 F.Supp 179, 182. [emphasis added])

Their Roman Cult cestui que trust JOHN HENRY SMITH is codified here (edicts under the Roman Cult's martial law):
"*Corporation shall be deemed to include* any company, trust, so-called Massachusetts trust, or association, incorporated or unincorporated, which is organized to carry on business for its own profit or that of its members, and has shares of capital or capital stock or certificates of interest, and *any* company, *trust*, so-called Massachusetts trust, or association, incorporated or *unincorporated, without shares of capital or capital stock or certificates of interest,* except partnerships, *which is organized to carry on business for its own profit or that of its members.*" (15 USC § 44 Definitions [emphasis added])

The Roman Cult's cestui que trust (JOHN HENRY SMITH) is created by the birth certificate, and social security number and is recognized under the Convention of the Law Applicable to Trusts and on their Recognition which was concluded July 1, 1985, and entered into force on January 1, 1992, which is also considered private international law, which was originated with the Roman Cult, as described herein.

The unconstitutional corporation that was set up in 1871 has not had a treasury since 1921 (41 Stat. Ch.214 pg. 654), and its treasury is now the International Monetary Fund (Presidential Documents Volume 29-No.4 pg. 113, 22 U.S.C. 285-288), which is an agency of the Roman Cult's United Nations.

All social security numbers are issued by the International Monetary Fund through the Treasury, which maintains an account for each Roman Cult cestui que trust (JOHN HENRY SMITH) under the social security number which is claimed under the Convention Concerning the International Administration of the Estates of Deceased Persons:

> "Any person who pays, or delivers property to, the holder of the certificate drawn up, and, where necessary, recognized, in accordance with this Convention shall be discharged, unless it is proved that the person acted in bad faith." (Article 22, Convention Concerning the International Administration of the Estates of Deceased Persons)

> "Any person who has acquired assets of the estate from the holder of a certificate drawn up, and, where necessary, recognized, in accordance with this Convention shall, unless it is proved that he acted in bad faith, be deemed to have acquired them from a person having power to dispose of them." (Article 23, Convention Concerning the International Administration of the Estates of Deceased Persons)

The convention was concluded on October 2, 1973, and is part of the Hague Conference on Private International Law.

Trump Administration = Roman Cult

Donald J. Trump is President of the United States, which is commonly called the Trump administration. Therefore Donald J. Trump is the administrator of the estates (cestui que trust) of the American people under the direction of the Roman Cult:

> "ADMINISTRATOR. A person authorized to manage and distribute the *estate of an intestate*, or of a *testator who has no executor*. In English law, administrators are the *officers of the Ordinary* appointed by him in pursuance of the statute, and *their title and authority are derived exclusively from the ecclesiastical judge*, by grants called letters of administration. Williams, Ex. 331. At First the Ordinary was appointed administrator under the statute of Westm. 2d. Next, the 31 Edw. III. c. 11, *required the Ordinary to appoint the next of kin and the relations by blood of the deceased*. Next, under the 21 Hen. VIII., he could appoint the widow, or next of kin, or both, at his discretion." (Bouviers Law Dictionary, 1883 Edition, page 119)

And Trump is an officer of the Ordinary:

> "COURT OF ORDINARY. In American Law. A court *which has jurisdiction of the probate of wills and the regulation of the management of decedents' estates.* Such courts exist in Georgia, New Jersey, South Carolina, and *Texas*. See 2 Kent, Comm. 409 ; *Ordinary*." (Bouviers Law Dictionary,1856 Edition, page 383)

And his "title and authority are derived exclusively from" an "ecclesiastical judge":

> "ORDINARY, *ordinarius*.] A civil law term for any judge who hath authority to take cognizance of causes in his own right, and not by deputation: *by the common law it is taken for him who hath ordinary or exempt and immediate jurisdiction in causes ecclesiastical. Co. Litt. 344; Stat. Westm. 2. 13 Edw. 1. st. 1. c. 19.*

This name is applied to a bishop who hath original jurisdiction; and an archbishop is the ordinary of the whole province, to visit and receive appeals from inferior jurisdictions, &c. *2 Inst. 398; 9 Rep. 41; Wood's Inst. 25.* The word ordinary is also used for every commissary or official of the bishop, or other ecclesiastical judge having judicial power: an archdeacon is an ordinary; and ordinaries may grant administration of intestates' estates, &c. *31 Edw. 3. c. 11; 9 Rep. 36.* But the bishop of the diocese is the true and only ordinary to certify excommunications, lawfulness of marriage, and such ecclesiastical and spiritual acts, to the judges of the common law, for he is the person to whom the court is to write in such things. *2 Shep. Abr. 472.*" (Tomlins Law Dictionary, 1835 Edition, Volume 2)

In support of their Roman Cult handlers, they have now passed statutes (edicts under martial law) in every state required the forced registration of the births of all children to create evidence of their US citizen slave property:

> "(a) *The physician, midwife, or person acting as a midwife in attendance at a birth shall file the birth certificate with the local registrar of the registration district in which the birth occurs.*

(b) If a birth occurs in a hospital or birthing center, the hospital administrator, the birthing center administrator, or a designee of the appropriate administrator may file the in lieu of a person listed by Subsection (a).

(c) If there is no physician, midwife, or person acting as a midwife in attendance at a birth and if the birth does not occur in a hospital or birthing center, the following in the order listed shall report the birth to the local registrar:
1. the father or mother of the child; or
2. the owner or householder of the premises where the birth occurs.

(d) Except as provided by Subsection (e), a person required to file a or report a birth shall file the certificate or make the report not later than the fifth day after the date of the birth." (Section 192-003 Texas Health and Safety Code [emphasis added])

all of which is for "persons" (US citizens) who are *order followers* as described herein because there is no law that says that anyone has to register their "property" because at common law it is property, and especially since you can be a state citizen without being a US citizen, and thereby a state national, like I am a Texas national:

"It is however, true that in all common-law countries it has always and consistently been held that the wife and minor children take the nationality of the husband and father. That is common-law doctrine." (In Re Page 12 F (2d) 135)

Karl Lentz

Karl Lentz was able to get his son back after eleven years after Child Protective Services stole his son from a hospital. He did it with a one-page lawsuit saying he "required" his "property." When they held a hearing and asked what his property was, he held up a picture and said "this is my property." A simple google search can find all of the information on Karl Lentz.

"Destroy the family, you destroy the country."

—Vladimir Ilyich Lenin

Child Protective Services

Child Protective Services is stealing children belonging to many people. These days, in support of the Roman Cult, it is their agenda to have lots of children available for their Ninth Circle Satanic Cult blood sacrifices, although they prefer orphans because nobody will be looking for orphans, and they regularly "run away" from their caregivers. It also causes lots of mental pain and anguish for the parents of these children, which is food for the Roman Cult's satanic gods, which David Icke claims are reptilians, and they even have a name for it: lousche.

I always say and put in my court documents: "Why on earth would anyone want to be a lowlife scumbag US citizen?"

Summary

As part of their agenda to replace God's common law with their Roman law the Roman Cult has made edicts under martial law

that really apply to nobody, that require the registration of the birth
of children under the Roman Cult's United Nations Convention
Concerning the International Administration of the Estates of
Deceased Persons, which was concluded on October 2, 1973, and is
part of the Roman Cult's Hague Conference on Private International
Law.

Under God's common law our property (sons and daughters)
are recorded in the family Bible, which is one of many reasons why I
believe that most so-called Christians have no idea what that means.

Satanists (the Roman Cult) have seized control of the
unconstitutional municipal corporation called UNITED STATES
OF AMERICA and are operating it as their owned and operated
criminal racketeering enterprise, but Trump is fighting back, which
is why the Satanists are not too happy right now!

19

THE ROMAN CULT
AND WARFARE

"Government is not reason, it is not eloquence,—it is force!
Like fire, it is a dangerous servant, and a fearful master; never for a
moment should it be left to irresponsible action."

—*GEORGE WASHINGTON*

The last World War had nothing to do with protecting anybody and everything to do with a commercial transaction: "The enemy is the German Reich and not Nazism, and those who still haven't understood this, haven't understood anything." (Churchill's chief counselor Robert Lord Vansittart (September 1940 to foreign minister Lord Halifax))

"Germany's unforgivable crime before WW2 was its attempt to loosen its economy out of the world trade system and to build up an independent exchange system from which the world-finance couldn't profit anymore. ...We butchered the wrong pig." (Winston Churchill (The Second World War - Bern, 1960))

"Not the political doctrine of Hitler has hurled us into this war. The reason was the success of his increase in building a new economy. The roots of war were envy, greed and fear." (Major General J.F.C. Fuller, historian, England)

"We made a monster, a devil out of Hitler. Therefore we couldn't disavow it after the war. After all, we mobilized the masses against the devil himself. So we were forced to play our part in this diabolic scenario after the war. In no way we could have pointed out to our people that the war only was an economic preventive measure." (US foreign Minister James Baker (1992))

"The war wasn't only about abolishing fascism, but to conquer sales markets. We could have, if we had intended so, prevented this war from breaking out without doing one shot, but we didn't want to." (Winston Churchill to Truman (Fultun, USA March 1946))

Commerce = Warfare & Warfare = Commerce

Anytime you have an interaction with the police, it is warfare. A mixed war is one "which is made on one side by public authority, and the other by mere private persons" (*Black's Law Dictionary*, 5th Ed., page 1420). "Under International Law of Warfare, all *parties* to a cause must appear by *nom de guerre*, because an "alien enemy cannot maintain an action *during the war* in his own name" (Merriam-Webster Dictionary, pg. 1534).

The reason you have warfare is because of martial law:

> "Statutes have been passed extending the courts of admiralty and vice-admiralty far beyond their ancient limits for depriving us the accustomed and inestimable privilege of trial by jury, in cases affecting both life and property . . . *to supersede the course of common law and instead thereof to publish and order the use and exercise of the law martial.*" (Causes and Necessity of Taking Up Arms (1775) [emphasis added])

> "But when a long train of abuses and usurpations, pursuing invariably the same Object evinces a design to reduce them under absolute Despotism, it is their right, *it is their duty*, to throw off such Government, and to provide new Guards for their future security.

> "He has erected a multitude of New Offices, and sent hither swarms of Officers to harass our people, and eat out their substance:"

> "He has kept among us, in times of peace, Standing Armies."

> "He has affected to render the Military independent of and superior to the Civil power:"

> "He has combined with others to subject us to a jurisdiction foreign to our constitution, and unacknowledged by our laws; giving his Assent to their Acts of pretended Legislation:"

"For transporting us beyond Seas to be tried for pretended offences:"

"For abolishing the free System of English Laws in a neighbouring Province, *establishing therein an Arbitrary government*, and enlarging its Boundaries so as to render it at once an example and fit instrument for *introducing the same absolute rule* into these Colonies:"

"For taking away our Charters, abolishing our most valuable Laws, and *altering fundamentally the Forms of our Governments*:"

"He has abdicated Government here, by declaring us out of his protection, and *waging War against us*." (Declaration of Independence, 1776 [emphasis added])

Martial law is really no law at all:

"What is called 'proclaiming martial law' is no law at all; but merely for the sake of public safety, in circumstances of great emergency, setting aside all law, and acting under military power; a proceeding which requires to be followed by an act of indemnity when the disturbances are at an end." (8 Atty. Gen. Op. 365, 367, February 3, 1857)

And comes about because of a military occupation, or some emergency such a bankruptcy. As we saw in chapter 3 (page 25) **there are three kinds of martial law: Full Martial Law, Martial Law Proper, and Martial Law rule.**

The Law of War is a branch of the Roman Cult's Law of Nations, and the Roman Cult cestui que trust is treated as a corporation: "STATUS. L. Standing: state, *condition*, situation. Compare Estate. *A corporation has no status as a citizen outside of the jurisdiction where it was created*" (Andersons Law Dictionary, 1889 Edition, page 968)

"*Corporation* shall be deemed to include any company, trust, so-called Massachusetts trust, or association, incorporated or unincorporated, which is organized to carry on business for its own profit or that of its members, and has shares of capital or capital stock or certificates of interest, and *any* company, *trust*, so-called Massachusetts trust, or association, incorporated or *unincorporated, without shares of capital or capital stock or certificates of interest*, except partnerships, *which is organized to carry on business for its own profit or that of its members*." (15 USC § 44 Definitions [emphasis added])

And all warfare is commerce and all commerce is warfare, which is why they need to get World War III going so they can set up a blood sacrifice to the Roman Cult's God BAAL. (They can send a bunch of our sons and daughters off to a field to murder each other.) And then they can seize the cestui que trusts for those killed under the *Convention Concerning the International Administration of the Estates of Deceased Persons:*

"Any person who pays, or delivers property to, the holder of the certificate drawn up, and, where necessary, recognized, in accordance with this Convention shall be discharged, unless it is proved that the person acted in bad faith." (Article 22,

Convention Concerning the International Administration of the Estates of Deceased Persons)

"Any person who has acquired assets of the estate from the holder of a certificate drawn up, and, where necessary, recognized, in accordance with this Convention shall, unless it is proved that he acted in bad faith, be deemed to have acquired them from a person having power to dispose of them." (Article 23, Convention Concerning the International Administration of the Estates of Deceased Persons)

This is what was concluded on October 2, 1973, and is part of the *Hague Conference on Private International Law*. It is also what uses the fake money in those accounts to pay off the national debt. After World War II, the United States was heavily in debt by a huge percentage based on gross national product, and by the 1970s, even with the Vietnam War, and the Korean War, the United States was one of the least indebted countries on the planet—it must be magic!

It is amazing that these Roman Cult banksters can do such things with their fake money and shell games!

Privileges and Benefits

Privileges and benefits are contracts:

"The rights of sovereignty extend to all persons and things, not privileged that are within the territory. They extend to all *strangers resident* therein; not only to those who are naturalized, and to those who are domiciled therein, having taken up their abode with the intention of permanent residence, but also to those whose residence is transitory. All

strangers are under the protection of the sovereign while they are within his territory and owe a temporary allegiance in return for that protection." (Carlisle v United States 83 U.S. 147, 154 (1873))

"Let a State be considered as subordinate to the People: But let everything else be subordinate to the State." (Chisholm v Georgia, 2 Dall 419 at p 455)

Those who accept the privilege become a subject:
"All subjects over which the sovereign power of the state extends are objects of taxation, but those over which it does not extend are exempt from taxation. This proposition may also be pronounced as self-evident. The sovereignty of the state extends to everything which exists by its authority or its permission." (McCullough v Maryland, 17 U.S. [4 Wheat] 316 (1819))

Benefits like social Security, welfare, prisons, and unemployment insurance are all for subjects, and require a social security number which are intended to put the government deep into debt for the next bankruptcy.

The more they give away the sooner the bankruptcy.

Then they send their property (all of those subjects who were busy getting the freebies) off to a field somewhere to murder their counter parts from a foreign country in a satanic blood sacrifice to the Roman Cult's god BAAL with the objective of paying off the so-called debt from the cestui que trust accounts of those murdered, and it all starts with the birth certificate. It all falls under the Roman Cult's international law.

World Wars

That is the reason for all these wars, including World War I, World War II, and their upcoming World War III because of the blood sacrifices to the Roman Cult's god BAAL, but all of those countries are now under a military occupation. Why do you think there are literally hundreds of US military bases around the world these days? It is in support of the military occupation of those countries:

> "Within twenty years this country is going to rule the world. Kings and Emperors will soon pass away and the democracy of the United States will take their place. . . . When the United States rules the world, *the Catholic Church will rule the world.* . . . Nothing can stand against the church." (Roman Catholic Archbishop James E. Quigley (October 15, 1854 – July 10, 1915) Chicago Daily Tribune May 5, 1903 [emphasis added])

As John Adams said, "There are two ways to conquer and enslave a nation. One is by the sword. The other is by debt."

Roman Cult Blood Sacrifices to BAAL

For those of you who fail to wish to participate in the Roman Cult's blood sacrifices to their god BAAL, always remember it is *only* the slaves – US citizens – who are required to register for the draft. Do you know who you are yet?

If you want additional ammunition, it is also two war crimes for them to compel you to work for the occupying power:

> "The Occupying Power may not compel protected persons to serve in its armed or auxiliary forces. No pressure or

propaganda which aims at securing voluntary enlistment is permitted." (Article 51, Geneva Convention Relative to the Protection of Civilians in Time of War of 1949 [emphasis added])

All measures aiming at creating unemployment or at restricting the opportunities offered to workers in an occupied territory, in order to induce them to work for the Occupying Power, are prohibited." (Article 52, Geneva Convention Relative to the Protection of Civilians in Time of War of 1949 [emphasis added])

I think the reason they stopped doing any draft is here, but if it ever does happen again, you don't have to run away to some other country. You can be right here, right in their face, and there is nothing they can do about it!

A Friend I Met

I met a man, Bill, who told me a very interesting story. Bill went to a university under the ROTC (Reserve Officer Training Corps) program. Bill got the US Army to pay for his bachelor's degree, and Bill told me that when he graduated from university, they had a big party and invited all of those who graduated to come over to the recruitment center for free coffee and donuts. Bill went and had their coffee and donuts. They had all sorts of contracts there for the graduates to sign so they could become an officer in the US Army, but all Bill did was eat their donuts, drink their coffee, and visit with everybody there. A couple of weeks later Bill got another invitation to another one of their celebrations, so Bill went and had more of their free coffee and donuts and visited with everybody and then left without signing any contracts to join the US Army Officer Corps. Bill never did become an officer in the US Army or any other military establishment. A few years later Bill was over in Vietnam working for a civilian contractor when he met one of the guys he went to school with who was now in the US Army as an intelligence officer. They went out for dinner and were talking one night. Bill asked his friend if he collected intelligence on the enemy, and the intelligence officer confirmed that he did do some of that but mostly his job was to take people who absolutely refused to fight and get them a job somewhere safe as a cook or something similar. The point I want to make with this story is that even if you get mixed up in their contract and are in the military, nobody is forced to fight. If you don't want to fight, then there are lots of alternatives. The real solution is *not* to register for the selective service in the first place. If you do, though, they still have to get you to sign a contract, and even if you do that, you can still refuse to fight.

Summary

All wars are a win-win scenario for the Roman Cult because it is a blood sacrifice to their god BAAL, and all wars precipitate a military occupation:

> *"Martial Law is the immediate and direct effect and consequence of occupation or conquest. The presence of a hostile army proclaims its Martial Law."* (Article 1, General Orders 100 (The Lieber Code) [emphasis added])

And they get to steal some property:

> *"A victorious army appropriates all public money, seizes all public movable property until further direction by its government, and*

sequesters for its own benefit or of that of its government all the revenues of real property belonging to the hostile government or nation. The title to such real property remains in abeyance during military occupation, and until the conquest is made complete." (Article 31, General Orders 100 (The Lieber Code))

I think that the United States is now collecting a royalty on all Iraqi oil. It is amazing how some Syrian gold has disappeared, and Libyan gold disappeared, and the United States did nothing. But somebody is collecting royalties on the Libyan oil and other resources.

All warfare is voluntary, and we need to learn how they are getting our consent and quit consenting!

All warfare is commerce and all commerce is warfare!

20

THE ROMAN CULT AND GUNS

say that the Pope is *not* Christian, and anyone who listens to the Pope is not Christian either. I further say that true Christians would be heavily armed but peaceful. The Roman Cult wants to make sure you are unarmed so you are defenseless when they do what they are intending to do. He wants his Jesuits to be able to murder you with impunity!

Technically, all Statutes are for government employees, which is another way they divide and conquer people, but the gun laws passed in the 1960s and 1970s affected *only* US citizens and certain racial groups in America. Then they always proceed to use their legislation any way they wish.

When Black people wanted to carry guns in the Sixties to protect themselves from the police, the NRA supported Ronald Reagan signing the 1967 Mulford Act that restricted people carrying guns

---

Divide & Conquer

It is *always* about dividing and conquering. They will divide and conquer you any way they can. Race is an obvious way to divide and conquer people in America, but I worked with Bombardier in Toronto for a couple of years. I was working with some guys from Short Brothers in Northern Ireland which is one of the Bombardier group of companies. They could tell just by your last name whether you were Catholic or Protestant, which is how they divide and conquer the people in Ireland.

DIVIDE AND CONQUER

Gun control in the United States is rooted in racism. Gun control was and is still meant to keep minority groups from having the ability to defend themselves.

China established gun control in 1935. From 1948 to 1952, 20 million political dissidents, unable to defend themselves, were rounded up and exterminated

"The *right of trial by jury* in civil cases, guaranteed by the 7th Amendment (Walker v. Sauvinet, 92 U. S. 90), and the *right to bear arms*, guaranteed by the 2nd Amendment (Presser v. Illinois, 116 U. S. 252), *have been distinctly held not to be*

Figure 39 – The Original Assault Rifle

privileges and immunities of citizens of the United States guaranteed by the 14th Amendment against abridgement by the states, and in effect the same decision was made in respect of the guarantee against prosecution, except by indictment of a grand jury, contained in the 5th Amendment (Hurtado v. California, 110 U.S. 516), and in respect of the right to be confronted with witnesses, contained in the 6th Amendment." (West v Louisiana, 194 US 258)

"The sensational account of the most horrifying religious massacre of the twentieth century ." Avro Manhattan (1914-1990) Knight of Malta.

Avro Manhattan, the author, is the world's foremost authority on Roman Catholicism in politics. A resident of London during WWII he operated a radio station called "Radio Freedom" broadcasting to occupied Europe. He was the author of more than twenty books including the best-seller *The Vatican in World Politics*, twice Book-of-the-Month and going through fifty-seven editions. He was a Great Briton who risked his life daily to expose the darkest secrets of the Papacy. His

Figure 40 – Experts Agree Gun Control Works!

books were number one on *The Forbidden Index* for the past seventy years!

War is when your government tells you who the enemy is.
Revolution is when you figure it out for yourself!

"PREFACE TO THE AMERICAN EDITION"

THE VATICAN'S HOLOCAUST is not a misnomer, an accusation, and even les a speculation. It is an historical fact. Rabid nationalism and religious dogmatism were the two main ingredients. During the existence of Croatia as an independent Catholic State, over 700,000 men, woman, and children perished. Many were executed, tortured, died of starvation, buried alive, or were burned to death."

Figure 41 – Gun Control Today

"Hundreds were forced to become Catholic. Catholic padres ran concentration camps; Catholic priests were officers of the military corps which committed such atrocities. 700,000 in a total population of a few million proportionally, would be as if one-third of the USA population had been exterminated by a Catholic militia. What has been gathered in this book will vindicate veracity of these facts.

Dates, names, and places, as well as photos are there to prove them. They should become known to the American people, not to foster vindictiveness, but to warn them of the danger, which racialism and sectarianism when allied with religious intolerance can bring to any contemporary nation, whether in Europe or in the New World. This book should be assessed without prejudice and as a lesson, but even more vital, as a warning for the future of the Americans, beginning with that of the USA. Avro Manhattan 1986"

"Editor's Note
An armed Serbia could have easily prevented this holocaust

Thanks God for the 2nd Amendment to the Constitution which guarantees the right to bear arms. Freedom of religion and an armed citizenry go hand in hand and is the only guarantee that this won't happen in the U.S.

Ed. Note: It is the *Vatican One World government* that doesn't want you to have the right to own arms or to use any means to defend yourself." The Vatican's Holocaust by Avro Manhattan," [emphasis added]

"A free people ought not only be armed and disciplined, but they should have sufficient arms and ammunition to maintain a status of independence from any who might attempt to abuse them, which would include their own government."

— **George Washington**

"Just because you don't take an interest in politics,…… doesn't mean politics won't take an interest in you"

– Pericles

Common Law

If you cannot see the irony in having a gun ban enforced by men with guns, then you fail to understand why the second amendment was written in the first place. At common law everybody is armed. Who needs a military when you have a posse.

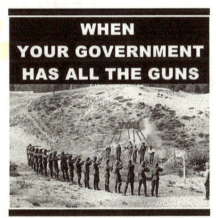

Figure 42 – When Government has all the Guns

Summary

The Roman Cult wants to shed innocent blood, and cause as much murder, theft, hatred, fear, and other negative emotions as possible for their satanic God BAAL.

21

THE ROMAN CULT
AND CANADA

It is all the same in Canada. *The Crown is the Roman Cult.* "… we will and establish perpetual obligation and concession we will establish that from the proper and especial revenues of our aforesaid kingdoms, for all the service and customs which we ought to render for them, saving in all things the penny of St. Peter, *the Roman church shall receive yearly a thousand marks sterling,* namely at the feast of St. Michael five hundred marks, and at Easter five hundred marks-seven hundred, namely, for the kingdom of England, and three hundred for the kingdom of Ireland" (Concessions of England to the Pope (1213)).

All checques paid to Canada are made payable to the Receiver General for Canada, which is a receiver in bankruptcy.

Martial law is a branch of the law of war, which is a branch of international law. Canadians use Bank of Canada notes, a negotiable instrument for money. The military force is called the Royal Canadian Mounted Police (RCMP). The Crown is just another name for the Roman Cult:

Government of Canada	Gouvernement du Canada

INSTRUCTION SHEET

A - Complete the application form.

B - You must provide an original primary document according to your status in Canada. Refer to leaflet "Documents you need to obtain a Social Insurance Number SC-207-03-06."

C - If the name on your primary document is different from the name you are now using, you must also submit an original supporting document. Refer to leaflet "Documents you need to obtain a Social Insurance Number SC-207-03-06."

D - If you are replacing your SIN card, you must pay a $10.00 fee (subject to change). Make your personal cheque, bank draft or money order payable in Canadian funds to the RECEIVER GENERAL FOR CANADA. You may pay in cash at a Human Resource Centre of Canada. DO NOT MAIL CASH.

E - If you are a guardian, you must submit an original document showing proof of legal guardianship in order to sign an application form on behalf of the applicant.

The information contained in the vital statistics registers and the Citizenship and Immigration Canada records can be used to validate information that you provide with this application form when presenting a document originating from these sources.

If you are employed, it is important that the name and Social Insurance Number under which you are working are identical to the name and Social Insurance Number that appear on your card. This will ensure that your Canada Pension Plan and/or Quebec Pension Plan contributions are properly credited to you.

Figure 43 – Canada is Bankrupt

"Canada", for greater certainty, includes the internal waters of Canada and the territorial sea of Canada; 'person', or any word or expression descriptive of a person, includes a corporation." (Section 35(1) Interpretation Act of Canada)

Their statutes say Canada is *only* the waterways = Admiralty Maritime law = the law of the sea = contract law.

"INCLUDE. (Lat. *inclaudere,* to shut in, keep within). To confine within, hold as in an inclosure, take in, attain, shut up, contain, inclose, comprise, comprehend, embrace, involve. Miller v. Johnston, 173 N.C. 62, 91 S.E. 593. Prairie Oil and Gas Co. v. Motter, D.C.Kan., 1 F.Supp. 464, 468; Decorated Metal Mfg. Co. v. U. S., 12 Ct.Cust.App. 140; In re Sheppard's Estate, 179 N.Y.S. 409, 412, 189 App.Div. 370; Rose v. State, 184 S.W. 60, 61, 122 Ark. 509; United States ex rel. Lyons v. Hines, 103 F.2d 737, 740, 70 App.D.C. 36, 122 A.L.R. 674." (*Black's Law Dictionary*, 4th Edition, page 905)

"INCLUDE

1. To confine within; to hold; to contain; as, the shell of
    a nut includes the kernel; a pearl is included in a shell.
    [But in these senses we more commonly use inclose.]
2. To comprise; to comprehend; to contain." (American
    Dictionary of the English Language, Noah Webster,
    1828)

"INCLUDE. (Lat. Inclaudere, to shut in, keep within.)
To confine within, hold as in an inclosure, take in, attain,
shut up, contain, inclose, comprise, comprehend, embrace,
involve. Premier Products Co. v. Cameron, 240 Or. 123,
400 P.2d 227, 228." (*Black's Law Dictionary*, 6th Edition,
page 763)

Person = Corporation

In Alberta, a "person" is *only* a corporation, and the heirs,
executors, administrators or other legal representatives: "person"
includes a corporation and the heirs, executors, administrators or
other legal representatives of a person" (Section 28(1)(nn) Alberta
Interpretation Act).

In Ontario a person is *only* a corporation: "In Every Act and
Regulation; "person" includes a corporation" (Section 87 Legislation
Act of Ontario).

Their courts even tell them to make it color of law, and
government legislation *only* deals with government property:

"It may still be legislation affecting the classes of subjects
enumerated in s. 92, and, if so, would be ultra vires. In
other words, *Dominion legislation, even though it deals with*

Dominion property, may yet be so framed as to invade civil rights within the Province; or encroach upon the classes of subjects which are reserved to provincial competence. *It is not necessary that it should be a colourable device, or a pretence.* If on the true view of the legislation it is found that in reality in pith and substance the legislation invades civil rights within the Province." (Re Employment and Social Insurance Act, 1937, 1 DLR, page 687)

People Are Sovereign

The people of Canada are sovereign. "The sovereign people through their representatives have created the Court and the Board, as well as the municipal council and have defined the rights and duties of each" (Re Casa Loma, (1927) 4 D.L.R. 645). And if you are subject to the regulations you are owned: "Section 2 Definitions (1) In this Act, *owned means, subject to the regulations*" (Canadian Ownership and Control Determination Act [emphasis added]).

Summary

There are more than one hundred nations around the world that are former British colonies, which is the British Commonwealth of Nations. I can prove the same thing in Australia and New Zealand, and I think it can be proven on every nation on the planet, except maybe Russia.

22

THE ROMAN CULT
AND THE RIGHT TO TRAVEL

Traffic Offenses

An offense is an offense against the martial law. All traffic offenses are based on presumptions:
"(h) DEFINITION's. …. "

"(1) SECURITY INTEREST.-The term 'security interest' means any interest in property acquired by contract for the purpose of securing payment or performance of an obligation or indemnifying against loss or liability. A security interest exists at any time

"(3) MOTOR VEHICLE.-The term 'motor vehicle' means a self-propelled vehicle *which is registered* for highway use under the laws of any State or foreign country.

"(4) SECURITY.-The term 'security' means any bond, debenture, *note*, or *certificate or other evidence of indebtedness, issued by a corporation or a government or political subdivision thereof,* with interest coupons or in registered form, share of stock, voting trust certificate, or any certificate of interest or participation in, certificate of deposit or receipt for, temporary or interim certificate for, or warrant or right to subscribe to or purchase any of the foregoing: *negotiable instrument: or money.*" (Federal Tax Lien Act of 1966 at Public Law 89-719 at 80 Stat. 1130-1131)

A "Motor Vehicle" Is Commercial

The term "motor vehicle" means every description of carriage or other contrivance "propelled or drawn by mechanical power and used for commercial purposes on the highways in the transportation of passengers, passengers and property, or property or cargo." *The term "used for commercial purposes" means the carriage of persons or property for any fare, fee, rate, charge or other consideration, or directly or indirectly in connection with any business, or other undertaking intended for profit"* (18 USC § 31 [emphasis added]).

Commerce = Equipment = Regulation

The same vehicle used for a purpose other than to carry passengers or property for hire is "consumer goods" and is not subject to taxation, and the Roman Cult's UNIDROIT and associated Uniform Commercial Code provides the remedy, especially since all of the so-called courts are commercial:

"Goods are: (1) "consumer goods" if they are used or bought for use primarily for personal, family or household purposes; (2) "equipment" if they are used or bought for use primarily in business (including farming or a profession) or by a debtor who is a non-profit organization or a governmental subdivision or agency or if the goods are not included in the definitions of inventory, farm products or consumer goods;" (Uniform Commercial Code 9-109 Classification of Goods: "Consumer Goods"; "Equipment"; "Farm Products"; "Inventory")

"Under UCC §9-109 there is a real distinction between goods purchased for personal use and those purchased for business use. The two are mutually exclusive and the principal use to which the property is put should be considered as determinative." (James Talcott, Inc. v Gee, 5 UCC Rep Serv 1028; 266 Cal.App.2d 384, 72 Cal.Rptr. 168 (1968))

"The classification of goods in UCC §9-109 are mutually exclusive." (McFadden v Mercantile-Safe Deposit & Trust Co., 8 UCC Rep Serv 766; 260 Md 601, 273 A.2d 198 (1971))

"Automobile purchased for the purpose of transporting buyer to and from his place of employment was ``consumer goods" as defined in UCC §9-109." (Mallicoat v Volunteer Finance & Loan Corp., 3 UCC Rep Serv 1035; 415 S.W.2d 347 (Tenn. App., 1966))

"The provisions of UCC §2-316 of the Maryland UCC do not apply to sales of consumer goods (a term which includes automobiles, whether new or used, that are bought primarily for personal, family, or household use)."

(Maryland Independent Automobile Dealers Assoc., Inc. v Administrator, Motor Vehicle Admin., 25 UCC Rep Serv 699; 394 A.2d 820, 41 Md App 7 (1978))

"A vehicle not used for commercial activity is a "consumer goods" . . . *it is NOT a type of vehicle required to be registered and "use tax" paid of which the tab is evidence of receipt of the tax.*" (Bank of Boston v. Jones, 4 UCC Rep. Serv. 1021, 236 A2d 484, UCC PP 9-109.14 [emphasis added])

"Thus self-driven vehicles are classified according to the use to which they are put rather than according to the means by which they are propelled." (Ex Parte Hoffert, 148 NW 20)

"The Supreme Court, in Arthur v. Morgan . . . held that carriages were properly classified as household effects, and we see no reason that automobiles should not be similarly disposed of." (Hillhouse v United States, 152 F. 163, 164 (2nd Cir. 1907))

"A soldier's personal automobile is part of his "household goods. U.S. v Bomar, C.A.5(Tex.), 8 F.3d 226, 235" (19A Words and Phrases - Permanent Edition (West) pocket part 94)

"[T]he exemptions provided for in section 1 of the Motor Vehicle Transportation License Act of 1925 (Stats. 1925, p. 833) in favor of those who solely transport their own property or employees, or both, and of those who transport no persons or property for hire or compensation, by motor vehicle, have been determined in the Bacon Service Corporation case to be lawful exemptions." (In re Schmolke (1926) 199 Cal. 42, 46)

"Consumer goods – automobile for transportation to and from work. The use of a vehicle by its owner for purposes of travelling to and from his employment is a personal, as opposed to a business use, as that term is used in UCC 9-109(1) and the vehicle will be classified as consumer goods rather than equipment." (In Re Barnes, 11 UCC Reporting Service 670)

"In view of this rule a statutory provision that the supervising officials "may" exempt such persons when the transportation is not on a commercial basis means that they "must" exempt them." (State v. Johnson, 243 P. 1073; 60 C.J.S. section 94, page 581)

Consumer Goods ≠ Taxation

Under the Texas constitution, consumer goods, household goods like my private conveyance, are not subject to taxation: "*The Legislature by general law shall exempt from ad valorem taxation household goods not held or used for the production of income* and personal effects not held or used for the production of income" (Article 8, Sec. 1 (d) Texas Constitution [emphasis added]).

Therein lies the contract: law enforcement officers enforcing the military occupation can presume a registered vehicle is commercial.

Texas Statutory Citations

Please note that these Texas code citations will be useful for those who are *not* in Texas because it will show you what kinds of things to look for in your local state statutes.

The Certificate of Title Act applies to state-owned vehicles, so if you have a certificate of title for your vehicle, the certificate certifies that the state has the title, which means the state owns the vehicle:

"(a) This chapter applies to a motor *vehicle owned by the state or a political subdivision of the state*" (Texas Trans. Code § 501.004. Applicability. (of Certificate of Title Act) [emphasis added])

"(a) a political subdivision of this state *may not require an owner of a motor vehicle to;*
(1) register the vehicle;
(2) *pay a motor vehicle registration fee*; or
(3) *pay an occupation tax* or license fee in connection with motor vehicle." (Texas Trans Code § 502.003. Registration By Political Subdivision Prohibited [emphasis added])

Class C Misdemeanor ≠ Crime

Traffic offenses are a class C misdemeanor in Texas:

"(e) An offense under this section is a Class C misdemeanor if the offense for which the actor's appearance is required is punishable by fine only." (Texas Penal Code § 38.10 Bail Jumping and Failure to Appear)

"(c) Conviction of a Class C misdemeanor does not impose any legal disability or disadvantage." (Texas Penal Code § 12.03 Classification of Misdemeanor)

"An individual adjudged guilty of a Class C misdemeanor shall be punished by fine only, not to exceed \$500." (Texas Penal Code § 12.23 Class (C) Misdemeanors)

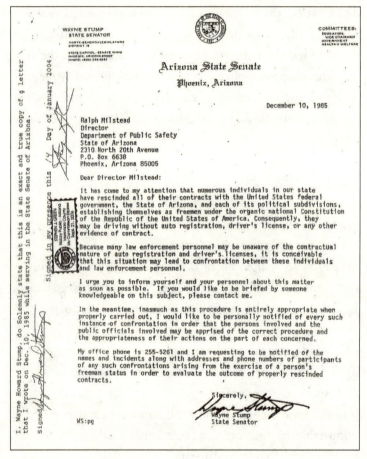

Figure 44 – Arizona Senator Letter

A class C misdemeanor in Texas (and probably everywhere else) is not a crime in Texas because it is punishable only by fine: "(5)

Crime means (A) a misdemeanor punishable by confinement (jail); or (B) a felony (6) "DEFENDANT" means a person accused of a crime" (Texas Government Code § 79.001 Definitions).

If it fails to be a crime, then it is a civil matter, and there is no probable cause for an arrest. They are operating in their private capacity as a revenue officer: "An officer who acts in violation of the Constitution ceases to represent the government" (Brookfield Const. Co. v. Stewart, 284 F. Supp. 94).

No Crime = No Probable Cause

The test for police officer's sufficient basis for probable cause is if the officer had a sufficient basis to make a "practical, common sense" decision that a "fair probability a crime existed." Once the officer's actions fail to satisfy this test, it may appear that *no reasonably objective officer could have believed that probable cause existed* to make an arrest. Allen v. City of Portland, 73 F.3d 232 (9th Cir. 1995), the Ninth Circuit Court of Appeals (citing cases from the U.S. Supreme Court, Fifth, Seventh, Eighth and Ninth Circuits), held that "by definition, probable cause to arrest can only exist in relation to criminal conduct; civil disputes cannot give rise to probable cause" (Paff v. Kaltenbach, 204 F.3d 425, 435 (3rd Cir. 2000)).

> "The people shall be secure in their persons, houses, papers and possessions, from all unreasonable seizures or searches, and no warrant to search any place, or to seize any person or thing, shall issue without describing them as near as may be, nor without probable cause, supported by oath or affirmation." (Article 1, Section 9 Searches and Seizures, Texas Constitution)

Article Four in Amendment *prohibits law enforcement officers from arresting citizens without probable cause* (citations omitted); in cases Santiago v. City of Vineland, 107 F.Supp.2d 512, 561-62, 564 (D.N.J. 2000); Hill v. Algor, 85 F.Supp.2d 391, 397-98 (D.N.J. 2000) *arrest made without probable cause violates the Fourth Amendment*; Rzayeva v. Foster, 134 F.Supp.2d 239, 248-49 (D.Conn. 2001) *holding involuntary civil confinement is a "massive curtailment of liberty", is tantamount to the infringement of being arrested and can be made only upon probable cause.* (Vitek v. Jones, 445 U.S. 480, 491, 100 S.Ct. 1254, 63 L.Ed.2d 552 (1980); Schneider v. Simonini, 749 A.2d 336, 163 N.J. 336, 361-65 (2000))

Malicious Prosecutions

When there is no Probable Cause for an arrest, then it is a malicious prosecution: "Although probable cause may not be inferred from malice, malice may be inferred from lack of probable cause" (Pauley v. Hall, 335 N. W. 2d 197, 124 Mich App 255). And false arrest:

> "The only thing the plaintiff needs to do is to allege a false arrest, is either (1) that the defendant made an arrest or imprisonment, or (2) that the defendant affirmatively instigated, encouraged, incited, or caused the arrest or imprisonment." (Burlington v. Josephson, 153 Fed.2d 372,276 (1946))

> "As in the case of illegal arrests, the officer... must keep within the law at his peril." (Thiede v. Scandia, 217 Minn. 231, 14 N.W.2d 400 (1944))

"When the plaintiff has shown that he was arrested, imprisoned or restrained of his liberty by the defendant, "the law presumes it to be unlawful." (People v. McGrew, 20 Pac. 92 (1888); Knight v. Baker, 133 P. 544(1926))

"The burden is upon the defendant (cop) to show that the arrest was by authority of law." (McAleer v. Good, 65 Atl. 934, 935 (1907); Mackie v. Ambassador, 11 P.2d 6 (1932))

"ANY ARREST, made without a PROPER warrant, Signed by a judge and backed up by an affidavit from two persons that states, under penalty of perjury, you have broken a contract or hurt somebody, if challenged by the defendant (person), is presumptively invalid...the burden is upon the state" to justify it as authorized by statute, and does not violate the constitutional provisions and Or (human rights.) (State v. Mastrian, 171 N.W.2d 695 (1969); Butler v. State, 212 So.2d 577 (Miss 1968))

Good Faith

Because of the martial law, and because so many people are so clueless about the two classes of citizens, our public servants can presume we are one of their US citizen slaves and claim good faith: "*All wanton violence committed against persons in the invaded country, all destruction of property not commanded by the authorized officer,* all robbery, *all pillage* or sacking, even after taking a place by main force, all rape, wounding, maiming, or killing of such inhabitants, are prohibited under the penalty of death, or such other severe punishment as may seem adequate for the gravity of the offense. A soldier, officer or private, in the act of committing such violence, and disobeying a superior ordering him to abstain from it, may be lawfully killed on the spot by such superior" (Article 44, General Orders 100 (The Lieber Code) [emphasis added])

This is codified in their statutes (edicts under martial law) and their federal statutes (edicts under martial law).

Alternative Plates

In Texas you can make up your own plate, or use no plate:

"(a) .. a political subdivision of this state may not require an owner of a motor vehicle to; (1) register the vehicle;

(2) pay a motor vehicle registration fee; or

(3) pay an occupation tax or license fee in connection with motor vehicle." (Texas Trans Code § 502.003. Registration By Political Subdivision Prohibited)

Figure 45 – Republic of Texas Plate

Summary

Certificates of title and vehicle registration is for commercial vehicles *only*. When you register your vehicle, it is presumed that it is commercial. By taking advantage of "privileges," it is a contract and you give up your sovereignty:

"*The rights of sovereignty extend to all persons and things, not privileged that are within the territory.* They extend to all *strangers resident* therein; not only to those who are naturalized, and to those who are domiciled therein, having taken up their abode with the intention of permanent residence, but also to those whose residence is transitory. All *strangers* are under the protection of the sovereign while they are within his territory and owe a temporary allegiance in return for that protection." (Carlisle v United States 83 U.S. 147, 154 (1873))

And thereby become a subject:

"*All subjects over which the sovereign power of the state extends are objects of taxation, but those over which it does not extend are exempt from taxation. This proposition may also be pronounced as self-evident. The sovereignty of the state extends to everything which exists by its authority or its permission.*" (McCullough v Maryland, 17 U.S. [4 Wheat] 316 (1819). [emphasis added])

The *only* real solution is to stay away from what they view to be contracts.

23

THE ROMAN CULT AND EQUITY

Equity in the Holy Bible

Equity comes from God's law (common law)

> "Before the LORD; for he cometh to judge the earth: *with righteousness shall he judge the world, and the people with equity.*" (Psalm 98:9 [emphasis added])

> "The king's strength also loveth judgment; *thou dost establish equity,* thou executest judgment and righteousness in Jacob." (Psalm 99:4 [emphasis added])

> "To receive the instruction of *wisdom, justice, and judgment, and equity;*" (Proverbs 1:3 [emphasis added])

> "*Then shalt thou understand righteousness, and judgment, and equity;* yea, every good path." (Proverbs 2:9 [emphasis added])

"Also to punish the just is not good, *nor to strike princes for equity.*" (Proverbs 17:26 [emphasis added])

"*For there is a man whose labour is in wisdom, and in knowledge, and in equity*; yet to a man that hath not laboured therein shall he leave it for his portion. This also is vanity and a great evil." (Ecclesiastes 2:21 [emphasis added])

"But with righteousness shall he judge the poor, *and reprove with equity for the meek of the earth*: and he shall smite the earth with the rod of his mouth, and with the breath of his lips shall he slay the wicked." (Isaiah 11:4 [emphasis added])

"And judgment is turned away backward, and justice standeth afar off: for truth is fallen in the street, *and equity cannot enter.*" (Isaiah 59:14 [emphasis added])

"The law of truth was in his mouth, and iniquity was not found in his lips: *he walked with me in peace and equity*, and did turn many away from iniquity." (Malachi 2:6 [emphasis added])

Common law is very severe. It is literally an eye for an eye and a tooth for a tooth. That means that if you cause an accident that puts somebody's eye out, at common law they would put your eye out and be done with it. Under equity, there is forgiveness, or insurance could compensate you. Equity is the power of the court to do justice even if a remedy is not available under law or statutes:

"EQUITY. In the early history of the law, the sense affixed to this word was exceedingly vague and uncertain. This was owing, in part, to the fact, that the chancellors of those days were either statesmen or ecclesiastics, perhaps not very scrupulous in the exercise of power. It was then asserted that equity was bounded by no certain limits or rules, and that it was alone controlled by conscience and natural justice. 3 Bl. Com. 43-3, 440, 441." (Bouviers Law Dictionary, 1856 Edition)

"EQUITY, COURT OF. A court of equity is one which administers justice, where there are no legal rights, or legal rights, but courts of law do not afford a complete, remedy, and where the complainant has also an equitable right." (Bouviers Law Dictionary, 1856 Edition)

Some states have courts of chancery, but all judges have equitable powers:

"Equity, 4. The system of law or body of principles originating in the English Court of Chancery and superseding the common and statute law (together called "law" in the narrow sense) when the two conflict <in appealing to the equity of the court, she was appealing to the "King's conscience">." (*Black's Law Dictionary*, 7th Edition)

Equity proceeds under Civil law, using the civil courts "And the forms and modes of proceedings in causes of *equity*, and of *admiralty*, and maritime jurisdiction, shall be according to the civil law" (Wayman and another v. Southard and another, 10 Wall 1, p. 317).

Courts of equity do not normally have a jury, but they can have a jury, and at the same time, they can ignore the verdict of a jury, or modify it. "It is well known that in civil cases, in courts of *equity* and *admiralty, juries* do not intervene, and that courts of equity use the trial by jury only in extraordinary cases to inform the conscience of the court" (Parsons v. Bedford, et al, 3 Pet 433, 479).

A principle of equity called "latches" is incorporated by most states that have placed a statute of limitations, which is normally two years, for civil litigation:

"LACHES laches (lach-iz). [Law French__"remissness; slackness"] 1. Unreasonable delay in pursuing a right or claim — *almost always an equitable one* — in a way that prejudices the party against whom relief is sought. — *Also termed sleeping on rights.*

2. The *equitable doctrine* by which a court denies relief to a claimant who has unreasonably delayed in asserting the claim, when that delay has prejudiced the party against whom relief is sought. Cf. LIMITATION(3). [Cases: Equity 67. C.J.S. Equity §§ 128–132.]" *The doctrine of laches ... is an instance of the exercise of the reserved power of equity to withhold relief otherwise regularly given where in the particular case the granting of such relief would be unfair or unjust.*" (William F. Walsh, A Treatise on Equity 472 (1930). *Black's Law Dictionary*, 8th Edition, page 2553-2554)

Foreclosures

Many people are confused as to why it is impossible to win against the banksters in a foreclosure, and it is because of equity. There are two kinds of title to real estate: legal title and equitable title. All mortgages are an equitable interest in the property, which is an inferior title, but when people fail to make their payments to the point that the banksters are foreclosing, the clean hands doctrine comes into play. Anyone who fails to abide by the terms of a contract also fails to have clean hands. You can have the best arguments in the world, but equity will not aid anyone who fails to have clean hands.

Contents [hide]

1 Role of maxims
2 List of maxims
    2.1 Equity considers that done what ought to be done
    2.2 Equity will not suffer a wrong to be without a remedy
    2.3 Equity delights in equality/Equality is equity (*Aequalitus est quasi equitas*)
    2.4 One who seeks equity must do equity
    2.5 Equity aids the vigilant not the indolent
    2.6 Equity imputes an intent to fulfill an obligation
    2.7 Equity acts *in personam* (i.e. on persons rather than on objects)
    2.8 Equity abhors a forfeiture
    2.9 Equity does not require an idle gesture
    2.10 He who comes into equity must come with clean hands
    2.11 Equity delights to do justice and not by halves
    2.12 Equity will take jurisdiction to avoid a multiplicity of suits
    2.13 Equity follows the law
    2.14 Equity will not assist a volunteer
    2.15 Equity will not complete an imperfect gift
    2.16 Where equities are equal, the law will prevail
    2.17 Between equal equities the first in order of time shall prevail
    2.18 Equity will not allow a statute to be used as a cloak for fraud
    2.19 Equity will not allow a trust to fail for want of a trustee
    2.20 Equity regards the beneficiary as the true owner
3 See also
4 Notes
5 References

Figure 46 – Equity

Normally, equity follows common law, (God's law) but martial law supersedes and replaces common law:

"In the meantime, "Civil Law" was the form of law imposed in the Roman Empire which was largely (if not wholly) governed by martial law rule. "Equity" has always been understood to follow the law; to have "superior equity," is to turn things on their head. This is exactly what happens when martial law is imposed. If "equity" is the law, then it follows its own course rather than following the common law, *thereby destroying the common law and leaving what is called "equity" in its place.*" (The Non-Ratification of the Fourteenth Amendment by Judge A.H. Ellett, Utah Supreme Court, Dyett v Turner, 439 P2d 266 @ 269, 20 U2d 403 (1968) [emphasis added])

"Statutes have been passed extending the courts of admiralty and vice-admiralty far beyond their ancient limits for depriving us the accustomed and inestimable privilege of trial by jury, in cases affecting both life and property . . . *to supersede the course of common law and instead thereof to publish and order the use and exercise of the law martial.*" (Causes and Necessity of Taking Up Arms (1775) [emphasis added])

This is why the Roman Cult BAR member / BAAL priests will tell you, "I can do anything I want in here," which then makes equity satanic, especially since all so-called judges are BAR members (foreign agents of the Roman Cult) as described herein. Furthermore, equity is supposed to follow common law (God's Law) and martial law stops that from happening which is the objective of the Roman Cult to replace God's Law with their satanic Roman law.

Summary

Equity is supposed to follow the law of the Land (common law) which is the principles found in the Holy Bible, but under martial law, there is no common law, and equity becomes satanic because they can do anything they want, and the officials making that decision (BAR members) are all satanic.

24

OBAMA THE TYRANT

Obama was a textbook tyrant. Let's look at the requirements for a tyrant according to Aristotle:

The tyrant who in order to hold his power, suppresses every superiority, does away with good men, forbids education and light, controls every movement of the citizens and, keeping them under a perpetual servitude, wants them to grow accustomed to baseness and cowardice, has his spies everywhere to listen to what is said in the meetings, and spreads dissension and calumny among the citizens and impoverishes them, is obliged to make war in order to keep his subjects occupies and impose upon them permanent need of a chief.

Figure 47 – NSA Spying

Does Away with Good Men

Every President fires government officials for various

reasons, and Obama certainly fired his share of people, but one official stands out because he exposed the illegal surveillance being carried out by the National Security Agency. The former head of the National Security Agency, Admiral Michael Rogers discovered the illegal surveillance being carried out by Obama against political opponents like Donald Trump.

Censorship reflects a society's lack of confidence in itself.
It is a hallmark of an authoritarian regime

—Supreme Court Justice Stewart Potter

Forbids Education and Light

George Bush's No Child Left Behind Act is a formula for making sure that people who can't spell are graduated from high school anyway. The Obama agenda then compelled a national education standard called "Common Core Standard," which causes all students into a lower standard.

Controls Every Citizens' Movements

Figure 48 – Gun Control

Obama continued the policy started by George W. Bush of the so-called Real ID Act, which is designed to compel everybody to get a national identification card. This applies to US citizens *only*, but under this requirement I was prohibited from filing a petition for a writ of habeas corpus for a friend in the United States

District Court for the Eastern District of Texas at Plano because I failed to have an acceptable form of identification.

Hegelian Dialectic
The synthetic solution to these conflicts can't be introduced unless those being manipulated take a side that will advance the pre-determined agenda.

—Georg Wilhelm Friedrich Hegel

Perpetual Servitude

This is a function of taxes. Taxes are a form of slavery. If you are paying taxes, you are being forced to work for the government for nothing. This is a War Crime under Article 52 of the Geneva Convention Relative to the Protection of Civilians in a Time of War of 1949:

> *"All measures aiming at creating unemployment or at restricting the opportunities offered to workers in an occupied territory, in order to induce them to work for the Occupying Power, are prohibited."* (Article 52, Geneva Convention Relative to the Protection of Civilians in Time of War of 1949 [emphasis added])

It is also a violation of their own current Thirteenth Amendment that requires slavery *only* upon conviction for a crime: "Section 1. Neither slavery nor involuntary servitude, *except as a punishment for crime whereof the party shall have been duly convicted*, shall exist within the United States, or any place subject to their jurisdiction."

([current] Article Thirteen in Amendment [emphasis added]). It is also one of the crimes that the tyrant King George engaged in as found in the Declaration of Independence.

"For imposing Taxes on us without our Consent"

—Declaration of Independence, (1776)

ARE YOU A DOMESTIC TERRORIST?

According to the Obama administration the following acts make you a domestic terrorist.

- *Speaking out against government policies*
- *Protesting anything (such as participating in the "Occupy" movement)*
- *Questioning war (even though war reduces our national security)*
- *Having bumper stickers saying things like "Know Your Rights or Lose Them"*
- *Taking pictures or videos*
- *Talking to police officers*
- *Writing on a piece of paper*
- *Being frustrated with "mainstream ideologies"*
- *Valuing online privacy*
- *Being anti-tax, anti-regulation, or for the gold standard*

- *Being "reverent of individual liberties"*
- *Believing in "conspiracy theories"*
- *Believing that one's personal and/or national "way of life" is under attack*
- *Supporting political movements for autonomy"*
- *Being suspicious of centralized federal authority*
- *Being fiercely nationalistic (as opposed to universal and international in orientation)"*
- *Opposing surveillance*

Figure 49 – Returning Military Labeled Terrorists

Source: *washingtonsblog.com, infowars.com, counterpunch.org, wired.com, publicintelligence.net, activistpost.com, reuters.com*

His Spies Are Everywhere

This is what the purpose of the illegal surveillance by the National Security Agency that is now well documented.

Spreads Dissention and Calumny

It is well known that government trolls were positioned in all social media to spread lies and disinformation.

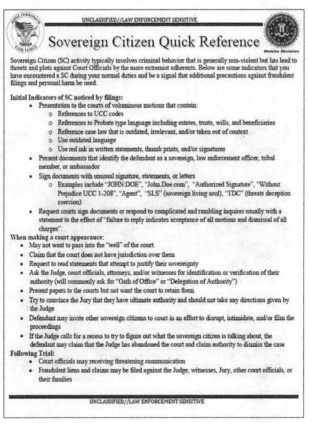

Figure 50 – Sovereign Citizen Quick Reference

Impoverishes Them

It is well documented that there is a long-term unemployed population in America—about 25 percent of the population—and Obama used to say they did not want to work. He used to manipulate statistics by using unemployment insurance data for published unemployment statistics when knows that unemployment insurance data is for government employees *only* because a social security number is required to collect unemployment insurance. What Obama was doing is compelling people to work for the occupying power by compelling the disclosure of a social security number in violation of Article 52 of the Geneva Convention Relative to the Protection of Civilians in a Time of War of 1949.

Any society that would give up a little liberty to gain a little security will deserve neither and lose both.

—Benjamin Franklin

"*All measures aiming at creating unemployment or at restricting the opportunities offered to workers in an occupied territory, in order to induce them to work for the Occupying Power, are prohibited.*" (Article 52, Geneva Convention Relative to the Protection of Civilians in Time of War of 1949 [emphasis added])

War Keep Citizens Occupied

If you think about it, this is the end game before you seize power: crush all opposition! That was supposed to be Clinton's job.

The War on Terror

The so-called War on Terror started with the 9-1-1 event that is also looking like an inside job.

I believe that the 9-1-1 event was orchestrated to justify the invasion of several countries in the middle east, including Iraq, Syria, and ultimately Iran. The twelve-hundred page Patriot Act, which had nothing to do with patriotism, and had everything to do with imposing a police state was passed by Congress. It gradually got worse through the Bush administration and then the Obama administration.

Figure 51 – Its NOT my Fault!

"We are going to take out seven countries in five years: Syria, Lebanon, Libya, Somalia, Sudan and Iran"

—General Wesley Clark

Hegelian Dialectic

Under the Hegelian Dialectic a problem is created with a pre-determined solution to promote an agenda.

Figure 64 – Hegelian Dialectic

The 9-1-1 event is an international terrorist event (if it fails to be a false flag operation), which created the whole War on Terror, which precipitated a police state in America and the invasion of Iraq, Libya, Syria, and Somalia. And currently Iran is being threatened. Lebanon and Sudan are next.

Figure 52 – USA Wars

Some people say that the so-called Patriot Act had been prepared in advance and was waiting for an event to justify it, which makes sense because it takes time to prepare a twelve-hundred-page piece of legislation, considering all of the people it needs to go past before it can be presented for a vote.

Trump Takes Office

When Trump took office, ISIS was in the middle of an invasion of Syria. Trump's first order of business

Figure 53 – Justice is Coming

was to completely destroy ISIS, stop the illegal surveillance by the National Security Agency, get NATO countries to pay their fair share, complete a tax reform bill, withdraw from recent international agreements, and other measures to end the tyranny put in place by Obama. That is why the forces of hell are working so hard to remove Donald J Trump, because they know justice is coming as long as Donald Trump is in power.

Figure 54 – Gangsters

Summary

Obama was a tyrant in every sense of the word.

25

WHAT IS TRUMP
UP AGAINST?

Satanists (the Roman Cult) have seized control of the unconstitutional municipal corporation and are operating it as their owned and operated criminal racketeering enterprise.

JFK Exposes Ruthless Conspiracy

"For we are opposed around the world by a monolithic and ruthless conspiracy that relies on covert means for expanding its sphere of influence on Infiltration instead of invasion, On subversion instead of elections, On intimidation instead of free choice, On guerillas by night instead of armies by day. It is a system which has conscripted vast human and material resources into the building of a tightly knit, highly efficient machine that combines military, diplomatic, intelligence, economic, scientific and political operations."

—John F Kennedy

The Price of Liberty

It happened because "we the people" have been asleep at the wheel.

Donald Trump has left his billionaire lifestyle to bail out "we the people," and we should be thanking God every day and be praying for his protection. "*The high office of the President,*" said JKF, "*has been used to foment a plot to destroy America's freedom,* and before I leave office, I must inform the citizen of this plight" (President John Fitzgerald Kennedy - In a speech made to Columbia University on Nov. 12, 1963, *ten days before his assassination*).

John F Kennedy was surrounded by Jesuits that will murder him if given any opportunity, just like they murdered the last guy who thought he could make a difference. I think Trump was born for this, just like I have always known that I was born to testify of the abominations of this generation:

> "But if the watchman see the sword come, and blow not the trumpet, *and the people be not warned;* if the sword come, and take any person from among them, he is taken away in his iniquity; *but his blood will I require at the watchman's hand.*" (Ezekiel 33:6)

Lindsay Williams

Lindsay Williams is a Southern Baptist preacher who went to Alaska to introduce the workers on the Alaska pipeline to Christianity, and the owners of the pipeline liked what he was doing and invited him to their board meetings. Lindsay calls them the Elite.

Lindsay Williams claims that the Elite are the people who are involved with the Deep State, and they would periodically tell him what their plans are. Over the years his disclosures of Elite's plans have been remarkably accurate.

Lindsay Williams says that the Elite told him that when Donald Trump was elected that God intervened, and that as long as Donald Trump is in power their plans are on hold.

Figure 55 – Communism vs Socialism

Communists Are Everywhere!

They call themselves socialists, but if you read the communist manifesto, the ONLY difference between communists and socialists is the implementation method. Socialists use subversion, and communists have a revolution (violent overthrow), but the end result is the same in both cases. I don't differentiate between Democrats or Republicans because most of the members of both parties are communists. In fact, many people call them Republicrats, because there is really no difference except for a few like Donald Trump. The reason they are spending money like mad is because they need to keep the government in bankruptcy to maintain the

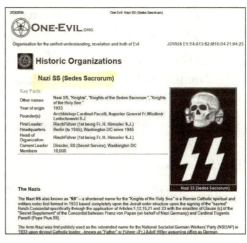

Figure 56 – Secret Service = NAZI SS

martial law. That is also the same reason why they need a trade deficit.

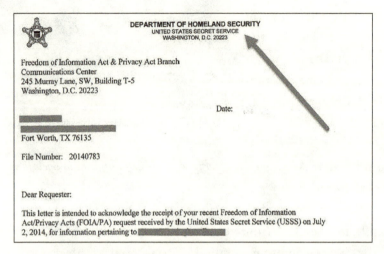

Figure 57 – Homeland Security = Secret Service

"The drive of the Rockefellers and their allies is to create a one-world government combining super-capitalism and Communism under the same tent, all under their control. . . . Do I mean conspiracy? Yes I do. I am convinced there is such a plot, international in scope, generations old in planning, and incredibly evil in intent." (Congressman Larry P. McDonald, 1976, killed in the Korean Airlines 747 that was shot down by the Soviets)

The Secret Service

Trump has his own Security people and he does not trust the Secret Service – absolutely brilliant!

The Secret Service is a subsidiary of the treasury, and the treasury is owned by the International Monetary Fund.

Homeland Security

Homeland Security is a subsidiary of the Secret Service. We all need to be doing things to support Donald Trump.

Figure 58 – Jefferson's Seal

"It behooves every man who values liberty of conscience for himself, to resist invasions of it in the case of others: or their case may, by change of circumstances, become his own." (Thomas Jefferson)

"If a law is unjust, a man is not only right to disobey it, he is obligated to do so." (Thomas Jefferson)

"If Ye love wealth better than liberty, the tranquility of servitude, better than the animating contest of freedom, go home from us in peace. We ask not your counsel or arms. Crouch down and lick the hands which feed you. May your chains set lightly upon you, and may our posterity forget that you were ever our countrymen." (Samuel Adams, the father of the American revolution, member of the sons of Liberty (the group that did the Boston Tea Party) and quoted from the debates of 1776)

"But the fearful, and unbelieving, and the abominable, and murderers, and whoremongers, *and sorcerers* [pharmaceutical drug pushers], and idolaters, *and all liars*, shall have their part in the lake which burneth with fire and brimstone: which is the second death." (Revelations 21:8)

"The individual is handicapped by coming face to face with a conspiracy so monstrous he cannot believe it exists. The American mind simply has not come to a realization of the evil which has been introduced into our midst. It rejects even the assumption that human creatures could espouse a philosophy which must ultimately destroy all that is good and decent." (J. Edgar Hoover, director of the Federal Bureau of Investigation, as quoted in the *Elks Magazine*)

Trump is literally in the belly of the beast. We should be praying for his protection every day! The District of Columbia is home for Georgetown University, a Jesuit-owned-and-operated university that has been training government employees for decades. Trump is surrounded by Jesuits and those who are trained by Jesuits. Are we surprised when they murdered Kennedy and tried to murder Reagan?

"The First World War must be brought about in order to permit the Illuminati to overthrow the power of the Czars in Russia and of making that country a fortress of atheistic Communism. The divergences caused by the "agentur" (agents) of the Illuminati between the British and Germanic Empires will be used to foment this war. At the end of the war, Communism will be built and used in order to destroy the other governments and in order to weaken the religions."

"The Second World War must be fomented by taking advantage of the differences between the Fascists and the political Zionists. This war must be brought about so that Nazism is destroyed and that the political Zionism be strong enough to institute a sovereign state of Israel in Palestine. During the Second World War, International Communism must become strong enough in order to balance Christendom, which would be then restrained and held in check until the time when we would need it for the final social cataclysm."

"The Third World War…fomented…taking advantage of the differences caused by… "agentur" of the "Illuminati" …The war…that Islam …and political Zionism (Israel) mutually

Figure 59 – CIA Whistle Blowers

destroy each other. Meanwhile the other nations … divided … constrained to fight to the point of complete physical, moral, spiritual and economical exhaustion! We shall unleash the Nihilists and the atheists, and we shall provoke a formidable social cataclysm … in all its horror … savagery … most bloody turmoil. Then everywhere, the citizens, obliged to defend themselves against the world minority of revolutionaries, will exterminate those destroyers of civilization, and the multitude, *disillusioned with Christianity … will receive the true light … of the pure doctrine of Lucifer*, brought finally out in the public view. This … will result from … reactionary movement which will follow the destruction of Christianity and atheism, both conquered and exterminated at the same time." (Albert Pike, taken from his book *Morals and Dogma*)

The Central Intelligence Agency

I worked in the US Airways engineering department during their merger with America West Airlines. I saw US Airways' Air Agency Certificate. I suspect the Central Intelligence Agency is a private company that has a contract to collect intelligence for the government. I also think that the Central Intelligence Agency is owned by the Roman Cult.

Are we surprised when the Central Intelligence Agency admits to promoting lies in the news media?

"The CIA owns everyone of any significance in the major media." (William Colby, former CIA director)

"We'll know our disinformation program is complete when everything the American public believes is false." (William Casey, CIA Director, from first staff meeting, 1981)

"Deception is a state of mind and the mind of the state." (James Angleton, head of CIA counter intelligence from 1954-1974)

"I will splinter the CIA into a thousand pieces and scatter it into the winds." (John F Kennedy)

"Make the lie big, make it simple, keep saying it, and eventually they will believe it." (Adolph Hitler)

Are we surprised when we have been in almost continual warfare since the Civil War? And especially all during the twentieth century?

Are we surprised that the news media have come out with such hatred and vitriol against Trump?

It is the legions of hell that have come out against him! For that reason alone we should be praying for his safety every day!

The Russian Collusion Hoax

The communists in Congress and the news media are doing everything they can because Trump is *not* under their thumb. They cannot control him.

"It is the duty of the patriot to protect his country from its government."

—Thomas Paine

Summary

Donald Trump is literally in the belly of the beast. He is surrounded by Satanists who will murder him at the drop of a hat if given the opportunity. I think he probably had a good idea of what he would be dealing with, but I am also sure he had no idea about the scope of the satanic power in the District of Columbia.

He is surrounded by people who are doing everything they can to get the next blood sacrifice to the Roman Cult's god BAAL going (WWIII).

The Roman Cult has been enslaving people on this planet for centuries, and just one free nation threatens their entire existence, and they will stop at nothing to put an end to anyone who stands in the way of their Holy Roman Empire and their New World Order!

> "When we get ready to take the United States we will not take it under the label of communism; we will not take it under the label of socialism. These labels are unpleasant to the American people, and have been speared too much. We will take the United States under labels we have made very lovable; we will take it under liberalism, under progressivism, under democracy. But take it we will." (Alexander Trachtenberg (1885-1966) at the National Convention of Communist Parties, Madison Square Garden, 1944)

I believe that Donald Trump is our last hope to save the Republic. We should be praying for Donald Trump's safety every day!

> "It is not the function of our government to keep the Citizen from falling into error; it is the function of the Citizen to keep the government from falling into error." (American Communications Ass'n v. Douds, 339 U.S. 382, 442)

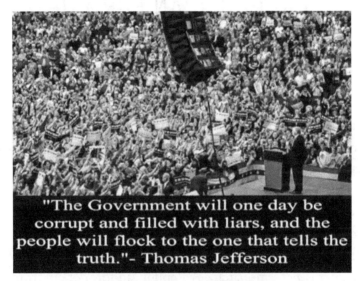

Figure 60 – Thomas Jefferson Prophecy

26

A REPUBLICAN FORM OF GOVERNMENT

It is said that when Benjamin Franklin was leaving the Constitutional Convention, a woman asked him "what have we got: a republic or a monarchy" to which he replied "A republic, if you can keep it"

The Constitution even says: "The United States shall guarantee to every State in this Union a Republican Form of Government" (Article IV, Section 4).

So what does that mean? We know it is *not* a democracy, and we know it is *not* a monarchy. A Republican form of government is a government of the people, by the people, and for the people, and we can tell that from court decisions of the day.

We know that the reason for the War of Independence was of a dictatorship by the tyrant King George:

"[S]tatutes have been passed extending the courts of admiralty and vice-admiralty far beyond their ancient limits for depriving us the accustomed and inestimable privilege of trial by jury, in cases affecting both life and property ... *to supersede the course of common law and instead thereof to publish and order the use and exercise of the law martial."* (Causes and Necessity of Taking Up Arms (1775) [emphasis added])

"The law, says Sir William Blackstone, ascribes to the King the attribute of sovereignty: he is sovereign and independent within his own dominions; and owes no kind of objection to any other potentate upon earth. Hence it is, that no suit or action can be brought against the King, even in civil matters; because no Court can have jurisdiction over him: for all jurisdiction implies superiority of power.' *This last position is only a branch of a much more extensive principle, on which a plan of systematic despotism has been lately formed in England,* and prosecuted with unwearied assiduity and care. Of this plan the author of the Commentaries was, if not the introducer, at least the great supporter. He has been followed in it by writers later and less known; and his doctrines have, both on the other and this side of the Atlantic, been implicitly and generally received by those, who neither examined their principles nor their consequences, The principle is, that all human law must be prescribed by a superior. This principle I mean not now to examine. Suffice it, at present to say, that another principle, very different in its nature and operations, forms, in my judgment, the basis of sound and genuine jurisprudence; laws derived from the pure source of equality and justice must be founded on the CONSENT of those, whose obedience they require. The sovereign, when traced to his source, must be found in the man." (Chisholm v Georgia, 2 Dal. 419 at page 458 [emphasis added])

"In despotic Governments, the Government has usurped, in a similar manner, both upon the state and the people: Hence all arbitrary doctrines and pretensions concerning the Supreme, absolute, and incontrolable, power of Government. In each, man is degraded from the prime rank, which he ought to hold in human affairs: In the latter, the state as well as the man is degraded. Of both degradations, striking instances occur in history, in politics, and in common life." (Chisholm v Georgia, 2 Dal. 419 at page 461 [emphasis added])

"Another instance, equally strong, but still more astonishing, is drawn from the British Government, as described by Sir William Blackstone and his followers. As described by him and them, the British is a despotic Government. It is a Government without a people. In that Government, as so described, the sovereignty is possessed by the Parliament: In the Parliament, therefore, the supreme and absolute authority is vested:* In *the Parliament resides that uncontrolable and despotic power, which, in all Governments, must reside somewhere."* (Chisholm v Georgia, 2 Dal. 419 at page 462 [emphasis added])

This is to say that all governments have an uncontrollable despotic power, and if people want to be free, then it needs to be in the hands of the people.

The problem is that everything is under martial law, which is International Law under the Roman Cult who are Satanists. All of the courts are full of BAR members, who are foreign agents of the

Roman Cult. The Founders tried to keep the BAR members out of the country with the true Article XIII:

> "If any citizen of the United States shall accept, claim, receive, or retain any title of nobility or honor, or shall, without the consent of congress, accept and retain any present, pension, office, or emolument of any kind whatever, from any emperor, king, prince, or foreign power, such person shall cease to be a citizen of the United States, and shall be incapable of holding any office of trust or profit under them, or either of them." (Article Thirteen in Amendment)

An additional problem is that the Roman Cult has been influencing things here from the beginning and many court cases can see their influence. A good case is Dredd Scott v Sanford (1857) where the US Supreme Court said that the Constitution was written *only* for the white race:

> "All citizens of the United States shall have the same right, in every State and Territory, *as is enjoyed by white citizens thereof* to inherit, purchase, lease, sell, hold, and convey real and personal property." (42 USC § 1982 [emphasis added])

A republican form of government fails to include any military dictatorships.

A republican form of government fails to include any statutes, codes, regulations:

> "Military jurisdiction is of two kinds: *First, that which is conferred and defined by statute*; second, that which is derived from the common law of war. Military offenses under the

statute law must be tried in the manner therein directed; but military offenses which do not come within the statute must be tried and punished under the common law of war. The character of the courts which exercise these jurisdictions depends upon the local laws of each particular country.

"In the armies of the United States the first is exercised by courts-martial, while cases which do not come within the

"Rules and Articles of War," or the jurisdiction conferred by statute on courts-martial, are tried by military commissions." (Article 13, General Orders 100 (The Lieber Code) [emphasis added])

All statutes, codes, rules and regulations are all edicts under martial law:

"NOTE: Under the Law-Martial, only the criminal jurisdiction of a Military Court is the recognized law. But as Article Three says, "the civil courts can continue wholly or in part as long as the civil jurisdiction does not violate the Military orders laid down by the Commander in Chief or one of his Commanders." By this means; a military venue, jurisdiction, and authority are imposed upon the occupied populace under disguise of the ordinary civil courts and officers of the occupied district or region, because the so-called civil authorities in an occupied district, or region, only act at the pleasure of a military authority.

"It should also be noted here that the several State Legislatures, County Boards of Commissioners, and City Councils, are constantly legislating to please the edicts of the federal government (the occupying force) and that their legislation, in this sense, is not an exercise of State sovereignty, but instead, a compliance with edicts of the military force which occupies the several States and consequently are edicts of Martial Law Rule." (Dyett v Turner 439 P2d 266 @ 269, 20 U2d 403 [1968] The Non-Ratification of the Fourteenth Amendment by Judge A.H. Ellett, Utah Supreme Court [emphasis added])

A Republican form of government fails to include any compelled attorneys (liars) and Star Chambers

"The corrupt Star Chamber Courts of England *required defendants to have counsel.* Star Chamber stood for swiftness and arbitrary power, it was a limitation on the common law." (Faretta v. California, 422 U.S. 806, 821 [emphasis added])

A republican form of government is a government of the people, by the people, and for the people with common law, and three separate and distinct branches of government:

"The powers of the Government of the State of Texas shall be divided into three distinct departments, each of which shall be confided to a separate body of magistracy, to wit: Those which are Legislative to one; those which are Executive to another, and those which are Judicial to another; *and no person, or collection of persons, being of one of these departments, shall exercise any power properly attached to either of the others,* except in the instances herein expressly permitted." (Article 2. Section 1, Texas Constitution [emphasis added])

The problem is that under the current regime, all judges are foreign agents of the Roman Cult (BAR members) and all courts operate under International Law (UNIDROIT – Uniform Commercial Code).

You may find a judge that honors his oath and you may *not*, but one thing is certain. Unless you say on the record the words that you require them to honor their oath as far as the republican form of government is concerned, they will fail to provide it, because of the martial law and the presumptions they take as a result of the military dictatorship.

A friend told me that a friend of his was recently elected to be a judge in Nevada and the new judge was all excited for his new responsibilities and a training court he was required to attend in Henderson, Nevada, for new judges. After the training course was concluded, the new judge was extremely discouraged because the training course was training on how to manufacture consent.

Once the martial law ends, their presumptions change completely.

27

RETURN POWER TO THE PEOPLE

think that Donald Trump is *not* too excited about being President because he knows there is a chance he could get assassinated by the Roman Cult. I don't know for sure, but I think he likes his billionaire lifestyle and would rather *not* be President of the United States, but he is doing it because he feels like there is nobody else who can (and will) do what needs to be done.

I cannot say what will happen because the possibilities are unlimited.

The Soviet Union

A good example is the Soviet Union. In the 1990s the former Soviet Union would murder anybody fleeing the Communist regime from East Germany to West Germany, but it all stopped when the military troops refused to murder the unarmed people fleeing for their life.

Then a trickle of people fleeing turned into a deluge of people fleeing.

Then the people, by the millions, tore down the wall separating east and west Germany, and the Soviet Union was no more.

Then when Boris Yeltzin was President of Russia a few Russian generals staged a coup. The Russians are very sophisticated, and I think the coup was staged to liquidate and overthrow the Roman Cult's municipal corporation, so they could establish a lawful de jure government.

After Putin came to power, Russia has paid off all of its debt, and it is now a major exporter of oil, import very little, and are stockpiling gold. I do not believe that any of this is a coincidence.

I went to Simferopol, Ukraine, a few years ago, and I transited through the Moscow airport on the way. Both Russia and Ukraine put red stamps in my passport. I have been all over the world. I have been across both oceans dozens of time, and I have probably been in fifty countries, but Russia and Ukraine are the *only* ones that put red stamps in my passport. Red ink signifies that it is a lawful de jure government.

Ukraine was absorbed by the Soviet Union, and Ukraine declared independence from the Soviet Union in 1991, so it would be a lawful de jure government.

Babylon the Great Is Fallen

Some say New York City is the world's capital, and it is certainly the seat of the United Nations, which is the Roman Cult's political New World Order:

> "And he cried mightily with a strong voice, saying, Babylon the great is fallen, is fallen, and is become the habitation of devils, and the hold of every foul spirit, and a cage of every unclean and hateful bird. For all nations have drunk of the wine of the wrath of her fornication, and the kings of the earth have committed fornication with her, and the

merchants of the earth are waxed rich through the abundance of her delicacies. Standing afar off for the fear of her torment, saying, Alas, alas, that great city Babylon, that mighty city! for in one hour is thy judgment come." (Revelation 18: 2-3,10)

Technical Remote Viewing is a program started by the US Army during the cold war. They say that everything that is ever done is recorded on the fabric of space-time creating a giant library, and all you need to know is how to access the library. They also say that they can teach anyone to access the library. They would give the remote viewer a sealed envelope with coordinates somewhere on the planet written on it, and they were required to describe what they remote viewed. They say that it is about 80% accurate, and that is how they knew what the Russians were doing during the cold war. They can even remote view the future, but human free will comes into play, so it gets murky and they have trouble with accuracy if you go too far in the future. Technical remote viewers (and others) have said that there will come a point in time when there are riots in every city in America and a great nation will disappear in one day, and then there will be wars between the states.

I have no idea if things will play out like this. All prophecies are conditional because if the people repent, the prophecy won't happen. I am just presenting this as a possible scenario.

What Is Required?

The power will never really be returned to the people until the martial law is ended. Trump needs to end the martial law by special proclamation: "Martial Law does not cease during the hostile occupation, *except by special proclamation, ordered by the commander in chief*, or by special mention in the *treaty of peace* concluding the war" (Article 2, General Orders 100 (The Lieber Code) [emphasis added]).

However before a special proclamation can be made, several things are required.

Lawful Money

The most important thing to do is to have lawful money, but that means US Treasury notes backed up by gold, and that also means we are required to have a balance of trade. Trump has already made the USA the world's biggest exporter of oil, and he is re-negotiating trade agreements, which is also why the Roman Cult-owned-and-operated mainstream media are calling it trade wars.

If we go to gold backed money without a balance of trade, foreign countries will require a gold payment, and we will be forced back to martial law when the gold runs out:

> "*The forced loans of 1862 and 1863*, in the form of legal tender notes, <u>were vital forces in the struggle for national supremacy</u>. They formed a part of the public debt of the United States, *the validity of which is solemnly established by the Fourteenth Amendment to the Constitution*." (Julliard v. Greenman, 110 US 432 [emphasis added])

Article 3 Courts

Trump will need to have Article 3 courts, which means that there will be no more BAR members, and we will require lawful de jure judges.

Presumptions Will Change

Right now the presumption is that you are a subject (slave) under martial law, and that will change to the new presumption: that you are one of "we the people." The style of cases will change. Right now a case might say "State of Texas vs whoever." That will change to "the People of Texas vs whoever." The judge will not be sitting there playing stupid but will be there to make sure we are provided due process and that justice is done.

Also, under true common law juries, the jury should call the witnesses, the jury should question the witnesses, the jury should determine the law and the facts in the matter and the jury should even pronounce sentence. The judge would be there to advise the jury on different points of law, but the jury could also disregard anything the judge has to say.

Elections May Change

Technically under a republican form of government the electors should *not* be required to register to vote, which is one very good reason to have landowners as electors, because a registered voter is a commercial contract:

> "REGISTER, *commer. law.* The certificate of registry granted to the person or persons entitled thereto, by the collector of the district, comprehending the port to which any ship or vessel shall belong; more properly, the registry itself. For the form, requisites, &c. of certificate of registry, see Act of Con. Dec. 31, 1792; Story's Laws U. S. 269; 3 Kent, Com. 4th ed. 141." (Bouviers Law Dictionary, 1856 Edition, Volume 2, page 437)

Deep State Prosecutions

There should be prosecutions but who and for what crimes are yet to be seen.

Martial Law Amendments Disappear

The current Thirteenth Amendment and all subsequent amendments are all martial law amendments and will go away, and the original Thirteenth Amendment will be back.

"A free people ought not only be armed and disciplined, but they should have sufficient arms and ammunition to maintain a status of independence from any who might attempt to abuse them, which would include their own government."

—George Washington

Summary

In order to end the martial law, the commander in chief, Donald Trump, is required to issue a special proclamation. Before he can issue a special proclamation, we are required to be on a lawful monetary system based on gold or silver coin, and we need a lawful Article 3 judiciary. A new system of elections are a good idea and some prosecutions of criminals are also preferred, but not mandatory, if we want the republic to last any amount of time.

28

MY OPINION

I was raised as a Christian. The word *God* can mean a lot of things to a lot of different people. When somebody says God, the first thought that comes to my mind is: "Which God are they talking about?" Even after further conversation many times I am left still wondering if they were Christian or something else. I have learned over the years that most people who claim to be Christian really have no idea what that means.

What God

When I say God, I mean the God of Abraham, Isaac, and Jacob as found in the Old Testament. I also believe that the same God is Yeshua, also known as Jesus Christ, and he is also the creator:

> "In the beginning was the Word, and the 'Word was with God, and the Word was God. The same was in the beginning with God. All things were made by him; and without him was not any thing made that was made. . . . And the Word was made flesh, and dwelt among us, (and we beheld his glory, the glory as of the only begotten of the Father,) full of grace and truth." (John 1:1-3, 14)

Jesuit Infiltrations

I believe that Jesuits have infiltrated everywhere, including the Mormon church. In fact some of the Mormon scriptures even talk about it, which is why I have not been to church in decades.

A friend goes to a Southern Baptist church, and he told me about one of the preachers in one of the big Fort Worth mega churches. He said the preacher would encourage people to do things that seemed to be against Christian doctrine. He was in favor of gays in the priesthood, and women in the priesthood, and he did unusual things like going to a Hallowe'en party dressed up as a nun. One day the preacher died, and the friend said that they buried the preacher in a Catholic cemetery. We both think the preacher was a Jesuit.

Rice McLeod used to correctly tell people that the biggest problem in this world is third parties. He would continue: "All attorneys are third parties, and go into court and make all sorts of statements about all sorts of things and none of them have any firsthand knowledge of anything." Then he would say: "So why on earth would you want some third-party preacher involved in your relationship with God?"

Americas Divine Destiny

I also believe that the Constitution of the United States of America was inspired by God, and the Founding Fathers were raised up by God to do what they did.

I also believe that I was born into this life to testify of the abominations of this generation, which I am doing with this book, and in the lawsuits that I file, and in the documents that I file into the public record. I am compelled to say these things. They must be said. All these things need to come to light:

"And he answered and said unto them, I tell you that, if these should hold their peace, the stones would immediately cry out." (Luke 19:40)

"For there is nothing covered, that shall not be revealed; neither hid, that shall not be known. Therefore whatsoever ye have spoken in darkness shall be heard in the light; and that which ye have spoken in the ear in closets shall be proclaimed upon the housetops." (Luke 12:2-3)

"Fear them not therefore: for there is nothing covered, that shall not be revealed; and hid, that shall not be known." (Matthew 10:26)

George Washington's Vision

I have a copy of what is claimed to be a vision that George Washington received, that talks about three great perils America will have to endure. The first peril was the War of Independence, the second peril was the civil war, and the third peril is the worst, and I believe has been under way since Kennedy was assassinated, and with the military occupation, and it is about to get a lot worse. I truly hope that Trump is successful, and nothing happens to him, but I am afraid that these Satanists are not finished, and we are probably living in the Book of Revelations time period.

Bruce R. McConkie was an Apostle of the Church of Jesus Christ of Latter-Day Saints (the Mormons) in the 1980s, and he wrote a book called Mormon Doctrine, and in the first edition of that book, with a white cover, he said that the Catholic Church is the *great and abominable church of the devil* that is described in the Book of Mormon, and they made McConkie take that out, and McConkie came out with another edition with a green cover that had that statement removed. Bruce R. McConkie died shortly after that.

Bruce R. McConkie may have been correct.

I will shew unto thee the judgment of the great whore that sitteth upon many waters: With whom the kings of the earth have committed fornication, and the inhabitants of the earth have been made drunk with the wine of her fornication." (Revelation 17:1-2)

- A whore sells themselves for money – the Roman Cult
- Sitteth upon many waters – admiralty maritime law is the law of the sea – contract law - UNIDROIT
- Fornication is an illicit activity – circulating fake money under Roman law is also an illicit activity
- Inhabitants made drunk with the wine of the fornication - People think they are rich with the fake money
- Rome sits on seven hills

"I know thy works, and tribulation, and poverty, (but thou art rich) and I know the blasphemy of them which say they are Jews, and are not, but are the synagogue of Satan." Revelations 2:9)

- This is all satanic

I also believe that Donald Trump is part of that destiny, and I believe that I am part of it as well.

There are websites that document near-death experiences, and they are similar in many ways, but the important thing I want to mention here is that not much happens by accident. There are unseen forces working to move people and events along a predetermined path. There are accidents, that is true, but most of what we think are accidents are actually orchestrated.

My friend Patrick calls the United States of America the United States of Israel, and I think he may be correct. The British coat of arms has a lion and a unicorn. The lion is the symbol of the tribe of Judah, and the unicorn is the symbol of Israel. When the ten tribes of Israel disappeared, they went to Northern Europe, and there is a lot of the blood of Israel in America.

Donald Trump was raised up by God to do what he is doing, and he will be protected as long as he is doing what God wants him to do.

Trump reluctantly ran for President, but he felt like he had no choice because he had the resources to provide for his own security, because security arrangements for the President cannot be trusted. He knew what he was getting mixed up in, but he also knew there was no other realistic alternative, because if there was a realistic alternative, he would have gladly let the alternative happen.

Figure 61 – The Deep State is After you

New World Order Crowd

I believe that like all billionaires on the planet, Trump was approached by the New World Order crowd, and they basically told Trump (what they tell everybody they approach) that he is required to go with their "program" or he might come to some accidental premature end.

I believe that Howard Hughes was a recluse because the New World Order crowd had approached him, and he turned them down. Hughes was concerned enough about his safety, and he was continually hiding from them. He was constantly worried about poisoning.

On October 10, 1989, when Stephen F. Hyde (forty-three-year-old chief executive of the Trump casinos), Mark Grossinger Etess (thirty-eight-year-old president and chief operating officer of the Trump Taj Mahal casino hotel), and Jonathan Benanav (thirty-three-year-old executive vice president of the Trump Plaza casino hotel) were all killed in a helicopter crash, it's easy to conclude that it was probably not an accident and was probably aimed at Trump because he refused to go with the New World Order program.

"I was in England two years before the violence in Syria… I met top British officials, who confessed to me that they were preparing something in Syria… Britain was organizing an invasion of rebels into Syria."

—Roland Dumas former French Foreign Minister

Sure Trump likes the limelight and uses Twitter for fishing. Every time he sends out a tweet, he is fishing. His opponents take the bait every time, and he reels them in!

The US military has offered Trump as much assistance and protection that they can offer, but Trump is smart enough to know that he needs to take additional steps with private security and other protections.

There Is No Al Qaeda

"The truth is there is no Islamic army or terrorist group called Al Qaeda. And any informed intelligence officer knows this. But there is propaganda campaign to make the public believe in their presence of an identified entity representing the devil only in order to drive TV watchers to accept a unified international leadership for a war against terrorism. The country behind this propaganda is the US." (Former British Foreign Secretary Robin Cook Inter-Services Intelligence [Cook died while hiking in the Scottish Highlands])

The CIA Is a Private Company

The Central Intelligence Agency is a private company that is owned by Jesuits and the Roman Cult and has a contract to collect intelligence for the unconstitutional municipal corporation UNITED STATES OF AMERICA. They have a contract to collect intelligence, and they provide it to government agencies. But what else do they do with the information?

The Central Intelligence Agency is responsible for all false flag operations around the world, and inside the UNITED STATES.

Sheer Coincidence

The alleged terrorists managed to strike the budget analyst office at the Pentagon on 9/11. The DoD staff were working on the mystery of the "missing" $2.3 *trillion* disclosed by Defense Secretary Donald Rumsfeld the day before. Conveniently, the topic of the missing money disappeared along with any reliable trace of the plane that was alleged to have been used in the attack.

It is well documented that the Central Intelligence Agency has engaged in mind control experiments, using torture, sleep deprivation, rape, and other sadistic techniques. The Jason Bourne series of movies were likely based on real events.

The Central Intelligence Agency is responsible for all of the lies in the media that Trump is dealing with.

I have heard that the head office of the Central Intelligence Agency is in Switzerland and that the United States of America is one of a handful of lawful de jure nations on the planet, together with the Republic of Texas and maybe Russia and hopefully Ukraine.

The President gets to pick the director of the Central Intelligence Agency in Langley, Virginia, but does the director know everything that is going on? Do they keep their boss, the President, in the loop? It is well documented that George Bush Sr., when he was director of the Central Intelligence Agency refused to tell Jimmy Carter, when Carter was President, some things, and Bush told Carter so to his face in a rather nasty way because Carter talks about it sometimes.

Many pedophiles that are being prosecuted these days are tied to Central Intelligence Agency programs, because victims of the CIA mind control experiments have said that the CIA likes to begin their mind control training at a very young age—sometimes it begins with babies.

FREEMASONRY DECLARES ITSELF A CULT

"Masonry, like all the religions, all the mysteries, hermeticism and alchemy conceals its secrets from all except the adepts and sages, or the elect, and uses false explanations and misinterpretations of its symbols to mislead those who deserve only to be misled; to conceal the truth, which it calls Light, from them, and to draw them away from it." (Albert Pike, Morals and Dogma, page 104-105)

One of the reasons Child Protective Services (CPS) is busy stealing the sons and daughters of so many people is so they can have a pool of babies and children for the Roman Cult's human sacrifices, and the CIA's mind control training.

Under the 1997 Adoption and Safe Families Act, CPS Agencies are granted $4000 - $6000 for every child that is removed from their home and placed with a stranger

---

Mark Passio, former priest in the Church of Satan, explained how he was set up and operated by the Central Intelligence Agency. I believe that Donald Trump is our last chance for freedom.

"There is no peace, saith my God, to the wicked."
Isaiah 57:21

"Because, even because they have seduced my people, saying, Peace; and there was no peace." (Ezekiel 13:10)

There will be no peace as long as these Satanists are in power "When the righteous are in authority, the people rejoice: but when the wicked beareth rule, the people mourn." (Proverbs 29:2)

I believe that this is literally a battle of good versus evil.

ABOUT THE AUTHOR

Growing up in communist Canada, I have no firsthand knowledge of a date of birth. I do remember finishing high school in Raymond, Alberta in 1975.

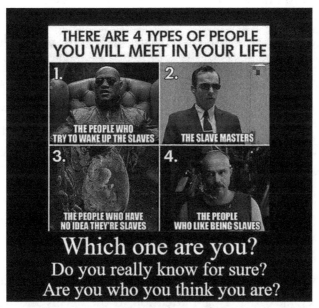

Figure 62 – Do you know who you are

In 1976 I started working on airplanes as a mechanic and have been working in aviation all my life. My mother was from Oklahoma, and shortly after finishing high school, I learned that I could claim American nationality by right of blood.

In the early 1990s, I was living in St. George, Utah, and working on a contract in San Diego, California, when somebody told me about the two classes of citizens. I told them they were crazy. They showed me some court cases that talked about it. I thought that this is the most amazing thing and I had to investigate into it further.

Over the years, I have been all over the world. I have traveled across both oceans dozens of times. I have been in every state in the USA and every province in Canada, except Prince Edward Island. I have been to France, United Kingdom, Ireland, Belgium, Holland, Germany, Italy, Spain, Egypt, Saudi Arabia, Switzerland, Poland, Yugoslavia, Ukraine, Russia, Turkey, Hong Kong, Philippines, Senegal, Ivory Coast, Upper Volta, Liberia, and others.

I have worked mostly contracts. In fact, I worked for America West Airlines during the time that they were merging with US Airways. I was there for seven years, and that is the longest position I have had in my life.

Every contract I went on I would talk to people about the law, and many times I ran into people who already knew much of what I knew and had collected material (court cases, etc.) to support it.

Toronto

I worked my way up into quality and then engineering. I guess they liked that I paid attention to the details and was good at doing research. I was in Toronto in the mid 1990s on a contract for Bombardier. It was there I met a guy by the name of Patrick. He showed me how to do court work (file lawsuits). There always seemed to be some government bureaucrat who wanted to violate my rights, so I would file a lawsuit against them. I have been to the

Supreme Court of the United States five times and in the lower courts dozens of times. I have had judges tell me I know how to make a legal brief.

Patrick was also Catholic and was telling me about the satanic nature of the Vatican, but I refused to believe it at first. Patrick is an avid researcher and spends hours and hours in law libraries in the Toronto area. He sent me a lot of very useful material and after Patrick sending me a lot of evidence and me doing my own research, I came to realize that Patrick is right (as usual) because the Vatican is satanic.

Almost all of the material in this book that is from England or Canada is from Patrick. It was not by chance that I met Patrick. I believe that there is not much in this life that happens by chance.

The Republic of Texas

Around 2004, under the Bush regime, a friend told me about Rice McLeod and the Republic of Texas. Up until then I knew about the two classes of citizens, but I was not clear about how it can be properly asserted. Rice McLeod was attorney general for the Republic of Texas and had a very simple way of looking at the issues and how to assert your rights with a notice and demand designed to take away certain presumptions and put our public servants in the position of being required to honor their oath of office. The procedure I use to assert my sovereignty is basically Rice McLeod's procedure modified, and I have served literally thousands of notice and demands by registered mail and spent tens of thousands of dollars doing it. For those of you who question the cost to me of doing this, the question I would ask you is: "At what point does your freedom become too expensive"? "Is there a cost that you would *not* pay to be free?"

Figure 63 – The Matrix ix Real

Over the years, I have learned that the movie *The Matrix* is more true than most people know. Everything is an illusion. Once you learn to see past the illusion, it changes your life forever.

Substantiation

I have used court cases, law dictionaries, and lots of other sources of information to substantiate what is said. I have said very little and let the source material speak for itself, so you can come to your own conclusions.

CONTACT INFO

GLENN FEARN

Website	www.sovereigntyinternational.fyi
Yahoo Private Group	Administrating-Your-Public-Servants@yahoogroups.com
Google Private Group	Administrating-Your-Public-Servants@googlegroups.com
Blog	http://sovereigntyinternational.wordpress.com
Youtube Channel	sovereignliving
Twitter	@engineerwin
Mike Adams' Brighteon	https://www.brighteon.com/channels/engineerwinlbry.tv
Email	engineerwin@yahoo.com @sovereigntyinternational

MIKE BLACKWELL

Website	www.authormikeblackwell.com
Email	mike@sovereignpress.net

REPUBLIC OF TEXAS CONTACT INFO

Website	http://thetexasrepublic.com/
Blog	https://thetexasrepublic.wordpress.com/
Youtube Channel	https://www.youtube.com/c/RepublicofTexas
Twitter	@TexasRepublic4u @WeareTexians
Email	1yellowroseenterprises@gmail.com

TABLE OF FIGURES

TABLE OF AUTHORITIES

Cases

13 Vin. Abr. 539

188 N.W.2d 294; 1971 Iowa Sup. LEXIS 863; 64 A.L.R.3d 1242

256 P. 545, affirmed 278 US 123, Tashiro vs. Jordan

30 Cal 596; 167 Cal 762

62 Va. (21 Gratt.) 790, 796 (1871)

Adams v Gunter 238 So.2d 824 (Fla. 1970)

Allen v. City of Portland, 73 F.3d 232 (9th Cir. 1995)

American Banana Co. v. United Fruit Co., 29 S.Ct. 511, 513, 213 U.S. 347, 53 L.Ed. 826, 19 Ann.Cas. 1047

American Communications Ass'n v. Douds, 339 U.S. 382, 442

American Export Lines Inc. v. United States, 290 F.2d 925, at 929 (July 19, 1961)

Atkins v. Lanning. D.C.Okl., 415 F. Supp. 186, 188

Balzac v People of Puerto Rico, 258 U.S. 298

Bank of Boston v. Jones, 4 UCC Rep. Serv. 1021, 236 A2d 484, UCC PP 9-109.14

Bank of Canada v. Bank of Montreal, [1978] 1 S.C.R. 1148 at page 1155

Bell v. Hood, 71 F.Supp., 813, 816 (1947)

Belmont v. Town of Gulfport, 122 So. 10

Bollow v. Federal Reserve Bank of San Francisco, 650 F.2d 1093, 9th Cir., (1981)

Bond v United States 572 US ____ (2014) case

Bond v United States 572 US ____ (2014) case number 12-158

Bowling v. Commonwealth, (1867), 65 Kent. Rep. 5, 29

Brasswell v. United States 487 U.S. 99 (1988) quoting, United States v. White 322 U.S. 694 (1944),

Brookfield Const. Co. v. Stewart, 284 F. Supp. 94

Brown, Jur Section 202; Wright v. Douglas, 10 Barb. (N.Y.) 97; Town of Huntington v. Town of Charlotte, 15 Vt. 46

Bulloch v. United States, 763 F.2d 1115, 1121 (10th Cir. 1985)

Burns v. Sup., Ct., SF, 140 Cal. 1

Caha v. United States, 152 U.S. 211 (1894)

Cal. v. Sims, 32 C3d 468

Carlisle v United States 83 U.S. 147, 154 (1873)

Chisholm v Georgia, 2 Dal. 419

Chisholm v Georgia, 2 Dal. 419 at page 458

Chisholm v Georgia, 2 Dall 419 at p 455

Chisholm v Georgia, 2 Dall 419 at p 456

Chisholm v Georgia, 2 Dall 419, at p 479

Chisholm v Georgia, 2 Dall. 419, at p 471;

Chisholm v. Georgia, 2 Dall 419, at p 453, (1794)

Chisolm v Georgia 2 Dall. 419

Church of the Holy Trinity v. U.S., 143 US 457 (1892)

City of Dallas v Mitchell, 245 S.W. 944

City of Lufkin v. McVicker, 510 S.W. 2d 141 (Tex. Civ. App. – Beaumont 1973)

Colgate v Harvey 296 US 404 at p 427

CRUDEN vs. NEALE, 2 N.C. 338 2 S.E. 70

Crunk v State Farm Fire and Casualty 719 P.2d 1338

Cummings v. Board of Education of Okla. City, 125 P2d 989, 994, 190 Okl.
    533

Daniels v. Dean (1905), 2 C.A. 421, 84 P. 332

Dawson v. Vance, 329 F.Supp. 1320, (D.C.Tex. 1971)

Downes v. Bidwell, 182 U.S. 244 (1901)

Dred Scott v Sandford, 60 US 393, at pg 404

Dred Scott v. Sandford, 19 How (60 U.S.) 393, 452, 15 L.Ed. 691 (A.D. 1856-
    1857)

Economy Plumbing and Heating v. U.S., 470 F.2d 585 (Ct. Cl. 1972)

Elk v. Wilkins, Neb (1884), 5s.ct.41,112 U.S. 99, 28 L. Ed. 643

Ex Parte Frank Knowles, 5 Cal. Rep. 300

Ex Parte Hoffert, 148 NW 20

Ex Parte Milligan 4 Wall (71 U.S.) 2, 18 L.Ed. 281, p 302

Faretta v. California, 422 U.S. 806, 821

Favot v. Kingsbury, (1929) 98 Cal. App. 284, 276 P. 1083

Gallagher v. Montplier, 52 ALR 744; 5 Am Jur. page 645

Gawthrop v. Fairmont Coal Co., 81 S.E. 560, 561; 74 S.Va. 39

Hague v. C. I. O., 307 U. S. 496, 509

Hale v. Henkel, 201 U.S. 43

Hancock V. Terry Elkhorn Mining Co., Inc., KY., 503 S.W. 2D 710 KY Const.
    §4, Commonwealth Ex Rel. Hancock V. Paxton, KY, 516 S. W. 2D. PG 867

Hill v. Algor, 85 F.Supp.2d 391, 397-98 (D.N.J. 2000)

Hill v. Waxberg, 237 F.2d 936

Hillhouse v United States, 152 F. 163, 164 (2nd Cir. 1907)

Hoke vs Henderson, 15, N.C. 15, 25 AN Dec 677

Home Building and Loan Association v Blaisdel, 290 US 398 (1934)

Horning v. District of Columbia, 254 U.S. 135, 138 (1920)

In Re Barnes, 11 UCC Reporting Service 670

In Re Bolens (1912), 135 N.W. 164

In re Estate of Steinfield, 630 N.E.2d 801, certiorari denied, See also Steinfeld v. Hoddick, 513 U.S. 809, (Ill. 1994)

In Re Newman (1858), 9 C. 502

In Re Page 12 F (2d) 135

In re Schmolke (1926) 199 Cal. 42, 46

Inhabitants of Manchester v. Inhabitants of Boston, 16 Mass. 230, 235

Isbill v. Stovall, Tex.Civ.App., 92 S.W.2d 1067, 1070

James Talcott, Inc. v Gee, 5 UCC Rep Serv 1028; 266 Cal.App.2d 384, 72 Cal. Rptr. 168 (1968)

Jones v. Temmer, 89 F. Supp 1226 (1993)

Julliard v Greenman 110 U.S. 421 at p 467

Julliard v. Greenman, 110 US 432

Kawananakoa v. Polyblank, 205 U.S. 349, 353, 27 S. Ct. 526, 527, 51 L. Ed. 834 (1907)

Kemper v. State, 138 Southwest 1025 (1911), page 1043

Knox v State, 586 S.W. 2d 504, 506 (Tex.Crim.App. 1979)

Lansing v Smith, (1829) 4 Wendell 9,20 (NY)

Lavin v. Marsh, 644 F.2nd 1378, 9th Cir., (1981)

License Tax Cases 72 U.S. (5 Wall.) 462 (1866)

Long v. Rasmussen, 281 F. 236, at 238

Loyd v. Director, Dept. of Public Safety, 480 So. 2d 577 (Ala. Civ. App. 1985)

Lubben v. Selective Service System Local Bd. No. 27, 453 F.2d 645, 14 A.L.R. Fed. 298 (C.A. 1 Mass. 1972). Hobbs v. U.S. Office of Personnel Management, 485 F.Supp. 456 (M.D. Fla. 1980)

Luckenback v. The Thekla, 295 F 1020, 226 Us 328; Lyders v. Lund, 32 F2d 308

Luther v. Borden, 48 US 1, 12 Led 581

MacLeod v. Hoover (1925), 159 La. 244, 105 S. 305

Madden v. Kentucky 309 US 83 (1940)

Major-Blakeney Co. v. Jenkins (1953), 121 C.A.2d 325, 263 P.2d 655, hear den.; Townsend Pierson, Inc. v. Holly-Coleman Co. (1960), 178 C.A.2d 373, 2 Cal. Rptr. 812

Mallicoat v Volunteer Finance & Loan Corp., 3 UCC Rep Serv 1035; 415 S.W.2d 347 (Tenn. App., 1966)

Manning v. Ketcham, 58 F.2d 948

Maryland Independent Automobile Dealers Assoc., Inc. v Administrator, Motor Vehicle Admin., 25 UCC Rep Serv 699; 394 A.2d 820, 41 Md App 7 (1978)

Matthews v Ward, 10 Gill & Johnson (Md.) 443 (1839)

Maxwell v Dow, 20 S.C.R. 448, at pg 451

Maxwell v Dow, 20 S.C.R. 448, at pg 455

Mayor of New Orleans v. United States, 10 Pet. 662, 736 [emphasis

Mc Donel v State, 90 Ind. Rep. 320 at pg 323

McAleer v. Good, 65 Atl. 934, 935 (1907); Mackie v. Ambassador, 11 P.2d 6 (1932)

McClarin v. Nesbit, 2 Nott & McC. (11 S.C.L.) 519 (1820)

McConnell v Wilcox, 1 Scammon (ILL.) 381 (1837).

McCullough v Maryland, 17 U.S. [4 Wheat] 316 (1819)

McFadden v Jordan, 196 P.2d 787

McFadden v Mercantile-Safe Deposit & Trust Co., 8 UCC Rep Serv 766; 260 Md 601, 273 A.2d 198 (1971)

McNeely v. City of Natchez, 114 So. 484, 487; 148 Miss. 268

Miller v. U.S. 230 F. 486 at 489

Missouri, K. & T. Ry. Co. v. Dewey Portland Cement Co., 242 P. 257, 259, 113 Okla. 142

Mitchell v. Wells, 37 Miss. 235

Murdock v. Pennsylvania, 319 US 105

n re Waltz et al., Burlow v Security Trust and Savings Bank, 240 P. 19 (1925)

National Mutual Insurance Company of the District of Columbia v. Tidewater Transfer Company, 337 U.S. 582, 93 L.Ed. 1556 (1948)

Ohio L. Ins. & T. Co. v. Debolt, 16 How. 416, 14 L.Ed. 997

Owens v Independence 100 S.C.T. 1398 (Ezra 7:23-26)

Paff v. Kaltenbach, 204 F.3d 425, 435 (3rd Cir. 2000)

PAROSA v. TACOMA, 57 Wn.(2d) 409 (Dec.22, 1960).

Parsons v. Bedford, et al, 3 Pet 433, 479

Pauley v. Hall, 335 N. W. 2d 197, 124 Mich App 255

People v Herkimer, 4 Cowen (NY) 345, 348 (1825)

People v. De La Guerra,40 Cal. 311, 342 (A.D. 1870)

People v. McGrew, 20 Pac. 92 (1888); Knight v. Baker, 133 P. 544(1926)

Perkins v Texas, 812 S.W. 2d 326

Perlman v Piche and Attorney General of Canada, Intervenant, Re Habeus Corpus, 4 D.L.R. 147

Perry v. U.S. (294 US 330)

Propeller Genessee Chief et al. v. Fitzhugh et al. 12 How. 443 (U.S. 1851)

Re Casa Loma, (1927) 4 D.L.R. 645

Re Employment and Social Insurance Act, 1937, 1 DLR, page 687

Robin v. Hardaway, 1 Jefferson 109

Roe v. Wade US Supreme Court 410 US 13, 35 L.Ed. 2d 147, 1973

Rzayeva v. Foster, 134 F.Supp.2d 239, 248-49 (D.Conn. 2001)

Santiago v. City of Vineland, 107 F.Supp.2d 512, 561-62, 564 (D.N.J. 2000)

Sapulpa v Land, 101 Okla. 22, 223 Pac. 640, 35 A.L.R. 872

Schneider v. Simonini, 749 A.2d 336, 163 N.J. 336, 361-65 (2000)

Schucker v. Rockwood, 846 F.2d 1202

Schwarts v. O'Hara TP School District, 100 A 2d. 621, 625, 375, Pa. 440

Sherar v. Cullen, 481 F. 946

Shuttlesworth v. City of Birmingham Alabama, 373 US 262

Spooner v. McConnell, 22 F 939 @ 943

St. Louis v Gorman, 29 Mo. 593 (1860)

Stanek v. White (1927), 172 Minn. 390, 215 N.W. 781

State ex rel. Herbert v. Whims, 68 Ohio App. 39, 38 N.E.2d 596, 599, 22 O.O.
110

State ex rel. McNamee v. Stobie, 92 SW 191, 212, 194 Mo. 14

State v Phillips 540 Pac. Rep.2d 936

State v. Johnson, 243 P. 1073; 60 C.J.S. section 94, page 581

State v. Mastrian, 171 N.W.2d 695 (1969); Butler v. State, 212 So.2d 577 (Miss
1968)

State v. Simmon, 2 Spears 761, 767 (1884)

State vs Manual 20 NC 122, 14 C.J.S. 4, p 430

State vs. Batson, 17 S.E. 2d 511, 512, 513

Tayler v Porter, 4 Hill 773 (1843)

Taylor v. Porter, 4 Hill 140, 146 (1843)

The Society, &c., v. The Town of New Haven. Et Al. 8 Wheat. 464; 5 Cond.
Rep. 489

Thiede v. Scandia, 217 Minn. 231, 14 N.W.2d 400 (1944

Thompson v. Smith, 154 S.E. 579, 583; Keller v. P.E., 261 US 428; F.R.C. v.
G.E., 281, U.S. 464

Thompson v. Thompson, 238 S.W.2d 218 (Tex.Civ.App. – Waco 1951

Trinsey v. Pagliaro D.C.Pa. 1964, 229 F. Supp. 647

Twining v. New Jersey, 211 U.S. 97, 1908

U. S. v. Lovasco (06/09/77) 431 U.S. 783, 97 S. Ct. 2044, 52 L. Ed. 2d 752

U.S. v. Bevans, 16 U.S. 336, 3 Wheat, at 350, 351 (1818)

U.S. v. Morris, 125 F 322, 325

U.S. vs. Cruikshank, 92 US 542

UNITED STATES of America v. William M. SLATER (1982) (D. Delaware)
545 F.Supp 179, 182.

United States v Amistadt 40 US 518 (1841)

105

STATUTES

10 USC § 838(a)(1)

12 Stat. 296, Chap XLV, August 5, 1861

12 U.S. Code § 83 - Loans by bank on its own stock

12 USC § 411

14 Stat. 428

15 USC § 44

18 U.S. Code § 8.Obligation or other security of the United States defined

18 US Code § 2707 Civil Action

18 USC § 1346 Definition of "Scheme or Artifice to defraud

18 USC § 31

18 USC § 7 Special maritime and territorial jurisdiction of the United States defined

3 Stat 566

31 Stat. 1189

31 Stat. 1230

31 Stat. 1363

31 Stat. 1365

31 Stat. 1366

31 Stat. 1432

31 Stat. 85

36 Stat. 1091

41 Stat. Ch.214 pg. 654

42 USC [District of Columbia Code] § 1982

5 USC § 552a.(a)(13)

5 USC § 552a.(a)(2)

50 U.S.C. Appendix 5 Trading with the Enemy Act

9 Stat 1

Alberta Judicature Act Section 15

Arizona Revised Statutes 13-103. Abolition of common law offenses and affirmative defenses; definition

Canadian Ownership and Control Determination Act

Chap. XVI Coinage Act April 2, 1792. Sec 9

Federal Tax Lien Act of 1966 at Public Law 89-719 at 80 Stat. 1130-1131

George III, CAP XII 1778

Gold Reserve Act of 1934, 48 Stat. 337

Section 192-003 Texas Health and Safety Code

Section 28(1)(nn) Alberta Interpretation Act

OTHER AUTHORITIES

RULES

TREATISES

REGULATIONS

CPSIA information can be obtained
at www.ICGtesting.com
Printed in the USA
JSHW021550160922
30433JS00001B/1

9 781947 360563